Kiev

THE BRADT CITY GUIDE

Andrew Evans

Bradt Travel Guides Ltd, UK
The Globe Pequot Press Inc, USA

First published 2004

Bradt Travel Guides Ltd
19 High Street, Chalfont St Peter, Bucks SL9 9QE, England; www.bradtguides.com
Published in the USA by The Globe Pequot Press Inc, 246 Goose Lane, PO Box 480,
Guilford, Connecticut 06437-0480

A catalogue record for this book is available from the British Library

ISBN-10: 1 84162 099 8
ISBN-13: 978 1 84162 099 2

Cover Kovnir's Belfry in the Kievan Cave Monastery (Mark Wadlow/Russia & Eastern Images)
Text photographs Andrew Evans *Maps* Steve Munns *Illustrations* Carole Vincer

Typeset from the author's disc by Wakewing
Printed and bound in Spain by Grafo SA, Bilbao

Author

Andrew Evans has been travelling regularly to Kiev since 1994, a city where he especially enjoys wandering the streets and meeting strangers. He completed his postgraduate work in Russian and East European Studies at Oxford University, where he wrote and lectured on Ukrainian politics, history and culture. His other books include *Ukraine: The Bradt Travel Guide*, and the *VegOut Guide to Washington, DC*.

FEEDBACK REQUEST

Dear Readers!

I can't think of any other city in Europe that is changing as fast as Kiev. The skyline alters with every return visit, and new hotels and restaurants open every month. I also love hearing about what others have experienced in Kiev – their impressions, likes and dislikes, and the new things they've found.

Some things we learn by experience, others by word of mouth. As much as I adore Kiev, and as much as I visit the city, I will never see and know everything about it. Therefore, I ask you kindly to share with me your experiences, insight, and advice. I love interesting letters and always appreciate good tips. Please address your letters or email to Andrew Evans, c/o Bradt Travel Guides, 19 High Street, Chalfont St Peter, Bucks SL9 9QE, England; email: info@bradt-travelguides.com. Your contributions will make life easier for future travellers to Kiev. I look forward to reading your feedback!

Cheers,

Andrew

Contents

Contents

Contents

Acknowledgements

Kiev is a city of three million people, and quite a handful of them helped me with this book, either directly or indirectly. Thank you to everyone who gave me directions, recommended cool places, drove me there, and provided me with valuable information. Thank you to the Tugai family (Andrei, Natasha, and Ilyushichka) – all Kiev natives whose friendship, warm spirit and honest advice continue to make me happy. A dear friend, Maksim Shiyan deserves a special thank you for his support, and for making sure I visited every club and pub possible; also, thank you to the wonderful Christiansen family for their hospitality and sharing personal experiences of Kiev. I am most appreciative of new friends at Kyiv Mohyla Academy whose welcome and knowledge made my recent travels to their city even richer. Also, I am very sincerely grateful to all the Ukrainian politicians (who shall remain nameless) and staff who offered me a more intimate vantage point of their lovely capital.

In England, much gratitude is due to Hilary Bradt for her vision of the world and for wanting something more from me. Thank you to Tricia Hayne for talking me into this one, and all the Bradt team for bringing the page to the shelf: Adrian Phillips, both of the Debbies, Selena Dickson, Adrian Dixon, Stewart J Wild and Sally Brock.

In Washington, DC a gigantic thank you to the Global Fairness Initiative for sending me back to Kiev so many times over such a short period; to Karen Tramontano and Sally Painter, who provided invaluable research material on so many different levels and blessed me with a more elegant take on Kiev; and to Steven Bennett and Annie Verderosa for laughing along with me. Thanks also to Dave Barber for letting me use his Mac.

As always, my deepest thanks to my family, who read the things I write and are always so encouraging.

And to Brian, for everything – ever patient, moving gently through piles of paper and books, giving great advice and needed support and pampering me through the production process.

Acknowledgements

How to Use this Book

Map references (eg: [1 B2]) for restaurants, hotels, and sites refer to the colour-map section at the end of the guide. The map number is listed first, followed by the grid reference on that map.

Prices quoted in the text were correct at the time of going to press; however, prices are known to fluctuate in Ukraine. I have listed prices, for the most part, in US dollars, except for some fairly stable museum entrance fees, which are listed in hrivna.

Email addresses and websites are listed when possible. *Chapter 13* also provides a list of websites relevant to travel in Kiev.

Streets are labelled in English on the map a) so you know how to ask others where things are, and b) so you can sound out the Cyrillic signs and recognise the streets on your map. Street names in Kiev change frequently – the ones used in this book were correct at the time of printing.

Hotel rates are individually explained for each establishment, but in most cases reflect single occupancy.

This book applies both **Russian and Ukrainian titles**, and is consistent in its application. Harbouring no desire to offend users of either language, I have made conscious decisions on what to call what, normally based on a word's general, long-term usage in British English (hence 'Kiev' and the 'Dnepr' river) versus widely used Ukrainian toponyms unknown in English (eg: Maidan Nezalezhnosti, Andriyivsky Uzviz). At present, the city of Kiev/Kyiv uses both languages interchangeably, so there is little need for allegiance to one or the other.

Transliteration is based in most part on generally accepted Cyrillic-Latin transliteration tables, with a few exceptions that have been edited to ease legibility for those unfamiliar with Slavic terms and names.

Introduction

If you fly into Kiev, the drive from Boryspil Airport into the city presents a fitting overture of what lies ahead. A super-smooth eight-lane highway (the newest and nicest in the country) cuts through a forest of pencil-thin birch trees, interspersed with spindly pines and white brick farmhouses where goats wander in summer and snow drifts in winter. Suddenly, a gigantic fluorescent yellow sign proclaims (in English) 'Welcome to Kiev' and the forest merges into a vast urban space of vehicles and construction. The methodical rows of apartment towers are now dotted with thousand-dollar satellite dishes and miniature churches topped with the signatory gold dome stand next to Ukrainian-brand fast-food joints. The view becomes stifled with giant billboards advertising new medications, brand-name cosmetics and mobile phone service providers. It's only after you've crossed the Dnepr river that you witness the rounded hills of Kiev beneath the silvery, sword-wielding motherland statue, next to golden specks of monasteries and churches.

The blend of the ancient with the recently outdated and the brand-spanking-new is not unique to Kiev, but the art of adjustment is. So many who travel to Kiev are secretly honing out signs of the Soviet times: the staunch glares, the emotionless bureaucracy, the dysfunctional plumbing. These and many more hints of the Soviet past may or may not be there, but Kiev has moved so far beyond such prejudices that it becomes the traveller's blessing to witness a city discovering the modernity of a globalised world while simultaneously recovering its most ancient ways.

Ten years ago, I made the same drive from Boryspil, but there was no smooth road – only bumps, holes and icy puddles. There were no golden domes upon the hillside – only ruins and broken frescos among the piles of bricks. Streetlights were shattered, the city was dark and people stayed off the streets. And yet those days of despair disappeared so quickly. Kiev moves steadily forward, and even the novelty of luxury and progress has worn off. The city's recent reincarnation is nothing new. In the 16 or so centuries that Kiev's been around, the city's been blown up, burned down, flooded, shelled and occupied so many times that historians have lost count. For this reason, Kiev differs tremendously from well-known tourist towns where skylines are set in stone and street names never change. Resilience and flexibility are the recognisable traits of Kiev's inhabitants, who should be praised for keeping the city's soul alive despite the waves of destruction and the waves of fads – be they political or economic. I am truly convinced that you could transport all three million Kievans to Moscow and that city would quickly turn into Kiev with all of its home-grown beauty and oddity.

For now, Kiev continues to be content with its current location, and those who know the city can't seem to leave it alone. You should feel special for having made it this far, and count yourself lucky for the early discovery. Kiev rewards both the curious and jaded with unexpected adventures and many true friends. May your visit be wondrous and smooth-going, but not too smooth. *Uspikha* ('good luck') and have fun!

KIEV AT A GLANCE

Location North Central Ukraine, Eastern Europe 50° north 30° east

Size 830 km² (319.3 square miles)

Geography Steppe embankment divided by Dnepr River

Population 3 million (49 million in Ukraine)

People Ethnic Ukrainian 78%, Russian 20%, other 2%

Languages Ukrainian and Russian

International dialling code +380 (Ukraine) 44 (Kiev)

Time GMT + 2 hours (7 hours ahead of New York City)

Electricity AC is 200 volts, frequency is 50 hertz

Public holidays January 1 (New Year's Day), January 7 (Orthodox Christmas), January 14 (Old New Year's Day), March 8 (Women's Day), May 1 (May Day), May 9 (Victory Day), August 24 (Independence Day, Ukraine), November 7 (Anniversary of the Great October Revolution)

Contexts

As one of Europe's more unassuming gems, Ukraine's capital earnestly welcomes visitors with a vision of stateliness and lasting energy. Surrounded by forest and spanning the steep green banks of the Dnepr river, Kiev's understated beauty comes out in a freeform skyline all its own: uniformly granite government buildings, ornate refurbished palaces, socialist skyscrapers topped with red stars, burgeoning shopping plazas beneath gigantic back-lit adverts, brick-and-mortar apartment towers, and within this medley, the dazzling gold from onion-shaped domes and cupolas topping dozens of historic Kiev churches. Ancient chestnut trees cloak the riverbank in green for half of the year, and in May, their distinctive white blossoms literally fill the bumpy cobblestone streets. During the winter months, when trees are bare, noses are red, and black crows linger as a single natural feature, Kiev still provides a thoughtful and poetic cityscape.

Kiev occupies a strange mental space in the world's mind: the few who know the city feel an intense affection for the place, while 'Kiev' remains otherwise unknown except for vague connotations of a distant eastern capital and a buttery piece of chicken. No songs or stories romanticise Kiev (in English) and so most people hark back to outdated Soviet-era recollections when Kiev completed the triad of great Slavic capitals – placed third after St Petersburg and Moscow. Fortunately, Kiev has experienced a much more tasteful and honest resurrection than the other two cities, and today the Ukrainian capital stands alone as the most ancient and least

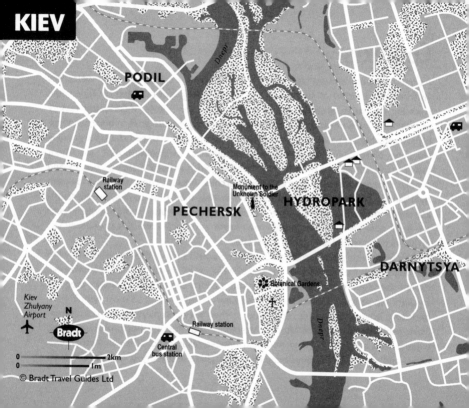

politicised of the three – upheld by a somewhat separate history and unique glory that both visitors and residents find so attractive.

What you experience depends on what you do. There is the Kiev of impressive monuments and sweeping vistas, delicate churches and historic statues – all of which fits nicely into a bus tour or a few days of guided walking. Then there is Kiev the Ukrainian capital – a realm of power that puts on a show of governance for this newly independent nation. Last, there is the *real* Kiev – comprising several highly individualised neighbourhoods, many of which are over a thousand years old and others that only just came into existence during the past 25 years. Kiev's separate districts proudly defend their separate personalities, defined over the centuries by who has lived (and died) there, and all that has transpired on those streets. Truly, getting to know this city requires a bit of targeted wandering.

Enjoying Kiev also means enjoying those who live in Kiev – few cities in the world are so defined by the people that call it home. Despite a population of three million, Kiev remains remarkably down-to-earth. Candid street scenes keep the observant person's neck turning and even the most seasoned of travellers can expect a visual adventure. Add to this spectacle the current, post-independence funk in which Kiev is still trying to find itself: accepting its proud heritage, turning the weight of the past into a novelty, and trying to create something cool and unique in the midst of capitalist bombardment. Keep in mind that no matter what you are doing in Kiev, your visit is part of the experiment.

Kiev is still the easiest city to travel to in Ukraine and has quickly become the number-one tourist and business destination in the country. For organised group tours, Kiev is almost always included as part of the itinerary, and there is no lack of things to see and do. Come prepared to participate.

HISTORY

Kiev is where it all began – Russia, Ukraine, and all that came with it. Simply 'seeing the sights' reveals a fair understanding of what's happened here and why. Truly, this city confesses a pretty turbulent past, but uses its very colourful and impressive history to reinforce the right to respect and a chance to build a new reputation as an independent capital.

The Slavs

Controversy will forever surround the question of how the Slavic tribes came to be a people, a debate fuelled by changing notions of national image today. By the 6th century AD, a definitive cultural and linguistic group was living in Eastern Europe and it is widely accepted that this was a mixed population of indigenous settlers and their nomadic overlords. Spreading across the expanses of western Eurasia, the Slavs evolved into three major groups of tribes. The South Slavs moved into the Balkans, the Western Slavs moved into modern-day Poland and central Europe, and the eastern Slavs moved into what is now Ukraine, Belarus and Russia.

Nature was the predominant force in the life of the eastern Slavic tribes. They produced grain in the fields and caught fish in the rivers and streams. In the forest they hunted game and collected honey and wax from beehives. In a land that was relatively flat, the eastern Slavs used the available hilltops to build protective fortresses. These fort cities were called *horodyshcha*, from whence comes the modern Ukrainian word for city: *horod*.

Legend tells us that Kiev started as such a *horod* in AD560, and that its founding was a family affair. Kyi, Schek and Koriv were three brothers of the Polianian tribe. Their sister (Lybed) is often shown standing at the helm of a Viking longboat with her three brothers rowing her gently onwards. She pointed out the spot that felt right, and each sibling settled on a separate hillside. A city emerged in between which they named after their eldest brother Kyi. Three hills in Kiev still bear their names today.

The Slavs found themselves conveniently located between two very different civilizations: the infamous Vikings to the north, and the eastern Christian capital of Constantinople to the south. The Vikings were especially keen to access the more extravagant goods of the Byzantine Empire and sought an alternate route to Constantinople rather than sail all the way around Europe. Cutting through the lands of the eastern Slavs seemed to be the best solution, and several of the local tribes were already paying tributes to the Varangians (the Slavic term for the Norse tribes). Through the years, the established route from the 'Varangians to the Greeks' went from the Baltic Sea over to Lake Ladoga, to Novgorod, along the

Lovat River, down the Dnepr, and across the Black Sea to Constantinople. Central to this proven route, the Kiev outpost swiftly grew into a vital trade centre, as it also corresponded to the east–west caravan routes that connected Europe to the Silk Road.

Kievan Rus

The civilisation of Kievan Rus officially began with the reign of the Varangian princes over Kiev and the surrounding regions in the latter half of the 9th century. As enterprising rulers, Askold and Dir used Kiev as a base from which to raid Constantinople in AD860, returning with enough booty to make other princes jealous. Prince Oleh (from northern Russia) snuck into Kiev, killed Askold and Dir, and crowned himself the very first prince over all of Rus, establishing Kiev as the capital of all lands between what is now modern-day St Petersburg and Moldova. Following a treaty of tax exemption from Byzantium, Kiev grew into one of Europe's most powerful cities (London was half the size at the time). The Byzantine Empire traded their gold, silk, exotic fruit and spices for the furs, wax, honey and slaves of Kievan Rus.

Prince Volodymyr's reign signifies the greatest advancement for Kievan Rus. He was the first ruler to establish a written code of law, adding stability through power transfer, tax collection, and a state religion. As the story goes, the Byzantine emperor was ingratiated to Volodymyr for his swift response to quell a rebellion within the Byzantine Empire. For a reward, the emperor offered him his daughter,

Contexts

the imperial princess, with just one catch. The marriage would take place as soon as Volodymyr converted to Christianity. Eventually, he was keen to strengthen his own empire and to integrate Kievan Rus with other surrounding empires. Volodymyr had noticed how the organised religions of the Jews, Christians and Muslims had furthered their own empires and served as an effective means of diplomacy. According to legend, Islam was rejected because of the Koran's specific restriction on drink, and Judaism was rejected for all of its restrictions.

In AD988, Volodymyr returned to Kiev with his new bride and a new state religion. In a monumental ritual, the people of Kiev were marched into the Dnepr, and the river's waters were blessed by Byzantine priests as the Prince watched from the bank. Kievan Rus was collectively baptised and the Slavic nation made Christian – pagan idols were torn down and new churches built in their place. Prince Yaroslav the Wise defended the city against a Pecheneg invasion in 1024 and built St Sophia's Cathedral in gratitude in 1051; Greek monks founded Kiev's Cave Monastery – the ecclesiastical centre of Russian Orthodoxy and the most visited site in Kiev today. Just upriver stands a statue of Prince Volodymyr, holding a tall cross in his hands.

The Golden Horde

Alas, Kiev's growing wealth was a constant target for raids. At the onset of the winter of 1240, the grandson of Genghis Khan – Batu Khan – came and decimated Kiev, bringing the last of Rus into the Mongols' military confederation, the Golden

History

Horde. The Mongols never colonised the region fully and respected the local culture and religion, even exempting the church from tribute. They put locals in places of power and had them do the dirty work of extracting each city's payment. It was a despotic realm and discipline was cruel. Unlike the Russians, the Mongols stayed in Ukrainian land for less than a century.

Lithuania and Poland

Kiev never did recover its seat of power, and was eventually annexed to the Lithuanian principality in 1362. Under the Magdeburg Law, Kiev was allowed the self-rule that prompted an urban development and cosmopolitanism similar to the cities of western Ukraine, but another Mongol invasion in 1482 cut the city down once again. It was not until 1569, following the Union of Lublin with Lithuania, that Poland began ruling Kiev and the city's demographic profile changed significantly with an influx of Poles and Jews.

The Cossacks

Polish landowners carried out a system of feudalism that exploited the western Ukrainian peasants and capitalised on the high grain yields from Ukraine's fertile soil. Uninspired by their lot in life, many peasants simply fled to the central Dnepr basin south of Kiev, the lands stretching across the plains north of the Black Sea. Here was a 'no man's land' of sorts, a shifting frontier, unregulated by any foreign nobility. Other peasants were sent to cultivate the area, sanctioned by the Polish nobles themselves. Hoping to increase grain production, the Polish–Lithuanian Commonwealth offered massive tracts of land rent-free for up to 20 years in the unsettled steppe of the east.

This system brought two benefits to Poland. More grain could be produced and bought at low prices and then sold to western Europe at a profit. Secondly, an effective buffer zone was in place, protecting the kingdom from the all-too-common invasions from the south. This borderland kept separate the civilised worlds of Poland, Lithuania and Muscovy from the barbaric Muslims of the Crimean Khanate and Ottoman Empire. This land was 'on the edge' of civilisation, or in the local language, 'U-krayi-na'.

A series of fortresses had been built to create a safety line for the Polish Commonwealth, stretching from the west all the way to Kiev. The land outside this line was called the *dike polye*, or the 'wild field'. Constant raids from the south made the *dike polye* a precarious place to settle. The Tatars of Crimea had been left behind in the receding tide of the Golden Horde and continued to launch attacks to the north. By the 1500s they controlled most of the Black Sea coast and its Greek and Genoese trading posts. Crimean Tatars and Ottoman Turks came at least yearly on slave-collecting sprees, robbing the settlers, wrecking farms, and severely depopulating the frontier.

Without the military protection of overlords, the locals began to take matters into their own hands. A new brand of fighter emerged, dedicated to protecting his crops, family and land from continuous invasion. The Cossacks became talented horse riders and disciplined warriors, earning their place as the genuine heroes of Ukrainian folklore. They gave the country its national costume and many of its folk songs and dances. Constantly training for battle, they still spent most of their time on the farm, gathering only when it was necessary to fend off invaders or else attack enemy cities. It was these enemies that christened them 'Cossack', the Turkic word for 'freeman' or 'adventurer'. They were outsiders, excluded from any of the surrounding civilisations, who in turn established their own loose-fitting system of rule of law and sword.

The rise of the Cossacks gave birth to the notion of an independent Ukrainian society, free from foreign bondage. Towns outside Kiev began to witness periodic uprisings against the Polish nobility. In Kiev, Cossack Pyotr Sahaydachny is remembered as a vital patron of the Ukrainian and Orthodox community, all the while keeping peace with Poland. Shortly thereafter, Cossack *hetman* (general) Bohdan Khmelnytsky drove the Poles out of the city, for which his statue stands on Sofiyska Ploscha today, astride a rearing horse. The moment of freedom from the Poles was short-lived for Kiev's inhabitants, since Khmelnytsky looked elsewhere for allies, and signed the Pereyaslav agreement with the Russian Tsar in 1654, bringing Kiev into Russian jurisdiction. At first Moscow's influence was minimal, a fact attributed to Cossack *hetman* Ivan Mazepa who had formed strong ties with Russia but guarded the city's autonomy. Mazepa funded a plethora of constructions in Kiev (including the walls and towers of the Pechersky Lavra) and donated the rest of his wealth to Kiev Mohyla Academy – the city's first university.

Contexts

The Russian Empire

Kiev's Russian fate was settled at the Battle of Poltava in 1709 when Tsar Peter I beat Mazepa and his Swedish allies, ending any hopes of Ukrainian autonomy. The culture and language of St Petersburg were the signs of the new élite and Russians were soon added to Kiev's ethnically diverse population. When Russia took control over right-bank Ukraine in 1793, Kiev was no longer the peripheral city of other empires, but a central metropolis, albeit in 'little Russia'. The Magdeburg Law was only revoked in 1835 and the autocratic government introduced a highly centralised legal system. Despite present-day anti-Russian sentiments, the period of Russian rule during the 18th and 19th centuries turned Kiev into a beautiful and booming modern city. Ukraine's sugar trade was the first of many large industries to be based in Kiev, and the fever of industrialisation spread quickly. In 1900, the population had reached 250,000; ten years later, it had doubled.

The Russian Revolution

Kiev's intellectual tradition and large labour population made it an important city in the dissent and popular revolt against the Russian tsar. With both nationalists and workers challenging St Petersburg's authority, Kiev was targeted by a collection of violent ultra-rightist groups to put down the revolutionaries. Known as the Black Hundreds, they indiscriminately beat and killed anyone who was not Tsarist, Orthodox or Russian. Blamed for the rise of revolutionary activity, the Jews suffered one of the bloodiest of pogroms in Ukraine.

History

Within days after news of the February Revolution of 1917 reached Kiev, the Ukrainian Nationalist Movement had mobilised. The Rada (parliament) was established in March, modelled after the Cossacks' self-governing assembly. It assumed the most representative body, and soon the Ukrainian Socialist Revolutionary Party joined, as well as the Peasant Congress. By May they had issued a list of requests to the provisional government who were now attempting to hold the empire together. The Rada demanded recognition of Ukraine's autonomy, separate Ukrainian army units, and Ukrainians to take up the civil posts in Ukraine. The Provisional Government ignored the document, embroiled in its own confusing struggle for authority. The Rada then published its First Universal Declaration that called for a *Sejm* – Ukraine's own national assembly with a sovereign General Secretariat. When it was granted them, Ukraine's ethnic Russians were outraged. Kiev's provisional government eventually collapsed, unable to deal with the conflicting aspirations of Ukrainians and Russians.

Soviet Ukraine

During the Russian Revolution and subsequent civil war, Kiev changed hands 18 times until the final Bolshevik victory in 1921. The capital of the Ukrainian SSR was moved from Kiev to Kharkiv, where there was greater support for the Bolsheviks, but then moved back to Kiev in 1934. Communist policies targeted some of Kiev's most beautiful buildings – including several churches of the Caves Monastery, as well as St Mikhayil's Monastery of the Golden Domes, which Stalin ordered blown up in 1937.

After Lenin's death, Stalin endorsed a policy of fast-pace collectivisation, which wreaked havoc on the Ukrainian countryside. After two years of grain requisitioning, most of Ukraine's food supply had been confiscated and the countryside was left to starve. Peasants ate rats, bark, leaves, dirt, and one another. Skeletal bodies were a common sight in city streets and whole villages died together. The famine of 1932–33 was the ultimate tragedy for the Ukrainian nation. Figures vary widely, but it is generally believed that over six million Ukrainians starved to death. The deliberate genocide went unnoticed in the West and in much of the Soviet Union, and is remembered as the Ukrainian nation's single greatest tragedy. A simple yet sobering monument to the famine stands outside St Mikhayil's Monastery in Kiev.

As the second largest 'republic' in the Soviet Union, Kiev wielded significant political power, but this was severely curtailed by Stalin's purges of the Ukrainian communist leadership and Kiev's intellectuals. Stalin's purges also made waves in Kiev, where scientists, church leaders, writers, editors, historians and musicians all disappeared as victims of the regime. The accused were shot or sent to the gulag prison camps of Siberia. In 1934, the Ukrainian Communist Party lost over 100,000 members in one year. New purges in 1937–38 eliminated the entire leadership of the Ukrainian Soviet Government and the Ukrainian Communist Party, an event that was carried out under the personal leadership of Khrushchev. The Stalinist terror introduced a paranoia that kept people circumspect for the remainder of the life of the Soviet Union.

World War II

The Nazi invasion reached Kiev by June of 1941. The defence of Ukraine's capital was perhaps less heroic than is portrayed by the city's memorials. Over half a million Red Army troops immediately surrendered to the Germans. Stalin had ordered the central thoroughfare booby-trapped before the retreat, exploding some of Kiev's most beautiful buildings upon the Nazis as they marched down Khreschatyk. The act of sabotage was answered by the mass execution of over 180,000 citizens of Kiev at Babi Yar, beginning with the Jews.

The three-year Nazi occupation of Kiev was brutal and exploitative. The collective farms of Ukraine were now feeding the Third Reich, and the Germans had a particular interest in such a fertile land. A common anecdote tells of trainloads of rich Ukrainian topsoil being shipped to Germany. All able Kiev citizens were ordered to work in munitions and supply factories for the duration of the war, and two million Ukrainians were exported to Germany as forced labour. These *Ostarbeiter* (Eastern workers) lived as slaves during the war, but were met with suspicion or imprisoned upon returning for their 'collaboration' in capitalist Germany.

Prior to the war, there were approximately one and a half million Jews in Ukraine. The majority of Ukraine's Jews were not sent to concentration camps, but were rather collected and shot and buried in mass graves. The 'final solution' was the annihilation of Ukraine's thousand-year-old Jewish community. By 1943 the Soviet Army returned to Ukraine, and the city was liberated in November of that year. It was estimated that half of Kiev's population had been killed.

Contexts

Perestroika and independence

Kiev's real heroism lies in the city's ultimate survival and total reconstruction following the war. Of all the cities in the USSR, Kiev was revered for its beauty, art, culture and especially people. Famous Kievans include Mikhail Bulgakov, Golda Meir, Mikhail Hrushevsky, Sholom Aleichem, Isaac Babel, and more recently Russian statesman Yevgeny Primakov and actress Milla Jovovich. Yet for all the 'famous' people born and raised in Kiev, there are hundreds more celebrities who have passed through Kiev on the way to their fortunes, and thousands more souls who brought the city back to life after every tragic episode without any recognition at all.

Following decades of stagnant, elderly leadership, the young reformer Mikhail Gorbachev claimed the highest seat in the Soviet Communist Party in 1985. Determined to overcome the clumsiness and rigidity of the Soviet Union, his policy of *glasnost* (openness) allowed more freedom of expression than ever seen before in the USSR. The reforms of *perestroika* (reconstruction) liberalised the economy and decentralised the political structure like never before.

On April 26 1986, the Chernobyl nuclear plant exploded 100km north of Kiev. The initial disaster was compounded by the reluctance of the government to confess the accident. Only after nearly a week did knowledge of the event reach the very people that were in the greatest danger – the citizens of Kiev. Hundreds died from the first heavy doses of radiation, but the real tragedy lay in the countless living with chronic ailments and the thousands of deformed children born in the following months. While the power plant was a Soviet enterprise, it was located in Ukraine and the Ukrainians found that they would suffer most for it. The Soviet government proved ineffectual in remedying the situation, and Chernobyl is still Ukraine's festering sore. The ecological damage is permanent, but the long-term effects on the people are still unknown. Chernobyl did much to catalyse an already intensive rise of national awareness and anti-Soviet sentiment. These nationalist feelings grew more vocal as people tested their boldness within the parameters of *glasnost*. In the summer of 1988, thousands gathered on several occasions in Lviv and Kiev with a variety of protests, lobbying mostly for Ukrainian autonomy. It was the last time the KGB arrested anyone for being pro-Ukrainian.

All over the Soviet Union, people from every republic were speaking their mind and their message was freedom, but not necessarily independence. In September 1989, the Ukrainian nationalist party *Rukh* was founded as an opposition to the communist party in Ukraine. Soon after, Gorbachev fired Ukraine's leading communist Shcherbytsky, after realising that repression of Ukrainian self-determination only hurt his position with the other republics. In 1990, democratic elections were permitted for the first time at the republican level. The Supreme Soviet, or *Verkhovna Rada* in Ukrainian, would be open to non-communist parties.

In 1990, thousands of Ukrainian students camped out on central Kiev's newly christened Maidan Nazelezhnosti (Place of Independence) and began a hunger strike calling for swift and major changes including a stop to military service outside Ukraine and a broad nationalisation of communist party property. Joined by politicians from *Rukh*, the demonstration was successful and the changes announced in the Rada.

Meanwhile in Moscow, communist hardliners were conspiring against the liberal reforms. In August of 1991, Gorbachev was vacationing with his family in Foros, Crimea, when he was put under house arrest and a state of emergency declared for the whole Soviet Union. The ringleaders of the coup sought to put the communist party back on track and prove Gorbachev a traitor. The Ukrainian communists could either comply and fall under a supposed new dictatorship, or support the 'democrats' in the party and split the Soviet Union. The Chairman of the Rada, Leonid Kravchuk, finally denounced the coup before it failed. The collapse of the central government in Moscow left Ukrainian communists to rush for a decision on total independence and keep some aspect of authority in their own territory. The voting was almost unanimous, and on August 24 1991, Ukraine was declared independent.

After a decade as the capital of an independent country, Kiev is establishing itself as the most prosperous and developed city in Europe-conscious Ukraine, but don't expect the rest of the country to look so flashy. A host of renovations make the city skyline a little more impressive each year, and a swift improvement in guest services has increased Kiev's esteem under international scrutiny. Kiev's post-Soviet makeover relies heavily on historical references (the birthplace of Slavic Orthodoxy, Kievan Rus and the patronage of the Cossacks) as well as a few slightly fuzzy aspirations towards 'Western' culture. Indeed, it is difficult to visit the city today

History

HOW DO YOU SPELL КИЇВ IN ENGLISH?

It seems too short a word to warrant so many spellings, but new transliterations of the ancient Cyrillic name include *Kyjiv*, *Kiyiv*, *Kyiv*, and the time-honoured *Kiev* (apostrophes and silent letters add exponential combinations). The inability to canonise a correct Latin spelling stems from contested Cyrillic spellings that would denote either a Russian or Ukrainian preference. It might seem pedantic, but since both Slavic cultures claim Kiev as their founding hearth, even spelling becomes a touchy subject. In this book and in most of the English-speaking world, the capital of Ukraine is *Kiev*, but to be politically sensitive, you would spell it out as the Ukrainian *Kyiv*. If you pride yourself as a cultural purist and want to pronounce the city's name 'right', go to the central train station and listen to the robotic female announcer list all the trains departing from *Kyh-Yeev*. Whoever she is, hers is the kindly voice of government-approved Ukrainian.

Contexts

without being impressed by the past, and yet, part of Kiev's modern appeal is its changing, organic nature. A rush towards newness and global acceptance has had both fortunate and unfortunate results, and visitors should come to Kiev today with the knowledge that they are part of the changes.

POLITICS
Government

Ukraine regained independence in 1991 and now functions as a constitutional democracy, led by a president and ruled by a 450-seat parliament, the *Verkhovna Rada*. Leonid Kravchuk won the first elections in 1991 but his presidency was troubled by incredible inflation and so much public unrest that elections were brought forward, and Leonid Kuchma was voted in as the new president in 1994, then re-elected in 1999 for a second five-year term. Initially Kuchma's presidency saw some improvements in the domestic economy, but he soon sacked the strongest reformers within his government and recoiled into an oligarchic regime fraught with serious corruption scandals.

Kuchma and his chief of staff are two of the wealthiest men in Europe, and in recent years their policies have leaned towards protecting their assets. While Kuchma should technically step down in autumn 2004, there has been some fear that he would arrange to stay in power for an undetermined length of time, or else appoint a successor that would grant him immunity from prosecution – much like the Yeltsin–Putin transition of power in Russia.

Kuchma's former prime minister, Viktor Yuschenko, now leads the 'Our Ukraine' block – the opposition block in the Rada who would see a free and fair electoral process oust the stagnant government and turn Ukraine towards real pro-Western policies. In the past, a general lack of party consolidation means gaining majority support for legislation is tough (30 parties were registered for the last parliamentary elections), and now a battle for power has led to the Rada being frequently blocked in order to prevent the majority from pursuing constitutional change.

Increased repression and a lack of freedom of speech led to major demonstrations in Kiev throughout the latter half of 2002, while the international community has become increasingly concerned by Ukraine's corrupt legal process. Freedom of the press has continued to suffer, and in February 2004, the Kuchma government shut down Radio Free Europe's Ukrainian service in yet another wave of oppression towards the media. Average Ukrainians now enjoy little access to an independent press, while already feeling somewhat disillusioned by their country's overall political process.

For the past years, Kiev's day-to-day problems have been managed by Mayor Oleksander Omelchenko. Like all mayors of capital cities, Omelchenko has experienced great difficulty in juggling the city's concerns with the interests of the national government which also happens to be based in Kiev.

With such a healthy dose of scandalous politicians and electoral apathy, Ukraine's political circus is not too different from most – only slightly less sophisticated in tactic. These early years of democratisation are an exciting time of change for Ukraine, and you are likely to see some form of politics up close and personal during your visit. Also keep in mind that Ukrainians do enjoy candid political discussion and will want to hear your impressions as a foreigner.

Contexts

Security

Ukraine has always occupied a difficult position in the world as the country is wedged between the superpower Russia, the expanding European Union and the Middle East. After independence from the Soviet Union, Ukraine sought distance from Russia through EU and NATO membership, but the process was delayed for lack of preparedness and lack of any real reform. Now it seems that Ukraine recognises the need for some partnership with Russia and the two countries continue their troubled friendship after putting to rest disputes regarding control over the prized Black Sea fleet and arrears in energy payments.

Ukraine signed an agreement with the United States in 1994 to get rid of its nuclear arsenal in return for US$1 billion in aid. The NATO–Ukraine charter was signed in 1997 as a treaty of co-operation in conflict prevention, but relations turned sour in 2002 when it was discovered that President Kuchma had illegally sold a Kolchuga nuclear-missile-detection system to Iraq. Ukraine still holds a sizeable arsenal of small arms, which, with the country's poor economic situation may give confidence to illegal arms dealers who fuel worldwide civil conflicts. This black mark on Ukraine's reputation was overlooked by some one year later when Ukraine declared itself a member of the US-led 'coalition of the willing' in Iraq, and sent soldiers to the Middle East.

ECONOMY

Within the context of the much larger Soviet Union, Ukraine was a highly co-dependent economy. The Ukrainian SSR produced raw industrial material and grain in exchange for the consumer goods and energy of the other republics, namely Russia. After independence, the country was left to its own devices in the global marketplace, hoping that a swift liberalisation would only effect a temporary inconvenience. Unlike Poland, where a year of 'shock therapy' was followed by steady economic growth, Ukrainians often claim they got the shock without the therapy.

The early 1990s were harsh years for Ukraine. A lack of institutional reform meant the command government continued to command with little regard for the 'invisible hand' of the free market. Because so many people had worked for the Soviet military industry or for factories producing uncompetitive goods, output collapsed and unemployment soared. Those who continued to work would sometimes go eight months (or more) without getting paid. In order to deal with these debts, the government simply printed more money, so that between 1993 and 1994 inflation reached 10,000%. Of all the former Soviet republics at the time, Ukraine was the poorest, and for a while even Russian roubles were coveted currency.

Shuffling through the pages of horrific statistics, international organisations bewailed Ukraine's impending doom, and yet people somehow survived year after year. Suddenly the experts began referring to Ukraine's pervasive shadow economy which encompassed elusive forms of black-market activity and the more innocent system of *blat*, a longstanding custom of exchanging favours for goods or services. Today, it is estimated that over half of Ukraine's money is kept outside the banking system.

Blatant corruption is also to blame for Ukraine's continuous economic setbacks. For a while, foreign investors completely stopped working in Ukraine due to the level of bureaucracy and criminal activity. There is some truth to stories about IMF and World Bank loans ending up in Swiss bank accounts since certain Ukrainian politicians have become internationally recognised billionaires overnight. At a lower level, some mafia-like organised crime groups rule large business networks in former industrial capitals. 'Privatisation' of Ukraine's economy constituted a few men divvying up Ukraine's natural resources and creating industrial monopolies. These oligarchs still control much of Ukraine's natural wealth and the country receives little benefit from sales of these exports.

The hrivna was introduced in September 1996 as the new currency by the then Prime Minister Viktor Yuschenko, and in the last few years has remained stable. Less corruption and the streamlining of Soviet-like bureaucracies would help to improve the economy, but things are much better today than they were five years ago. In 2002 Ukraine ranked 80th (out of 173) in the United Nations Development Programme's (UNDP) Human Development Index, up 20 places from the previous year. In 1998, Ukraine's GDP per capita was only US$750 a year and today the figure has risen to US$4,000; however actual distribution of wealth is another matter as pensions and wages are still extremely low. In January 2003, a bill was passed to increase the minimum monthly wage from 185UAH (US$34) to 237UAH (US$45), but a decent, livable salary in Kiev would be around US$300 a month. Pensioners and dependents on the state still suffer most, and many must supplement their incomes by doing physical labour. Early 2004 saw continued demonstrations for a rise in the minimum wage.

Economy

The most positive change has been tax law reform, which has sparked a nationwide movement of entrepreneurs. For nearly a decade, small businesses were subject to random tax collections that favoured the corrupt and bankrupted start-ups. Now, the new laws only require business owners to pay a base fee every month, after which they keep all profits. It seems simple, but the change has been revolutionary for Ukraine and now you will see all types of private enterprises flourishing, though most are less than three years old. Ukrainians who emigrated to the USA, Britain, or Portugal have also begun to return with hard currency in hand, ready to start businesses or invest, but despite any external show of prosperity, life is a day-to-day struggle for most. The adults you will meet have probably seen their life savings disappear and have gone hungry (or seen their children go hungry), but Ukrainians are survivors at heart and pulling through tough times is nothing new.

As Ukraine's capital and biggest city, Kiev has been the largest recipient of foreign direct investment, government spending, and developmental aid. 'Business' has become a primary occupation, and you'll notice the city is buzzing with a recent workaholic fever that seems slightly out of place in comparison with the rest of the country. Kiev natives are busy with commerce.

PEOPLE

Anyone who's been to Ukraine knows that getting to know people is far more important than visiting any prescribed sights. Long after you've forgotten the name of some church you saw in the city, you will recall individuals and their stories, even

Contexts

if your conversations were carried on by made-up sign language. Kiev's inhabitants are far more fascinating than most of the stuff that gets pointed out to you from a tour-bus window.

Kyivlyanin refers to all who call Kiev home, a diverse gathering of three million people who share a firm attachment to these twisted streets on the Dnepr's banks. The population is more exotic than it thinks it is – come with few expectations but watch closely. Kiev's native species include bleary-eyed government officials, cunning taxi drivers, disinterested soldiers, fragile grandmothers, quiet protestors, amateur fashion models, lively street artists, passionate students, thick-necked *byznessmeny*, Roma fortune tellers, picture-perfect families, black-cloaked monks, and a lot of free-roaming kids. (Add to the landscape a new breed of ex-pats and immigrants from all over the world.)

Whereas Ukraine is traditionally known as a land of rural peasants, the capital has always embodied the exception to that rule. Kiev has been home to Ukraine's urban elite from the very beginning – a favoured attitude that flourishes to this day. Despite any disparaging view the uninitiated may hold towards Kiev (Soviet, grey, and miserable), the city has been chasing its style ever since independence. You'll find that people here truly appreciate fine things, be it art, music, or expensive designer clothing. They like going out to the theatre, the movies, to eat, and to simply *gulyat* – a verb that includes every activity from leisurely strolling through a park to slam dancing in a nightclub. A tendency towards melodrama makes the day-to-day a little more exciting in Kiev.

People

GRANNIES

Out and about in Kiev, and in all sorts of weather, you'll see an abundance of old ladies engaged in hard labour, digging holes, sweeping streets, carrying Atlas-sized bundles, and fervently selling things. Why so many grannies? In World War II, the Soviet Union lost over 20 million citizens, the majority of whom were male soldiers. Their sisters, widows and mothers survived, and now make up the majority of the elderly population. No other demographic group in Ukraine has endured as much as these women. After the devastation of the war, they spent their 20s and 30s rebuilding the country, and the rest of their working years keeping the USSR going. They retired just in time for Ukrainian independence and then watched their entire pension devalued repeatedly. Today, most female pensioners receive around US$30 a month and are left with no other choice but to go back to work. Enterprising grannies in their 70s and 80s have had to find ways to supplement their income, usually through very hard work. Many will sell roasted sunflower seeds, flowers, herbs and anything else out on the street. Others undertake hard-labour jobs that pay little but at least pay, and it is not uncommon to see old women carrying pickaxes, shovels or large buckets to a construction site or through the market. *Bábushka* (grandmother) is the respectful term used to address all elderly women (*babulya* or *babusya* in

Ukrainain, or simply *baba*). *Babushki* hold a vital role in Ukrainian culture and society, since most young mothers are expected to work, and traditionally, young married couples live with the bride's parents. In consequence, nearly all Ukrainian children are raised by their grandmothers. Naturally, Ukrainians think fondly of their grandmothers, and will constantly quote them as a source of wisdom. Grandmothers are responsible for telling grandchildren stories, teaching them folk songs, religion and how to dance. Perhaps detrimental to their own image, grandmothers warn recalcitrant grandchildren of *baba yaga*, an evil grandmother witch who eats children and lives in a house with chicken legs deep in the Ukrainian forest (it works to keep children in their beds).

Grannies also feel compelled to feed others: their families and their guests. Nothing compares to the privilege of eating a meal prepared by a real live *babushka*. For visitors to Ukraine, grannies also present a rare access to living history. Most have lived under the Stalinist regime, some have fought as partisans, and others have built tanks in factories or conducted scientific research in Siberia. They *all* know how to survive. Buying their sunflower seeds or flowers is a nice way to keep the grandmothers in business and if you ever want to give a gift, just think of what your own grandmother would like.

City slickers or not, all Ukrainians live closely to the earth. Every season has meaning, as does the blossoming of each plant. Like the rest of the country, Kiev's inhabitants tend to smallholdings outside the city (*pod kievom*) where they live in small summer cottages (*dacha*) and grow vegetables. Until recently, most Kievans survived the winter by eating food they had produced themselves, and many still do. Pick out any random, middle-aged man or woman off the street in Kiev, and they'll have a firmer grasp of organic farming than their counterparts in Paris or Moscow.

Families play a key role in Ukrainian life. Members of an extended family depend on one another as a strong support network that goes far beyond the limitations of the West's independence and rugged individualism. Grandparents may raise children, young people look after the elderly and food and cash are shared all around. As with so many societies, Ukrainian families vest their resources and brightest hopes in the young.

Ukrainians like to have a good time by eating and drinking, singing songs, and telling stories and jokes. They like to talk lots and most have a natural intellectual bent that's manifest in their conversational musings. By custom, Ukrainians are very hospitable and will gladly open their home to a stranger they have only just met and trusted. Guests are always offered some sort of refreshment – at least tea, if not a meal. You may think that as a foreigner, your presence in Kiev is routine, but most Ukrainians are keen to engage with the outside world, which you represent. Talking to random people brings them the satisfaction of learning and friendship, and should do the same for you.

Contexts

RELIGION
Orthodoxy

For most Ukrainians, Orthodoxy and nationality are one and the same, a dual force that has come to define Kiev, especially during the present Ukrainian renaissance. Ukrainian Orthodoxy asserts that theirs is the original Church of ancient Kievan Rus, brought to them by the Apostle Andrew, and that the union of Slavic culture and Christianity was destined to occur in Ukraine. By nature, Ukrainian Orthodoxy is also highly mystical and meditative, and Ukrainians employ the outer rituals of prayer, fast and iconography as methods towards a deeper spiritual process. The religion's philosophy is based largely on the writings of the early Christians and Gnostics of the wider Middle East, as well as a millennium of Slavic monastic work.

Orthodox **saints** (*svyaty*) are the holiest of religious symbols and most churches will hold at least one body of a saint, a physical remnant or an icon. Different saints perform different functions; for instance, Nikolai the Miracle Worker is popular in times of need or emergency. People will visit his icon in the church, pray to it and post a candle near it. Posting candles is both a sign of faith and an offering, and every church will sell different sizes of long beeswax candles for different degrees of prayer.

Icons are central to Orthodox worship and are much more than a picture of a favourite saint. Painted on wood or covered with gold and silver-plating, blessed icons carry holy powers of protection, healing and fortune. Believers visit and pray to icons in churches and monasteries and most taxi or bus drivers will keep an icon on their rear-view mirror or dashboard to protect their vehicle from accidents. In homes, icons are placed in the top of the farthest corner opposite the door of a room to bless and protect the family's space.

Traditional Orthodox church buildings are built in the shape of a Greek cross. Those from the Byzantine era were made of stone with the typical rounded domes of the period (like St Sophia's in Kiev). Kiev's wooden churches were lost to invasion and stone construction, but in other parts of Ukraine, and in Kiev's Pirogov village, traditional churches from the 15th to the 17th centuries are usually built from wooden beams criss-crossed in log cabin style and fitted only with joints and pegs (no nails). Younger cathedrals are larger and made of stone, brick and mosaic with the onion-shaped domes normally associated with Orthodoxy. On the inside, most churches have a highly decorated *iconostas*, covered with images of the saints and closing off the back apse of the church. Only priests are allowed behind this sacred wall.

A normal Orthodox Sunday mass lasts about two and a half hours. Prayers are chanted and a small choir sings out chilling responses while aromatic *ladan* (incense) smoke fills the church. You'll notice there are no chairs inside, and that is because it is a sin to pray or worship sitting down. Instead, believers will stand or periodically prostrate themselves on the ground. All-night vigils and extra-long church services are not unusual, and the faithful will continue to stand for up to seven hours. Shorter services during morning and evening weekdays are easier times to visit. Taking part in an Orthodox church service is an amazing experience and travellers should make it a priority during their stay in Kiev. The problem is that most churches do not appreciate having tourists running around untethered during a sacrament. Only visit churches with a spirit of reverence: men should remove their hats and women are supposed to cover their heads. Even if the church's interior is beautiful, taking photographs indoors (especially during a service) is very offensive. You can avoid conspicuousness by buying a candle and lighting it in front of your favourite icon as you are walking around the church.

The Soviet era was a time of severe religious repression, and Kiev's religious skyline was severely damaged during the reigns of Stalin and Khrushchev. Today however, Orthodoxy has become the most important sign of Ukrainian patriotism and independence, so that although society tends to divides itself among *verushy* and *neverushy* (believers and non-believers), the allegiance to Orthodoxy and country transcends theistic beliefs and the churches are remarkably full. Kiev's oldest churches were the first to be rebuilt and remodelled, so that much of the religious architecture that tourists will see in Kiev was only renovated in the last five years. Historically, Ukraine has always been considered a very spiritual country (within the context of Russian Orthodoxy). In the USSR, Ukraine had more churches than all the other republics put together and a majority of Orthodox clergymen were Ukrainian. Kiev's Pechersky Lavra (Caves Monastery) is considered by many as the holiest site in Russian/Ukrainian Orthodoxy, and in 2004 Russian President Vladimir Putin made a highly publicised pilgrimage to the Caves to pray and light candles to the Orthodox saints. In terms of numbers of physical churches, Ukrainian

Religion

Orthodoxy is the largest Orthodox Church in the world, however three separate Ukrainian Churches consider themselves the Ukrainian Orthodox Church, and the government recognises four:

Ukrainian Orthodox Church (Moscow Patriarchate)

Throughout the Russian Empire and the Soviet Union, 'the Church' and 'Christianity' fell under the jurisdiction of Moscow, taking on a very political structure. After independence, the Ukrainian Orthodox Church that still recognised Moscow's ecclesiastical authority was named as such, and it is still the largest Church in the country today. Followers exist all over, but the Church's presence is largest in Russian-speaking areas of the east and Crimea, although it still owns churches throughout the country. Traditionally, all services are read in Old Church Slavonic. The Moscow-allegiant Church owns and has its headquarters at Kiev's Caves Monastery, a point of dispute for Ukraine's other Orthodox groups.

Ukrainian Orthodox Church (Kiev Patriarchate)

In an attempt to break away from Russian influence after independence, the Ukrainian Metropolitan (with the government's help) formed an independent Orthodox Church in 1992 with the intent to offer a centrist version of Ukrainian culture that coincided with the political movement towards Ukrainian unity. The Moscow Patriarch excommunicated the Kiev Patriarch for his rebellion and both Churches still bicker about property and territory. St Mikhayil's Monastery of the

Golden Domes and St Vladimir's Cathedral in Kiev are this Church's most prominent pieces of real estate.

Greek Catholics (Uniate)

During the centuries of Polish rule in western Ukraine, the Orthodox believers made a symbolic compromise in order to appease the government and preserve their culture. The Ruthenians agreed to pay allegiance to the Pope in Rome, but they would keep their Ukrainian Orthodox doctrine and service. The Church was made illegal in 1946 but officially reinstated when Gorbachev met with the Pope in 1989. Greek Catholic beliefs tend towards a mixture of old Byzantine and Galician folk culture with the traditional Catholic catechism. Concentrated in western Ukraine and the Carpathians, Greek Catholics tend to promote a strong nationalist culture. As yet, there is no official presence of this Church in Kiev, and the Church is headquartered at St George's Cathedral in Lviv. To identify a Greek Catholic church, look for any tapestry or picture of the Pope and the absence of the habitual Orthodox iconostas. In western Ukraine, Roman Catholics are called 'Polish Catholics'.

Ukrainian Autocephalous Orthodox Church (UAOC)

During the window of Ukrainian independence at the time of the Russian Civil War, nationally conscious Ukrainian believers sought autocephaly (self-rule) from the Russian Church, believing they should be able to worship in their own language. The

Church was formed in 1919, but later fell victim to Stalin's early repression of nationalities and was declared illegal in 1930. The Autocephalous survived in exile, mainly through the Ukrainian Diaspora in North America, although the Church was said to meet frequently in western Ukraine in clandestine forest gatherings. The state gave official recognition to the Church in 1993 but there is little visible presence in Kiev. Like the Greek Catholic, the Autocephalous is concentrated in western Ukraine and is known as the most nationalist of Ukraine's Churches.

Other beliefs

Kiev's Jewish heritage dates back to the 10th century and has always been an important element in Kiev's historical experience, while Kiev has been an important point in Jewish experience. Many scholars believe that Judaism came to Europe from the Middle East via Ukraine. In the 19th century there were over three million Jews in Ukraine, while today there remain about 250,000, about half of whom live in Kiev. Jewish religious life centres around Kiev's two main working synagogues (see pages 259–60).

As a modern capital, Ukraine's other religions all have some official presence in Kiev city. Baptists constitute Ukraine's traditional form of evangelical Christianity, brought by missionaries over a hundred years ago, and since independence, Ukraine has seen a flood of missionary activity and a significant rise in religious pluralism, so that most western-Christian denominations have established churches in the city. Islam holds a visible presence in Crimea, a minority which Kiev officially accepts. Among certain groups of Ukrainians, Slavic paganism has also come back into open practice, although with due respect, most Ukrainian spirituality is already deeply rooted in early pagan practices.

The supernatural

Despite a national pride of all things scientific and factual, a world of superstition rules the lives of many Ukrainians. Be prepared to pick up a few of your own during your travels.

Orthodoxy and the trappings of organised religion have done little to hide the Ukrainian cultural connection between the natural and supernatural spheres, and between the pagan and Christian. According to Ukrainian tradition, all forms of nature have a spiritual personality: there are spirits in the fields and in the trees and evil water nymphs in the rivers called *rusalky*. The spiritual world can either help or harm, but most people just notice the harm.

The *nechysta sila* (unclean power) is the cause of all wickedness, evil and human woes and can only be avoided through spiritual *zaschyta* (protection) that stems from a combination of Christian and pagan customs. In rural Ukraine, for example, during Christmas an axe is placed outside the door to ward off evil spirits. The headache of supernatural ailments is the evil eye, which can affect you in a number of ways: depression, fatigue, toothache, quarrelling with your spouse, bad luck or spoiled food. Wicked people can pass on the evil eye just by looking at you, as can nice people who simply look at you in the wrong way (with jealousy or

Religion

condescension). The best protection against the evil eye is by wearing small mirrors under your clothing (front and back) that reflect 'the eye' back to the sender.

Ekstrasensa is the Ukrainian/Russian version of spiritual foresight or ESP. The gifted (usually older women and *babushki*) can look into the future and work things for or against someone's favour through black or white magic. Rituals are based on physical manifestations of metaphysical ideas and usually involve Orthodox icons, bibles and crosses. The use of herbal medicine is also normally combined with some sort of supernatural healing or with the help of 'bio-energy'.

Sophisticated and cosmopolitan Kiev may seem immune to backwoods folklore, but stay in the area long enough, and you'll discover this city adheres to its own version of dealing with life's uncertainties.

CULTURE AND FESTIVALS
Symbols

Ukraine's official coat of arms is a gold **trident** (*tryzub*) on a blue field, probably linked to the Greek god of the sea, Poseidon. Prince Rurik of Kievan Rus was said to use the same symbol and old coins and bricks from the period of Prince Vladimir are also decorated with the trident. In the small bursts of independence in 1918 and in the Carpathians during 1939, the trident was re-adopted to show separatism from ruling powers. During the late Soviet period, nationalist demonstrators would flash 'trident' hand symbols with their three middle fingers held apart. The national emblem was made official in 1992. You will see it everywhere and on everything.

Plants, animals and trees are also important symbols for Ukrainians. The **sunflower** has always been used to represent Ukraine, and if you visit in summer, you will see why. The *lipa* (lime tree or linden) is considered the most important and symbolic of Ukrainian trees, and Ukrainians use the flowers and leaves for all kinds of herbal remedies. The **sickle** of the Soviet flag actually comes from Ukraine where it has always been an important symbol of the country's traditional agricultural lifestyle. Ukraine's own **flag** does look a lot like the Ukrainian landscape: a light blue sky over a golden field of wheat or sunflowers. The origins however date back to the Habsburg monarchy in 1848 when the Supreme Ruthenian Council adopted the flag of a golden lion on a blue background. The lion eventually disappeared but the colours stayed. Cossack flags were generally red and white, and various nationalist peasant and anarchist bands have used banners of red, green and black. The original flag of Kiev differs from all others and pictures the Archangel Michael with sword in hand, an important symbol of the holy warrior defending Kiev, the seat of Christianity, against heathen invasion.

National dress

The Ukrainian national costume is typically worn only for festivals and ceremonies (like weddings) but is the prominent display of culture for many. Traditionally, women wear a white embroidered tunic over which a scarlet woven *platya* (skirt) is wrapped and secured with a colourful belt. The ensemble is completed with leather boots, a flowered head wreath with long coloured ribbons and several red,

THE UKRAINIAN CALENDAR

Names for the months in Ukrainian bear no relevance to the Roman calendar, although Russian has adapted the Latin names. The Ukrainian year follows nature's tempo as a simple but poetic remark to earth's changes.

English	Ukrainian	Root & meaning
January	Sichen	*cut*; a cutting wind
February	Lyuti	*fierce*; cold and biting
March	Berezen	*birch*; the birch forests begin to bud
April	Kviten	*flowers* blossom
May	Traven	the *grass* grows
June	Cherven	*worms* crawl from the earth
July	Lypen	the *lime tree* blossoms; flowers are collected for tea
August	Serpen	*sickle*; the harvest begins
September	Veresen	the *heather* blossoms
October	Zhovten	*yellow*; wheat fields and forest leaves turn yellow
November	Lystopad	literally, *falling leaves*
December	Hruden	*balls* of snow fall

Contexts

clay, beaded necklaces. Men wear baggy Cossack-style trousers tucked into low boots, a long silk sash belt and the traditional *rubakha*, an open cotton shirt with intricate embroidery around the neck. A recent fad has Ukrainian businessmen substituting the sober shirt and tie of the West with the more colourful *rubakha*.

Rural folk costumes aside, Kiev's inhabitants have insisted on becoming total victims to fashion. Year round, Boulevard Khreschatyk serves as a catwalk on which artistic and stunning (and sometimes disastrous) combinations of leather, lace and fur are paraded before the more modest elements of the public. Enjoy the show, as this is Kiev's national dress in the making.

Art

Kiev has long been the home of struggling artists and passionate painters, but with Kiev's political past, few have made it into Western art's hall of fame. Today, Kiev's art world is becoming an important centre for creative expression.

Classic romantic painting did not feature as strongly in Ukraine as it did among the European élite of Paris and St Petersburg, but there are a few important exceptions. Repin and Aivozovsky are the most renowned Ukrainian painters, and you'll find most art museums have at least one of their pieces, along with well-intentioned collections of other Ukrainian-themed paintings. Soviet Ukrainian propaganda is only now being widely considered an art form, with its colourful posters and sober messages. A few permanent exhibits of Soviet artwork exist in Kiev and some souvenir shops also sell prints.

The most traditional form of Ukrainian painting is that of a floral motif, usually painted on black lacquered platters or, in some areas, around the doorways and windows of homes. Colours are always bright, and the designs symmetrical and full.

Although religious in significance, icon-painting is very much the ultimate Ukrainian form of rendering human images. Figures or faces of Christ, Mary, the Apostles and Saints are painted on wood and sometimes decorated with gold. Important Orthodox icon-painting schools existed in Kiev, which have set the standard for most Slavic icon imagery today. Many famous icons are attributed to either Kiev's Vydubytsky or Caves Monastery. In homes, icons are placed in the corner of a room, usually opposite the door, and a small sheaf of wheat is placed underneath to ensure peace and prosperity for that home. Traditionally, this sheaf was cut from the last sheaf of good grain and tied with a ribbon during *Obzhynky*, the Harvest Festival.

Handicrafts

Ukraine's greatest artistic expression comes alive in the everyday experience of work and survival. For example, the large tile stoves of traditional Ukrainian homes were always the warmest part of the house. In winter, a family would spend most of the day (and night) on top of the warmed tiles. For a few centuries, painted stove tiles were revered as a high art form.

Eggs hold all kinds of symbolic meanings for Ukrainians, and eggs are often used in fortune-telling and folk cures. The quintessential Ukrainian craft is the decoration of **pysanky,** or Easter eggs. After blowing out the contents through a small hole in the shell, melted wax and different coloured dyes are used in a batik-like process to produce a layered pattern of intricate designs. Traditional patterns are usually geometric or show basic representations of flowers or animals. Like all Ukrainian art, *pysanky* vary from region to region, and the craft has been kept alive largely by the Diaspora.

Rushniki are the most basic art-form in Ukraine but the most widespread in tradition. Calling them 'hand towels' doesn't do them justice, although technically that's what they are. The long white cloths are embroidered with bands on either end in simple geometric patterns. Traditional designs and colours differ by region. Mothers are supposed to embroider *rushniki* for their sons before they leave home, and a young bride will be sure to embroider enough for her trousseau. In Ukrainian homes, the cloths are used for special occasions: holiday meals, for holding newborn children or for a christening, for weddings, for welcoming guests with bread and salt, and for shrouds at funerals. In many Ukrainian churches, *rushniki* are draped over the icons and altars.

Rather than cover the whole piece of material, Ukrainian embroidery only decorates the edges of simple white cloth with colourful geometric designs crossstitched around the wrists, hems and neckline. Designs vary, but besides triangular and diagonal shapes, crosses, flowers and leaves are traditional. In the Carpathians, animal shapes hold special meaning.

Ukrainian woodcarving is either intentionally crude and rough, or else incredibly refined and inlaid with beads or shells. Small shaped boxes and lids are customary, along with bowls, plates, spoons, combs and pipes. Pottery is another important Ukrainian folk-art form. Black, charcoal-fired pots are traditional.

Literature

Taras Shevchenko is Ukraine's national hero and eternal poet laureate who wrote *Kobzar*, esteemed as the greatest written work in the Ukrainian language. His statue and portrait are ubiquitous and, as a rule, children memorise his poetry at school. Nikolai Gogol, who wrote *Dead Souls* and *An Inspector Calls* is better known in the West. His short stories take place in Ukraine's countryside and describe well the superstitious world of Ukrainians. Lesya Ukrayinka, whose pen-name means 'Ukrainian forest', started the writers' circle called the 'Pleiades' and wrote lyrical poetry in Ukrainian while there was a ban on the language. Most cities have streets named after her, if not a memorial. Writers like Kotlyarevsky and Kotsyubinsky also wrote during a time of linguistic repression and their homes now stand as national shrines. Ukrainian literary canon also includes Russian writers like Pushkin and Chekhov who wrote and lived in Ukraine for part of their lives. Ukrainians hold writers in high esteem and every town will boast about the famous men and women who might have stayed there. Few people know that the English/Polish writer Joseph Conrad was actually born in Ukraine, and Balzac spent a good deal of time in the country. Kiev was also home to writers Isaac Babel and Mikhail Bulgakov, and the latter's novel *The White Guard* re-tells life in Kiev during the Russian Civil War.

Contexts

Ukraine enjoys a 98% literacy rate and the people enjoy reading. Writing and reciting poetry is also a national hobby. Owning books is a status symbol and most individuals harbour vast libraries in the smallest of apartments with Ukrainian, Russian and international literature. Soviet culture also permitted the reading of approved Western writers, namely Ernest Hemingway, John Steinbeck, Jack London and Sir Arthur Conan Doyle, so you will hear them mentioned often.

Folk dancing

At weddings, holidays, festivals or any day, dancing is a very important part of celebrating. Folk dances are normally conducted by large groups of paired couples, but different dances have evolved from specific regional terrains. The wide spread of the Ukrainian steppe influenced the unique style of folk dancing that involves running, leaping and people forming extensive circles. Dances from the mountainous Carpathians are performed in small circles and involve more fancy footwork and jumping on the spot. Ukraine's national dance is the *hopak*, a very energetic ensemble where women spin and encircle the men, who perform a number of difficult acrobatic stunts in the front, including the well-known squat kicks and split jumps of the Cossacks. Traditional Cossack dances excluded women and the *hopak* was originally a stage for physical competition between the warriors. Now, nearly every folk dance performance will include at least part of the *hopak* in a charged mood of dancing, clapping and very fast music. Larger folk dance troupes tend to be based in Kiev, western Ukraine and around Poltava, where so many Ukrainian dances originated.

Music

Ukrainians sing when they are very happy and when they are very sad. It seems as though the centuries of upheaval favoured the preservation of songs to any other kind of material culture, and if there is anything that brings Ukrainians together, it is their music. Today most Ukrainians sing at large gatherings: birthday parties, weddings and holidays. Once started, they can sing for hours and everyone in the room (of all ages) will know all the lyrics and the accompanying harmony.

The traditional Ukrainian instrument is the large tear-shaped *bandura,* normally with 60 strings. Strummed like a harp and tuned like a guitar, the *bandura's* music has an enchanting sound. Once played by the Cossacks, today you see buskers playing them in the streets and subway stations. Traditionally, blind children were taught to play and sing historical and religious songs in order that they might have an occupation. Named *kobzari* for the lute-like *kobzar* they played, these bards walked from village to village playing on request in exchange for food and alms. Many of the songs you hear date back to the era of the *kobzari* with a series of short stanzas that tell a staggered story, sometimes through dialogue. It is not uncommon for a set tune to have over a dozen verses, with repeated choruses in between. The music is always in a minor key, which adds a melancholy tone.

Ukrainian folk songs are normally about love, vodka, or love and vodka. Some are ironic and humorous, but most are wistful or solemn. *'Kozak Viyizhdzhaye'* is the dialogue of a weeping girl and her Cossack, who is about to ride off into the unprotected 'wild field' of Ukraine. She begs to go with him, and in each verse he asks her what she will eat, where she will sleep, what she will do in far off Ukraine? In '*Oi Verbo, Verbo!*' a young maiden sings to a weeping willow tree, telling of her betrothal to the town drunkard and her plans to run away on a horse. Today, most people sing with a classic Russian guitar, accordion or without any accompaniment. Soviet folk songs also add to the national repertoire, and almost every adult male can sing you a song about being homesick and lonely out on the eastern front.

If you want to buy some good folk music, check the tables on the Maidan Nezalezhnosti in Kiev. Most of these sellers are from western Ukraine and are showing their patriotism by acquainting tourists with Ukrainian culture. Mariya Burmaka is one of the greatest Ukrainian folk singers, and her earlier cassettes add a fitting soundtrack to the landscape. Nina Matviyenko is best known for her haunting voice and pre-Christian folksongs, and most music dealers will have her recordings, as well as those of folk singer Mariya Mykolaychyk.

Traditional religious music is integral to Ukrainian culture and there are few sounds more celestial than an Orthodox choir singing. The singers normally stand in a small balcony at the back of the church by the entrance and respond to the priest throughout the service. Most churches and monasteries will have recordings of Orthodox chants and singing for sale.

Ukraine's national anthem is entitled '*She Ne Vmerla Ukrayina*' ('Ukraine is yet alive') and is meant to reinforce the country's perseverance through suffering. The anthem is played morning and night on the national radio station in the same fashion as the old Soviet anthem.

Ukrainian pop music is going full force in its artistic licence, sometimes mixing folk elements into modern beats. I recommend Iryna Bilyk, and of course Ruslana, who won the Eurovision Song contest for Ukraine in 2004. The Russian techno music you hear in taxis, marketplaces and long bus rides has a giveaway polka bass line that will stay in your head long after you've left the country.

Holidays

Most traditional Ukrainian holidays fit into a meticulous Orthodox calendar which changes from year to year. **Easter** is the most important of these holidays, and in Ukrainian Orthodoxy, believers will fast for the Lenten period by abstaining from meat and dairy products. All-night church services (standing!) and ritual parades around the church at midnight mark the beginning of the *Velyky Dehn* ('Great Day') and the festivities begin. Tall, yeasty sweet cakes called *paskhy* are baked at home and then brought in to the priest for blessing, along with other food and decorated Easter eggs. The traditional greeting is *Yisus Voskres!* ('Christ is Risen!'), to which you are expected to reply *Va Istynno Voskres!* ('Truly, He is Risen!')

Ukrainian **Christmas** is a colourful and mystical holiday, celebrated quite differently from most Christian cultures. On Christmas Eve, a single youth will travel from house to house singing *kolyadki,* cheerful Ukrainian carols to wish a good evening and good health to neighbours and friends. Singers will stand beneath the main window of the house brandishing large sacks and continue singing loudly until the window is opened and the homeowner drops Christmas treats into the bags. The practice goes on well into the night. In the home, a meal of 12 dishes is often served to symbolise the 12 Apostles. A single candle is set inside a special braided bread loaf called *kolach* and the family eats *kutya*, a semi-sweet mixture of cooked wheat, honey and poppy seeds eaten only on Christmas Eve.

New Year became the most important holiday of the year during the Soviet era, where emphasis on the first of January detracted from any national or religious recognition of Orthodox Christmas on the seventh. Christmas trees (*yolka* in Russian, *yalynka* in Ukrainian) are put up for New Year and children receive gifts from *Dyed Moroz* (Father Frost) who wears dark blue robes and is accompanied by his helper, the princess *Snigorichka* (Little Snowflake). The evening is marked by a gigantic meal that is meant to last all night long with heavy drinking, singing and dancing (in that order).

In Kiev, the public display of holidays in the city centre reflects massive Soviet-style celebrations. During the combined winter holiday of Christmas and New Year, Kiev gets decked out in lights, a giant Christmas tree is set up near the Maidan Nezalezhnosti, and staged amusements go on for weeks beforehand. Wintry music gets blared through the streets by loudspeaker and then the whole city shuts down for two weeks.

Ukraine's most important summer holiday takes place on midsummer's eve from July 6 until the morning of July 7, but is not hugely celebrated in Kiev. **Ivana Kupala** began as the pagan festival in honour of the deity of the summer, *Kupalo*, but the holiday's connotation was shifted towards Christianity's John the Baptist, hence *Ivana* (St John's) *Kupala* (Bathing) and the festival's common translation St

Culture and festivals

John's Eve. Ritual cleansing through fire and water are the main objectives of the evening. In the early evening, medicinal herbs are gathered and couples search for a special fern that is meant to promise them happiness. Unmarried women are supposed to weave a head wreath of leaves and flowers (*vynok*), place a candle in its centre, and set it into a flowing river. If the wreath floats, she will be married within the next year, if it sinks she will not (*vynok* symbolises love and protection, from whence comes the Ukrainian word for marriage, *vynchaniya*). During the night of Ivana Kupala, participants immerse themselves completely in a lake or stream, and then later, a roaring bonfire is lit and men and women hold hands and leap over the flames. The fire is meant to heal all ailments, and the couples who keep their clasp held through the flames will stay together. Ukrainians celebrate Ivana Kupala more than any other pre-Christian holiday.

The summer holiday to witness in Kiev is Ukrainian **Independence Day**, on August 24. The deliberate spectacle of parades, fanfare, banners, folk music and long speeches is a real celebration, but has also become a serious time for political reflection in these early years of independent Ukraine's history in the making.

The Soviet holidays of May 1 (Labour Day) and May 9 (Victory Day) are still widely celebrated with big military parades and fireworks. November 7 (October Revolution) is recognised but most businesses stay open. May 8 (International Women's Day) is celebrated much like Mother's Day in the West. Flowers and cards are presented to women of all ages, and men are supposed to cook for their wives/mothers/girlfriends/sisters. Several other holidays have been born from a combination of current political exigencies for Ukrainian-ness in the city, traditional or Orthodox cultural roots, and the lustre of Soviet fanfare. For example, *Maslinitsya*, the Orthodox equivalent of Shrove Tuesday comes in February, and in Kiev, the whole city comes out to eat pancakes in the streets and hear folk songs. Mourning for the Great Famine of 1932–33 (*Holodomor*) has also become an annual event in Kiev.

Weekends are also an important celebration for Kiev, and a lot of people come down to the centre to *gulyat* – stroll through the streets and hang out. The main street of Khreschatyk is closed from 12.00 to 22.00 on Saturday, from 10.00 to 21.00 on Sunday, and becomes quite busy as a pedestrian zone packed with balloon sellers, outdoor performers and shoppers.

GEOGRAPHY AND WEATHER

Kiev's very beginnings and continual existence can be attributed to its position as a free-moving crossroads of land, river, and sea routes between Europe, Asia and the Middle East. Ukraine's natural landscape comprises a vast steppe that rises and falls with only the slightest change in elevation. The Dnepr river runs south, dividing the country into two equal halves – Ukraine's traditional left and right bank territories (judged by the reference point of someone facing south). The city of Kiev spans both sides of these steep banks at a point where the river passes through several narrow channels that swirl around a series of flat sandy islands. Kiev's complex physical geography has granted the city its steep winding streets and famous

UKRAINE VERSUS RUSSIA

Ukraine is NOT Russia. Just like Canada is not America, and Scotland is not England, Ukraine is too often defined by the shadow of its powerful neighbour, Russia. The last decade exhibits Ukraine's longest recognised independence, attributed by many to keeping Russia at bay in the post-Soviet era. In Ukraine, attitudes towards Russia range from friendly association to deep animosity, although most families embody the microcosm of a bi-national relationship: one parent might be Russian, the other is Ukrainian, and relatives can be found on both sides of the border. In general, the two countries are neither too distantly related for total cultural separation, nor different enough to make it difficult to get along.

For now, Ukraine's recognised independence from Russia is the most important fact in the relationship and many Ukrainians now embrace everything that sets Ukraine apart from Russia. People will be quick to tell you that Russian civilisation was actually founded in Kiev, that Ukrainian is the older and more sophisticated Slavic language, and that famous Russian writers, or great Soviet leaders, were born and bred in Ukraine. Ukrainians like to consider their homeland inhabited by the more spirited and unconventional of the Slavs.

The current government-sanctioned cultural renaissance promotes all things Ukrainian, while Russian is somewhat politically incorrect. At school, children make cut-out paper sunflowers and learn Ukrainian folk dances. All official government business is conducted in the Ukrainian language and most place names have been changed, if only by one letter. This separate national consciousness has energised society somewhat, but has also led to feelings of self-alienation for those whose culture is more closely linked to Russia. The slang term Russians use for a Ukrainian is *Khokhol*, from the Tatar words for blue and yellow. In return, the Ukrainians will refer (rudely) to Russians as *Kotsap*, meaning 'little goat', but having the same effect as 'jackass' in English. Hopefully, a more comfortable cultural balance will emerge, but travellers should be sensitive to the past struggle of Ukrainian cultural survival as they witness the present show of nationalism.

Since both of these barely conflicting cultures claim Kiev as their own, extremists come to Kiev to make a stance. On a given day in Kiev, you may see the blue and gold of Ukrainian nationalists claiming Ukraine for the Ukrainians, or you may happen upon the red flags of those nostalgic for Russia. Kievans themselves however have become a lot more relaxed about the whole issue. The up-and-coming generation speak Ukrainian and Russian interchangeably, and think it's 'cool' to be patriotic. Remember that whatever you find Ukraine to be, it is not Russia, and it is the intertwining of the two histories and cultures that makes Kiev such a fascinating place to explore.

individual neighbourhoods. A few pointed hills offered fortification for the original, and therefore oldest parts of Kiev, while the floodplain north of the city allowed for the even city blocks of the Podil and Obolon.

Kiev's climate is continental, meaning cold, white winters and fairly hot summers. Spring and autumn are short and mild but sunny. The uninformed often lump Kiev with Moscow and St Petersburg, imagining a frozen, unforgiving city, but inside the Soviet Union and Russian Empire, Ukraine was fondly known as 'the warmer place', and Kiev 'the southern capital'. Average July temperatures hover around 24°C, and average January temperatures normally won't dip below −6°C.

Planning

2

KIEV – A PRACTICAL OVERVIEW

It never pays to make too vigorous a plan prior to your journey to a new place, especially one as unpredictable as Kiev. Plans tend to invoke expectations, and expectations often lead to disappointment. I've noticed that the travellers who complain the most about Kiev are those who tend to plan out every little detail of their trip in advance, and then proceed through a series of mini-breakdowns when a museum is closed or there's no milk for their tea. Instead, you should expect real adventure and variability in Kiev. Go ahead and make a hotel reservation, and have a think about what you would like to have happen on your trip, but then just accept Kiev as it comes to you. Schedules can disappear and previous non-interests will become interesting and urgent. Be flexible and watch closely. Typically, it's only after you leave Kiev that your mind lets you link together all the people, buildings and scenes that you've witnessed.

On the flip side, don't come in search of pain and hardship in 'destitute' Ukraine. The post-Soviet doldrums never lasted long in this town, and for the time being, the city's moving full tilt towards illusions of high-life, modernity and 'European' glamour. Those travellers looking to rough it and collect war stories will definitely find it in Kiev, but no more than you can find the same in New York or London.

In becoming acquainted with the city, think about the city's history. Kiev's layout is sensible, but still harbours the eclectic beauty of a city built in stages: first on a cluster of hills, then on a lower flood plain, then the addition of a military fortress to the south, and finally an expansion on the plains across the river, and far-reaching Soviet residential spaces on all sides. There is a compact city centre, full of all the cultural, historic, and commercial attractions necessary to tourists. Staying in the centre will bring you up close and personal with some of Kiev's greatest attractions, and will make your stay very user-friendly. On the downside, some visitors to Kiev find they spend most of their trip running up and down Khreschatyk, never really knowing the city. Surrounding that centre are older, well-defined neighbourhoods, each with its own personality. Just south of Khreschatyk you'll find the stately, rich quarter of Lypki, the mansions of which have been transformed into government buildings. Further south is the ancient quarter of Pechersk, a name that refers to the 'Caves'. Pechersk is home to Kiev's most famous tourist attraction, the Caves Monastery, as well as the old military fortress, the city's biggest Soviet memorials, and a lot of long, quiet streets. To the northwest of Kiev's centre is Podil, a jubilant quarter, still rich with pre-Soviet architecture and an old city, bohemian air that still lingers. Kiev's left bank (livoberezhna) is predominantly residential, consisting of massive city blocks and towering apartment buildings that go on for miles and miles. The people who live there and the people who visit there feel as if it's a whole different city, but it's the 'real Kiev'. Several other residential neighbourhoods will bring you the full experience of everyday life in Kiev: Obolon, Vynohrad and Petrivka. A highly effective public transportation system links it all together, making travel within the city practically painless, if long. Remember that Kiev is a very big city, and that it can take a long time to travel across, especially with traffic.

Kiev's composite structure means savvy travellers will compartmentalise their movements. Bouncing from one end to the other, even on the subway, becomes tiresome and time-intensive. If you're around long enough, stake out an area of the city and dedicate some time to just that area. Then move on to the next. It sounds simple, but most people want to 'do' Kiev in a day or two and zip from one sight to the next. Instead of seeing all of Kiev, they see a lot of Kiev's traffic.

WHEN TO VISIT

In short, May. Every person in Kiev will go on and on about how beautiful Kiev is in May, when the chestnuts bloom, the sun begins to shine, and the trees put out their greenery. Truly, this one month is a beautiful time to enjoy the city, so if you can arrange your trip as such, then do. Common misconceptions have some falsely believing that Ukraine borders on Siberia and that Kiev is a frozen wasteland for much of the year. Ukraine actually has four distinct seasons like most of the northern hemisphere, and each provides a distinct backdrop to the city. Travelling from June to September does promise warmth, sunshine, long days, green fields, leaves on the trees and lots of fresh fruit in the markets. Tourist facilities will also be in full swing and the more colourful cultural festivals take place towards the end of the summer season. Keep in mind that Kiev gets hotter than you'd expect and air conditioning is still a rare luxury. Spring and autumn are generally warm and mild

When to visit

(but short), and the October harvest is the most picturesque moment for the areas just outside Kiev. Snow covers the ground from late November until April and the prettiest snowfall occurs in late December. January and February are Kiev's coldest months and you will be forced to plan your travel schedule to correspond with less than seven hours of hazy daylight. Travelling in the dead of winter requires a lot more patience, but the Ukrainians do it, so why not you?

You should also consider holidays and festivals you may want to observe during your visit. Orthodox Easter (the weekend following Catholic Easter) is the biggest religious holiday of the year with lots of public display and ritual. May celebrations (the 1st and the 9th) involve massive parades in Kiev that still demonstrate the heavy tradition of Soviet military fervour. For the most Ukrainian of Ukrainian events, Ivana Kupala falls at the end of the first week of July and is celebrated more passionately in western Ukraine. August visitors to eastern Ukraine will witness the sunflower fields in full bloom. The Christmas/New Year holiday is the very worst time to be in Kiev for business or tourism, since the city shuts down for nearly two weeks, everything is booked up and everyone is inebriated. If you have come to the city expressly to celebrate Christmas or New Year, sit tight and join in the party.

HIGHLIGHTS AND ITINERARIES

What you see and do obviously depends on how much time you have and how much you like to delve into a place (and what you like). The organised tour groups that market Ukraine will normally spend two to three days in Kiev, which is enough to get a feel for the place and see all the designated tourist spots. The average business trip to Kiev takes under a week, and normally allows a half-day of freedom, and perhaps a couple of evenings. Either way, the one-stop shopping approach to Kiev does little credit to this city or to the traveller.

Kiev's Caves Monastery is the city's number one tourist attraction by number of tourists who go there. Wandering through this extensive religious complex should fill about half of one day. St Sophia's Cathedral (which is actually a museum) should also be a priority, as should St Vladimir's Cathedral, for its incredible beauty. Check out what's in the vicinity (museums, shops, and restaurants) that interest you, and work them into your schedule.

A suggested itinerary could be:

Day 1 Orientation in the city centre. Have a walk around the Maidan Nezalezhnosti, see St Vladimir's, the Golden Gate, St Sophia's and St Mikhayil's, and Bessarabsky Rynok.

Day 2 Kievo-Pecherska Lavra (Caves Monastery), continue south to Rodyna Mat, and the Great Patriotic War Museum; then to Vidubytsky monastery if you still want more.

Day 3 Pirohiv village, Kiev's synagogues, Babi Yar, Andriyivsky Uzviz and Podil.

Most people agree that one of the highlights of their time in Kiev is the opera or ballet. Make it a priority to see a show. If you want to be different from everyone else, spend a day just hanging out in Podil. Your experience will be completely

Highlights and itineraries

separate from what happens up on the hills, but you will come away with better mental snapshots than the rest. If you long for quiet, then visit Vydubytsky Monastery – a fascinating place hidden away in the forest with sparse and silent monks. If you long for people and action, hang out at the main railway station around six in the evening. Nowhere in Kiev exudes more energy. If you're blessed with a slightly longer time in Kiev, or if this is a repeat trip and you've already seen the sights, then venture onwards. Go to Chernobyl, Pereyaslav Khmelnytsky or Uman. If you feel you've been in Kiev far too long and nothing seems interesting any more, then head out to Hydropark for a day, or start visiting the city's 101 churches.

No matter where you go in the world, some basic travel rules apply. On average, human beings can handle up to three museums per day. Any more is overkill and makes you think the place you're visiting is boring. If you can only squeeze in one museum on your whole trip, make it the Museum of One Street on Andriyivsky Uzviz. No other museum tells you more about Kiev in so few words. If you've got some more time and the weather's nice, head out to Pirohiv Village on the south side of the city. The outdoor museum-village is wonderfully refreshing and pretty self-explanatory. It's also the number one place to visit if you're travelling with children (or teenagers). Kiev's art museums are all wonderful, but if your time is limited, don't push it. Visit the National Museum, with its Ukrainian and Soviet collections, or just visit one of the modern galleries on Andriyivsky Uzviz.

IF YOU'VE JUST GOT ONE DAY IN KIEV...

If all you have is a single day in Ukraine's capital – then so be it. Be sure to make it memorable and wear comfortable walking shoes. Start the day by stepping into one of Kiev's Orthodox church services, if only for a minute. If you yearn for the city's 'culture', the singing and devotion you'll witness here comes closest. Choose two or three main attractions that interest you and experience them fully. If you're under orders to return home with armloads of 'something from Kiev' than be sure to hit Andriyivsky Uzviz, and enjoy the history of the place betwixt purchases. Then, come evening, take in a show. You should only feel that you've missed out if you haven't heard church bells ringing, taken in the squalor of a marketplace, made eye contact with a stray dog, had a good long gaze at the Dnepr river, been mesmerised by some hidden piece of architecture, had a ride on the metro, smelled fresh-baked black bread, and applauded a ballerina.

TOUR OPERATORS
UK

Interchange Interchange House, 27 Stafford Rd, Croydon, Surrey CR0 4NG; tel: 020 8681 3612; fax: 020 8760 0031; email: gordon@interchange.uk.com; web: www.interchange.uk.com

Intourist 7 Wellington Terrace, Notting Hill, London W2 4LW; tel: 0870 112 1232; email: info@intourist.co.uk; web: www.intourist.co.uk. Also offices in Manchester and Glasgow.
Regent Holidays 15 John St; Bristol BS1 2HR; tel: 0117 921 1711; fax: 0117 925 4866; email: www.regent-holidays.co.uk
Russia House Gospel Court, Borough High St, London SE1 1HH; tel: 020 7403 9922; fax: 020 7403 9933; email: www.russiahouse@btinternet.com ; web: www.the-russiahouse.net
Ukraine Travel Falcon House, Victoria St, Chadderton, Lancs OL9 0HB; tel: 0161 652 5050; fax: 0161 633 0825; email: info@ukraine.co.uk; web: www.ukraine.co.uk. Custom-made trips for Ukraine, specialist travel and visa support.

US

MIR Corporation 85 Washington St, Suite 210, Seattle, WA 98104; tel: 206 624 7289; fax: 206 624 7360; email: info@mircorp.com; web: www.mircorp.com. Small, specialist groups – cultural programmes, ancestral-village trips, tailor-made tours.
Scope Travel 1605 Springfield Av, Maplewood, NJ 07040; tel: 973 378 8998 or 1 800 242 7267; fax: 973 378 7903; email: info@scopetravel.com; web: www.scopetravel.com

Canada

Chumak Travel Agency 52 Mabelle Av, Suite 1215, Toronto, Ontario M9A 4X9; tel/fax: 416 234 5604; email: ukrainetour@ukrainetour.com; web: www.ukrainetour.com. Open since Ukrainian independence, specialising in professional, private and student travel, tours and visas.

RJ's Tours 11708 135A St; Edmonton, Alberta T5M 1L5; tel: 780 415 5633; fax: 780 415 5633; email: rjstours@tourukraine.com; web: www.rjstours.shawbiz.ca. Cruises and large escorted group tours.

RED TAPE

Ukraine has turned bureaucracy into an art-form that never fails to amaze Ukrainians and foreigners alike. Suspicion, indifference and micro-management are holdovers from the Soviet age and ticket-taker attitudes still prevail. Regulations and procedures habitually change as well. As long as you don't think like a consumer and come with a lot of patience, you'll get by just fine.

All Ukrainians are issued with identification passports at age 16 and this is the document police want to see when they ask for *bumahy* (papers). Your passport is your 'papers' so never go anywhere without it on your person, as you will be asked to show it. Obviously, you should keep a photocopy of your passport's front page and Ukrainian visa separate from your passport, as well as any other valuable forms or information: it makes getting a new passport much easier. Because independent travel is such a new concept, lone foreigners will appear suspect to various authority figures: police, ticket sellers, guards and soldiers. Only police have the authority to see your passport and they are under international obligation to return it immediately. As long as you have a valid visa, there is no problem. If you find that you do get called into a police station or they want to search your bags, nonchalant co-operation is the best policy, but don't be afraid to put up a reasonable fuss (for instance, there is no need for anyone to open your camera). These days, people would rather chat with foreign travellers than arrest them, so a frank and friendly demeanour will help any situation.

Rarely does any of this scaremongering apply to Kiev, a city with plenty of foreigners and enough action to keep the police otherwise engaged. I know of no visitors who have ever had a run-in with the law in Kiev, even when they deserved it. Dealing with bureaucratic attitudes down to the lowest level (even in the market) is probably Kiev's most annoying feature.

Visas

Besides the Cyrillic alphabet, a pesky visa is the number one deterrent that keeps travellers from venturing into Ukraine. Visitors rightfully comment that a country so lovely should be more accessible, yet fail to acknowledge that Ukraine is presently more accessible than it ever has been. Hopefully, the situation will continue to improve for tourists.

Citizens of Poland, Russia and the countries of the former Soviet Union (except Turkmenistan) are exempt; everybody else needs a visa, obtained in advance from a Ukrainian embassy or consulate.

Overall, few visa applications are ever rejected, but the process can be lengthy, tedious and expensive. Travellers must submit the visa application form with a passport still valid for six months (after your *return* from Ukraine), two passport-size photographs and the initial fee, payable by money order only: £50 (US$90) for the normal ten-day processing, double that for 'speedy' three-day processing. Visas are based on purpose of visit – Tourist, Business, Private or Transit – and each requires different forms and/or additional fees.

Tourist visas are the most obvious choice and require an additional letter of invitation from a Ukrainian or a foreign country tourist agency, or confirmation from a hotel. If they are licensed, they can issue an invitation letter (for which you will be charged). Usual procedure has the Ukrainian party faxing the official invitation to your country's embassy and presenting you with a confirmation number to be matched with your visa application. Organised tours often take care of all this for you.

A convenient sidestep to the tourist rigmarole is the private visa, designed for foreigners visiting friends or family in Ukraine. Simply state the name and address of the person you are going to visit and where you might travel. If you don't know anybody in Ukraine, make some friends beforehand. Citizens of the EU, Canada, USA, Japan, Switzerland, Slovakia and Turkey **do not** require an invitation letter when applying for a private or business visa, cutting out the biggest headache of the application process. A private visa is also the best option for independent travellers, since you are not committed to a specific itinerary and the process is easier when applying on your own.

Visas are generally issued for three months, or for six months if you are from a favoured nation (above). It used to be that foreigners were required to register at the OVIR (Ministry of Interior's Office of Visas and Registration) within three days of entering any city, but this is only an issue if you are planning on staying in one area

Red tape

for longer than six months. If you seek to extend your visa, you must apply well in advance at the local OVIR office.

Travellers passing overland between Russia and Europe require the quicker and cheaper transit visas, which usually give you four days in the country. Applications require proof (another visa or one-way ticket) that you will be moving on. If you are planning on leaving and re-entering, make sure to apply for a double- or multiple-entry visa, which adds significant cost but offers a safety measure for chronic wanderers. Visas are issued in person at the embassy or by mail and consist of a full-page sticker in your passport. You'll find that your visa becomes a constant reference during your travels as all hotel registrations and ticket purchases must take down your visa number (someone out there is tracking your movements!), and many need to see the page in order to know how to spell your name in Cyrillic.

Immigration and customs

Both processes can be long and unfriendly, although as with everything, it's getting better as democracy progresses. Slow queues and a lot of questioning are just part of the drill, but as long as you have your visa and don't look too suspicious, you will be allowed in. Present yourself in the simplest manner and declare a specific goal or itinerary, even if you do plan on taking to the open road.

Customs can be a more demanding process. On your flight to Kiev, or upon entering the country, you will be issued with a customs declaration form that you will need to fill in with your details. You *must* have the form when you leave, so keep it somewhere safe throughout your trip. The declaration is mainly to assess how much cash you are bringing into the country and what you end up taking out (see *Money*). Everyone has their own way of dealing with border guards and customs agents, so there is no single word of advice applicable to the Ukrainian *tamozhniki*, although, in general, it helps to be honest and open, but not too honest and open. Certain objects will catch the eye of customs officials, in particular artwork and some electronic data or media materials. If you have brought your own video camera with you and made videos during your stay in Kiev, the videocassettes will be considered suspicious and you must normally be issued with a clearance statement. In my experience, this has only been a problem with large quantities of videocassettes.

After losing a valuable amount to souvenir hunters, the Ukrainian government now prohibits the export of any national art treasures without special permission. These include antique icons, rugs and dishes, some Soviet medals, and coins. Most Ukrainian dealers are aware of the law and only sell goods that can be exported, and there tends to be one official at customs who knows what is legal and what's not. When you are buying artwork in Kiev, ask the dealer for the government certificate of authenticity which you can present at customs if asked. For questions, check out www.customs.gov.ua.

EMBASSIES
Australia Consulate of Ukraine, Level 3 Edgecliff Centre, 203–233 New South Head Rd, Edgecliff NSW 2027; tel/fax: 61 293 285429

Embassies

Belarus Starovilenska 51, 220002 Minsk; tel: 375 17 283 1990; fax: 375 17 283 19980

Belgium 30 Av Albert Lancaster, 1180 Bruxelles; tel: 322 379 21 00; fax: 322 379 21 79

Canada Embassy of Ukraine, Consular Section, 331 Metcalfe St, Ottawa, Ontario K2P 1S3; tel: 613 230 8015; fax: 613 230 2655; web: www.infoukes.com/ukremb; Consulate General of Toronto, 2120 Bloor St West, Toronto, Ontario M6S 1M8; tel: 416 763 3114; fax: 416 763 2323; web: www.ukrconsulate.com

Czech Republic De Gaulla 29, Prague 6; tel: 42 02 33 342000; fax: 42 02 33 344366

France 21 Av de Saxe, 75007 Paris; tel: 33 1 43 06 07 37; fax: 33 1 43 06 02 94

Germany Albrechtstrasse 26, 10117 Berlin; tel: 49 30 288 87 116; fax: 49 30 288 87 163; web: www.botschaft-ukraine.de

Hungary Stefania 77, Budapest H-1143; tel: 36 1 422 41 20; fax: 36 1 220 98 73

Israel 50 Yirmiyahu, 62594 Tel Aviv; tel: 97 23 602 1952; fax: 97 23 604 2512; web: www.ukraine-embassy.co.il

Japan 3-15-6 Nishi Azabu, Minato-ku, Tokyo 106-0046; tel: 81 3 5474 9770; fax: 81 3 5474 9772; web: ukremb-japan.gov.ua

Poland Aleja Szucha 7, 00580 Warsaw; tel: 48 22 625 0127; fax: 48 22 629 8103; web: www.ukraine-poland.com

Moldova Sfatul Taril 55, 277004 Chisinau; tel: 373 2 582 151; fax: 373 2 585 108

Romania Calea Dorobantilor 16, Sector 1 Bucharest; tel: 40 1211 6986; fax: 40 1211 6949

Russia Leontievsky 18, Moscow 103009; tel: 7 095 229 1079; fax: 7 095 924 8469

Slovakia Radvanska 35, 811 Bratislava 01; tel: 42 12 5920 28 11; fax: 42 12 5441 26 51

Turkey Sancak Mahalessi 206 Solak N 17, Yildiz Cankaya, Ankara 06550; tel: 90 312 441
5499; fax: 90 312 440 6815
UK Embassy of Ukraine, Consular Department, 78 Kensington Park Rd, London, W11 2PL;
tel: 020 7243 8923; fax: 020 7727 3567; Consulate in Edinburgh, 8 Windsor St, Edinburgh
EH7 5JR; tel: 0131 556 0023; fax: 0131 557 3460
USA Embassy of Ukraine, 3350 M St NW, Washington DC 20007; tel: 1 202 333 0606; fax:
1 202 333 0817; web: www.ukremb.com; Consulate General of Ukraine in New York, 240
East 49th St, New York, NY 10017; tel: 1 212 371 5690

GETTING THERE AND AWAY
By air
Even though it's technically part of Europe, the airline industry has long perceived
Kiev as a long-haul destination, although a gradual increase in direct flights shows a
slight change in these attitudes. Today, most major European carriers fly to Kiev at
least once a week, connecting western Europe and North America to Ukraine.
Aerosvit is Ukraine's largest international airline and offers the best connections
between international flights and domestic destinations in Ukraine, but they do not
fly to many western European cities. Ukraine International Airlines flies to most
European capitals and code-shares with several western European airlines (ie: has
agreements whereby a ticket with one company allows flight on another company's
plane, and vice versa).

From Europe

Austrian Airlines has been flying to Ukraine the longest of any European carrier, and now offers a regular service to Kiev twice-daily via Vienna. British Airways flies five days a week direct from London Heathrow to Kiev Borispol, as does Air France from Paris Charles de Gaulle, Lufthansa from Frankfurt and Munich, and KLM from Schiphol. Prices vary, but expect to pay at least £250 (US$400) for any round-trip flight from London to Kiev (three hours). Cheaper tickets can sometimes be found on East European carriers. Czech Airlines flies every day to Kiev Zhulyany with an optional stopover in Prague, Lithuanian Airlines offers similar deals via Vilnius, and LOT Polish Airlines has sporadic connections to Kiev. Another alternative is flying with Turkish Airlines, with connections every other day from Istanbul to Kiev (two hours).

Often when purchasing Austrian Airlines and Lufthansa tickets to Kiev, your flight to Kiev will be on a UIA (Ukraine International Airlines) flight. UIA flights travel direct to all major European capitals, including Berlin, Paris, Lisbon, London, Helsinki, Rome, Madrid and Zurich – but not necessarily on their own planes.

From North America

For now, the only direct flights from North America to Ukraine are on Aerosvit, which offers regular flights from Toronto and New York City's JFK to Kiev. Prices range from US$500 to US$600). Otherwise, Austrian Airlines, British Airways, KLM and Lufthansa offer the most competitive and comfortable transatlantic connections to Ukraine via their respective hubs. Travellers tend to leave Canada or the US the night before and arrive in Ukraine the following afternoon, with around a two-hour layover somewhere in western Europe. A return economy class ticket to Kiev from North America ranges in price from US$650 to US$1,000.

Other routes

Various Ukrainian airlines and charter flights service all the recent hotspots for Ukrainian travellers. Aerosvit has started a regular service to and from Delhi, Bangkok, and several locations in the Middle East (Abu Dhabi, Cairo, Damascus). For travellers from Australia, New Zealand, and Southeast Asia, Singapore Airlines advertises the best connection to Kiev from Sydney and Auckland via Frankfurt on the Star Alliance. Business travellers from Japan and China tend to favour Austrian Airlines' Tokyo-Vienna-Kiev route. Transaero, Aeroflot and Siberia Airlines connect Kiev to cities all across Russia's 12 time zones and Central Asia. Aeroflot is also the official airline of the former communist world, and its stopover in Moscow is still the cheapest way to travel between Kiev and India, Africa, or China (the flight to Kiev from Moscow only takes an hour). Keep in mind that flying Aeroflot from long-haul destinations will require a troublesome airport change in Moscow and perhaps an overnight layover, but it is still the easiest transit from places like Angola, Cuba and Guinea-Bissau.

Airline offices in Kiev

Aeroflot Saksahanskovo 112A; tel: 044 245 4359
Aerosvit Chervonoarmiyska 9/2; tel: 044 490 3490

Austrian Airlines Chervonoarmiyska 9/2; tel: 044 244 3540

British Airways Yarsolaviv Val 5; tel: 044 490 6060; web: www.britishairways.com/ukraine

Czech Airlines Ivan Franka 36; tel: 044 246 5627; web: www.czechairlines.com

KLM Ivana Franka 34/33, 2nd floor; tel: 044 490 2490; email: klm.Ukraine@klm.com; web: www.klm.com.ua

KyiAvia Peremohy 2; tel: 044 490 4902

Lithuanian Airlines Dmitrivska 1; tel: 044 490 4907; email: info-ukraine@lal.lt

LOT Polish Airlines Ivana Franko 36; tel: 044 246 5620; web: www.lot.com

Lufthansa Khmelnytskovo 52; tel: 044 490 3800; email: kiev@lufthansa.com.ua

Malev Hungarian Airlines Hospitalna 12г; tel: 044 247 8672; web: www.malev.hu

Transaero Chervonoarmiyska 9/2, Office 1; tel: 044 490 6565

Turkish Airlines Horodotskovo 4; tel: 044 229 1550; web: www.turkishairlines.com

Ukraine International Airlines Peremohy 14; tel: 044 461 5050

Borispol Airport Бориспіль

Kiev Borispol has a bad reputation, which it only half deserves. A major refurbishment has helped improve things, but the entry process can still seem a bit tangled and highly chaotic. Upon arriving, passengers are herded into several very long and very slow queues that creep towards a row of surly guards waiting to stamp your visa. During daytime rushes, your bags will be waiting for you after the first checkpoint, having long beaten you to the spot. With bags in hand, enter the green line at customs. Only enter the red line if you are a) told to, or b) carrying large conspicuous boxes, in which case you'll be told to, or c) have something to declare which you have marked on your form. You'll have already been given a customs declaration form before landing, which should be filled out clearly and honestly (paying more attention to detail than normal). Hand it over to a customs officer, and be fully prepared to have your bags rummaged through. Once you've been waved on (making sure you have your customs form stamped and in your possession) you will exit into the main hall, where there is an information booth if you're feeling a little bit overwhelmed. The shortest time anyone gets through this process is one hour, which used to sound long and inconvenient, but is becoming the norm everywhere.

The Ukrainian answer to all the hustle and bustle is a newly introduced VIP service, where foreign visitors can circumvent the dismal wait by paying up prior to arriving. As a Very Important Person at Borispol, someone will be waiting right by the exit of the plane with your name on a placard. You'll be whisked off to the separate VIP Service Hall and allowed to quickly pass through, receiving a 'free gift' commemorating Kiev. When departing under the auspices of the VIP service, you'll wait for your flight in the private lounge without any hassle, and then be driven in a minivan directly to your plane, just as the flight begins to board. As advertised, the US$100 fee helps save time and 'reduces scrutiny' by customs officers. If it seems appalling to pay someone else US$100 in order to be treated civilly, that's because it *is* appalling, but then so are the queues for the proletariat. Usually the VIP service is an option offered with group tours, and your contact in Ukraine will know how to arrange the VIP pick-up, but if you are travelling on your own, contact your airline or the Borispol Information Service; tel: 044 296 7243.

Borispol Airport has come a long way since its spartan Soviet existence. Planes all leave from the main terminal which now boasts a bona-fide Irish pub and a sleek duty-free shop that competes well with any other airport shop that sells perfume and giant Toblerone.

Zhulyany Airport Жуляни

The lesser of Kiev's two airports is actually an easier location to fly in to since it is closer to the city centre and therefore more accessible by public transportation and city taxis (see pages 130–2). Traditionally, the smaller city airport has dealt mainly with domestic air traffic, although technically, any flights from former Eastern bloc countries will come in here (Aeroflot and Czech Airlines both have international flights to Zhulyany).

Overland

Ukraine is much closer than people realise, so that travelling across Europe to get there sounds more daunting that it actually is. From a North American perspective, the trip from Paris to Kiev is the same as driving from New York to Denver, or Toronto to Calgary. The route across Germany and Poland is the quickest, but many would argue that crossing the Czech Republic and Slovakia or Hungary is much more beautiful. Either way, going overland can be a romantic endeavour and fairly inexpensive.

By bus

Numerous bus companies travel from western Europe directly to Ukraine, most of which are Ukrainian companies offering a direct service from Germany, Belgium, France and the UK to Kiev and Lviv (ie: Lviv Inturtrans; email: info@lviv-inturtrans.com.ua; web: www.lviv-inturtrans.com.ua). Eurolines shares tickets on their one Antwerp–Kiev bus that can be joined from London, although this costs more than going to a Polish destination and then continuing on Ukrainian transport (www.eurolines.com).

The bus journey to Kiev from London takes two days and two nights, so you must consider whether the money you're saving is worth sitting upright for 48 hours and being forced to watch the latest Hollywood blockbusters dubbed into Polish. From the UK, the very cheapest way to get to Ukraine is on a two-day Eurolines bus from London Victoria to Rzeszow, Poland, usually costing £80 return (US$140). From Rzeszow there are frequent buses that cross the border to Lviv (three hours). Other options are quicker buses that travel to Warsaw or Krakow, and then you can continue to Kiev on an overnight train.

By car

Everyone should drive across Europe at least once in their lifetime, and the trip from England to Kiev by car always promises to be a bit of an adventure (but see pages 134–7). For many, all is well until they get inside the country. If you have the option of bringing an old car that you don't mind losing, then do. The most direct route to Kiev is from Brussels: follow the E-40 east and just keep driving across Germany via Cologne and Leipzig to the border at Görlitz; in Poland drive via Wrocław, Krakow and Przemyśl to the German–Polish border at Shehini. The E-40 continues in Ukraine through Rivne and on to Kiev. (Stay on the road to Kharkiv and you'll end up in Kazakhstan and eventually Beijing.) Take note that many of the roads in Poland are not paved and will do damage to your car's chassis and shock absorbers. Alternative routes to Kiev from Europe travel through Slovakia and Hungary, which are also 'easy' border posts that are accustomed to lots of European traffic. When entering by car from Romania, Moldova, Russia or Belarus, remember that all roads lead to Kiev. *Chapter 4* has a section on driving in Kiev.

By rail

Ukrainian trains still travel from all of the former Eastern bloc capitals, and this can be a more creative way to make your entrance into Kiev. Direct overnight trains from Berlin, Belgrade, Budapest, Bucharest, Warsaw, Krakow, Bratislava, Prague and Sofia all go to Kiev. With central European travel pretty standardised these days, budget-conscious travellers can save cash by combining a cheap flight or bus to Berlin or Prague followed by an overnight train to Kiev. The fast train from Berlin Zoo Station to Warsaw Central takes only five hours and costs around US$20, and from Warsaw there are daily trains to Kiev (20 hours) for around US$50 single. There's also the daily direct train from Berlin to Kiev (24 hours) which effectively instils a historical mood. The most exciting part of the train ride to Kiev is at the Polish–Ukrainian border, when the carriages are suspended (with you still inside them) and the wheels changed to fit a different gauge.

There are so many trains between Russia and Ukraine it's not worth listing them all, but this is the most convenient way of getting into Ukraine from the north. The dozen or so Moscow trains usually pass through Kiev (14 hours) on their way to Crimea and the Black Sea coast. A dozen more trains travel in from Russia's east and the Caucasus. Some might consider beginning or finishing their Trans-Siberian excursion in Ukraine, as there are regular trains between Vladivostok and Kiev. There are also plenty of trains from the Baltic States, however, most travel through Belarus, requiring a tricky transit visa and a lot of bureaucracy. It's only worth doing if you intend to spend some time visiting Belarus. Otherwise, go through Russia or Poland. Remember that a US$5 surcharge is added when buying international rail tickets in Ukraine.

HEALTH

Despite US State Department warnings and exaggerated tales, Ukraine is not the dreaded third-world country it is often made out to be. Every country has its bugs to which travellers will always be more susceptible. As the sophisticated capital, Kiev is the safest place to travel in Ukraine, and also features the best medical facilities in the country.

Immunisations

Although there are no specific vaccinations required for Ukraine, it is recommended that visitors should be up-to-date with **tetanus** and **diphtheria** (every ten years), **typhoid** and **hepatitis A**. A single dose of hepatitis A vaccine (eg: Havrix Monodose, Avaxim) lasts for one year. It can be boosted after this time to provide cover for at least ten years. The vaccine is best taken at least two weeks before travel but can be taken even the day before, as the incubation period of hepatitis A is at least two weeks. The vaccine has replaced immunoglobulin, which should no longer be used.

The newer typhoid vaccines (eg: Typhim Vi) are about 80% effective and last for three years. It is worth taking, unless time is short and your trip is one week or less. For trips of four weeks or more you should also consider vaccination against **polio** (every ten years), **hepatitis B** and **rabies**. Hepatitis B is especially relevant if you are working in a hospital or with children, and rabies vaccination is recommended if you are handling animals or are likely to be more than 24 hours from medical facilities. Ideally three doses of each are needed and should be taken at least three weeks before travel. However, if time is short then two doses, or even one of either, is better than nothing at all. For hepatitis B, only Engerix B is currently licensed for the rapid course.

Tuberculosis (TB) has reached epidemic proportions in Ukraine during the last decade, and it is known to be a highly persistent strain of the disease. The BCG vaccination for tuberculosis is routinely given in the UK between the ages of 11 and 13, whereas in the USA only high-risk individuals are vaccinated as a matter of course. If you have not been vaccinated, and are over 35, it is probably not worth having, as there is some doubt as to its efficacy. But don't worry, tuberculosis needs prolonged close contact with an infected individual and is still treatable. Symptoms of active TB include a permanent, crackling or dry persistent cough, fever (most often at night), fatigue and weight loss. Avoid long contact with anyone who coughs all the time, and if you think you may have been infected, or else you've spent a long time in Ukraine, get a TB test as a precaution. Treatment includes a long-term daily medication ritual, so the sooner you begin the better.

Tick-borne encephalitis is common in the Ukrainian forest (but practically non-existent in Kiev) and can also be transmitted through unpasteurised dairy products. Travellers at risk include anyone visiting the Ukrainian countryside from April to August, but you should only consider being vaccinated if you are going into the country for more than three weeks or if you intend to spend most of your time in the woods. In the UK, vaccine is available only on a named-patient basis, so has to be pre-ordered. A new, faster schedule allows the three doses needed to be given over a four-week period. Whether or not you are vaccinated you should always take general precautions against ticks: wear loose, long-sleeved shirts, long trousers that cover your limbs and are tucked into your socks or boots, and a hat. You should also use a tick repellent with DEET. At the end of the day, check for ticks on your body and hair. This is easier to do with another person as the ticks are small and hard to see. It is especially important to check the heads of children, who are more likely to get ticks from overhead branches.

Health

Travel clinics and health information

A full list of current travel clinic websites worldwide is available on www.istm.org. For other journey preparation information, consult www.tripprep.com. Information about various medications may be found on www.emedicine.com/wild/topiclisthtm.

UK

Berkeley Travel Clinic 32 Berkeley St, London W1J 8EL (near Green Park tube station); tel: 020 7629 6233

British Airways Travel Clinic and Immunisation Service There are two BA clinics in London, both on tel: 0845 600 2236; web: www.britishairways.com/travel/HEALTHCLININTRO. Appointments only at 101 Cheapside; or walk-in service Mon–Sat at 213 Piccadilly

Cambridge Travel Clinic 48a Mill Rd, Cambridge CB1 2AS; tel: 01223 367362; fax: 01223 368021; email: mkedward@cambridgetravelclinic.co.uk.; web: www.cambridgetravelclinic.co.uk. Open 12.00–19.00 Tue–Fri, 10.00–16.00 Sat.

Edinburgh Travel Clinic Regional Infectious Diseases Unit, Ward 41 OPD, Western General Hospital, Crewe Rd South, Edinburgh EH4 2UX; tel: 0131 537 2822. Travel helpline open 09.00–12.00 weekdays. Provides inoculations and advises on travel-related health risks.

Fleet Street Travel Clinic 29 Fleet St, London EC4Y 1AA; tel: 020 7353 5678; web: www.fleetstreet.com. Injections, travel products and latest advice.

Hospital for Tropical Diseases Travel Clinic Mortimer Market Centre, 2nd Floor, Capper St (off Tottenham Ct Rd), London WC1E 6AU; tel: 020 7388 9600; web: www.thehtd.org. Offers consultations and advice, and is able to provide all necessary drugs and vaccines for travellers. Runs a healthline (09061 337733) for country-specific information and health hazards.

MASTA (Medical Advisory Service for Travellers Abroad), at the London School of Hygiene and Tropical Medicine, Keppel St, London WC1E 7HT; tel: 09068 224100. This is a premium-line number, charged at 60p per minute. For a fee, they will provide an individually tailored health brief, with up-to-date information on how to stay healthy, inoculations and what to bring.

MASTA pre-travel clinics Tel: 01276 685040. Call for the nearest; there are currently 30 in Britain.

NHS travel website, www.fitfortravel.scot.nhs.uk, provides country-by-country advice on immunisation, and a list of relevant health organisations.

Nomad Travel Store 3–4 Wellington Terrace, Turnpike Lane, London N8 0PX; tel: 020 8889 7014; fax: 020 8889 9528; email: sales@nomadtravel.co.uk; web: www.nomadtravel.co.uk. Also at 40 Bernard St, London WC1N 1LJ; tel: 020 7833 4114; fax: 020 7833 4470 and 43 Queens Rd, Bristol BS8 1QH; tel: 0117 922 6567; fax: 0117 922 7789. As well as dispensing health advice, Nomad stocks anti-bug devices, and an excellent range of adventure travel gear.

Thames Medical 157 Waterloo Rd, London SE1 8US; tel: 020 7902 9000. Competitively priced, one-stop travel health service. All profits go to their affiliated company, InterHealth, which provides health care for overseas workers on Christian projects.

Trailfinders Immunisation Centre 194 Kensington High St, London W8 7RG; tel: 020 7938 3999.

Health

Travelpharm The Travelpharm website, www.travelpharm.com, offers up-to-date guidance on travel-related health matters and has a range of medications available through their online mini-pharmacy.

USA

Centers for Disease Control 1600 Clifton Rd, Atlanta, GA 30333; tel: 888 232 3228 (toll-free and available 24 hours) or 800 311 3435; fax: 877 FYI TRIP; web: www.cdc.gov/travel. The central source of travel information in the USA. Each summer they publish the invaluable *Health Information for International Travel*, available from the Division of Quarantine at the above address.

Connaught Laboratories PO Box 187, Swiftwater, PA 18370; tel: 800 822 2463.

IAMAT (International Association for Medical Assistance to Travelers) 417 Center St, Lewiston, NY 14092; tel: 716 754 4883; email: info@iamat.org; web: www.iamat.org. A non-profit organisation that provides lists of English-speaking doctors abroad.

Canada

IAMAT (International Association for Medical Assistance to Travellers) Suite 1, 1287 St Clair Av W, Toronto, Ontario M6E 1B8; tel: 416 652 0137; web: www.iamat.org

TMVC (Travel Doctors Group) Sulphur Springs Rd, Ancaster, Ontario; tel: 905 648 1112; web: www.tmvc.com.au

Australia, New Zealand, Thailand

TMVC Tel: 1300 65 88 44; web: www.tmvc.com.au. Twenty-two clinics in Australia, New Zealand and Thailand, including:

Auckland Canterbury Arcade, 170 Queen St, Auckland; tel: 9 373 3531

Brisbane Dr Deborah Mills, Qantas Domestic Building, 6th floor, 247 Adelaide St, Brisbane, QLD 4000; tel: 7 3221 9066; fax: 7 3321 7076

Melbourne Dr Sonny Lau, 393 Little Bourke St, 2nd floor, Melbourne, VIC 3000; tel: 3 9602 5788; fax: 3 9670 8394

Sydney Dr Mandy Hu, Dymocks Building, 7th Floor, 428 George St, Sydney, NSW 2000; tel: 2 221 7133; fax: 2 221 8401

IAMAT PO Box 5049, Christchurch 5, New Zealand; web: www.iamat.org

South Africa

SAA-Netcare Travel Clinics PO Box 786692, Sandton 2146; fax: 011 883 6152; web: www.travelclinic.co.za or www.malaria.co.za. Clinics throughout South Africa.

TMVC 113 DF Malan Drive, Roosevelt Park, Johannesburg; tel: 011 888 7488; web: www.tmvc.com.au. Consult the website for details of clinics in South Africa.

Switzerland

IAMAT 57 Voirets, 1212 Grand Lancy, Geneva; web: www.iamat.org

First-aid kit

A traveller's basic first-aid kit could sensibly include the following:

- antiseptic wipes
- plasters/band-aids, and blister plasters for after long walks
- wound dressings such as Melolin, and tape
- sterilised syringes and needles
- insect repellent; antihistamine cream
- antiseptic cream
- oral rehydration sachets

In Kiev

'Don't drink the water' fully applies to Ukraine and is the best advice to follow for a healthy stay in Kiev. Never mind the lead pipes, dodgy sewage systems and a menagerie of gastro-intestinal ailments, the water tastes bad and will make you sick. Drink bottled or boiled water only; tea and hot drinks served in restaurants are safe.

Accept that you will get diarrhoea at some point and then you won't be so unhappy when you do, although good hygiene practices such as scrubbing your hands regularly with soap may help prevent infection. New food and new bacteria are the usual cause in Ukraine and the condition should only last 24 hours. Even if you are taking anti-diarrhoea tablets like Imodium-D, be sure to drink lots of clear fluids to avoid dehydration. Rehydration sachets can be purchased in most pharmacies, but you can make the solution yourself with a teaspoon of salt, eight teaspoons of sugar and a litre of safe water. Bacillary dysentery usually fails to settle after 24 hours, and the diarrhoea may contain blood and/or slime or you may have a fever. This may be difficult to distinguish from amoebic dysentery. The latter is a much more serious ailment passed by contaminated food or water and human contact. Besides severe and bloody diarrhoea, there may be constant vomiting, stomach pains and a high fever. Another unpleasant, but rare, illness is giardiasis, caused by the protozoon *Giardia lamblia*. This gut infection includes greasy, bulky and often pale stools, stomach cramps and characteristic 'eggy' burps. It requires prompt treatment, otherwise chronic infection may occur. Replenish all your lost fluids by drinking about four litres of rehydration fluid a day. Doctors in Ukraine will also prescribe anti-biotic treatments, and in Kiev you will always be near medical facilities, however you may still want to bring your own supply. Ciprofloxacin (one 500mg tablet repeated 6–12 hours later) will usually work for bacillary dysentery. Suspected amoebic dysentery or giardiasis should be treated with 2g of Tinidazole (Fasigyn) taken as four 500mg tablets in one go, repeated seven days later if symptoms persist. If your tummy feels fine, but your stool appears dark red, don't panic – you are probably eating a lot more beets (*borscht*) than you are accustomed to.

Chernobyl
Chernobyl does not pose a serious health threat for travellers in Ukraine unless you plan on camping next to the reactor for an extended period of time. The general

advice cautions against eating local food known to contain radiation, namely mushrooms and berries gathered from the Polissyan woods. Also, avoid freshwater fish from rivers as they are known to carry worms.

Animals

In Kiev, stray dogs move about in large packs and scavenge for food. Even if you think they are cute little puppies and others seem to be feeding them scraps of food, these are wild animals that have been known to attack individuals. They also carry disease, rabies being the most obvious risk. Whether or not you are vaccinated, you are at risk of contracting rabies from being bitten, scratched or licked over open wounds. Wash the affected area immediately with soap and water then apply an antiseptic (or alcohol if you don't possess any antiseptic), then go as soon as you can for medical help. Having pre-exposure rabies vaccine (see above) will reduce the number of post-treatment doses required. If you have had at least two doses of vaccine then you will not need rabies immunoglobulin (RIG). The latter is expensive and often unavailable, so will offset the cost of being vaccinated before departure. Rabies, if contracted and untreated, is always fatal and a horrific way to die.

In cheaper hotels, bedbugs can be a problem, known for the rows of small red bites you'll find in the morning. Bedbugs do not spread disease and there's not much you can do about them, but calamine lotion or a proprietary antihistamine cream such as Anthisan can reduce any itching.

AIDS

AIDS is spreading in Ukraine, mainly through intravenous drug use and prostitution. Be wise in your behaviour. It makes sense to buy condoms before you leave to guarantee their quality, although most kiosks and shops in Ukraine sell foreign-brand condoms.

Ukrainian health care

Socialised medicine once supported a culture of efficient, long-term treatment, but with the current economic situation and severe supply shortages, the quality of care has dropped significantly. Ukrainian doctors are for the most part highly skilled, but paid miserably low salaries. Most continue to work with the incentive of receiving underhand gifts of cash or in kind for medical services rendered. In my experience, travellers are welcome at public hospitals and will often be given priority. Be prepared to pay for any service, but don't be surprised if they refuse; there is some prestige in treating a foreigner. Ukraine does have a reciprocal health care agreement with the UK, so most medical treatment is free. This may also apply to dental treatment, but you will have to pay for prescribed medicine.

Drunk doctors are a known problem in Ukraine's depressed state, so you might think to check their state of sobriety before they begin to operate. Several private clinics have emerged in the larger cities, especially Kiev, where the staff speak English and the quality of care is comparable to that in the West.

When Ukrainians go to the hospital, they are often expected to bring their own

Health

supplies along, including gauze, syringes and even anaesthetic. Travelling with a small first-aid kit is always a good idea, and it is also wise to take packaged syringes and needles in case you need an injection. These days, Ukrainian pharmacies are well stocked with high-quality medicine and medical supplies. Pharmacists work as over-the-counter doctors. Simply pointing or explaining an ailment in gestures will usually get you the right medicine or ointment.

Ukrainian folk medicine is a fascinating topic and you won't leave the country without being offered some sort of home remedy, some of which involves the supernatural. *Babushki* gather dried herbs and sell them on the street as medicine. List your symptoms and they'll mix a tea infusion that can cure anything (they say). Mustard plants, powder or plasters are also effective for soothing chest colds.

Cold weather

Ukrainian winters are colder than might be expected, so bundle up with lots of layers and make sure to cover your hands, ears and head, where you lose the most heat. After a while, you'll find your body gets used to the cold, but pay attention to signs like chattering teeth. After being outdoors, drink hot tea or eat hot *borscht*: it can help prevent catching cold.

Frostbite is a serious condition where the flesh has actually frozen. The first signs include a 'pins and needles' sensation and white skin. Go inside and warm the affected area with lukewarm water and slowly increase the temperature until feeling returns. Be smart about walking on frozen rivers and lakes. Ukrainians will not step out on the Dnepr's ice floe unless the temperature has been continuously below 0°C for at least five days. You can usually see which ice is safe for recreation by all the footprints and fishing holes there. If you do fall through, get indoors, remove the wet (but frozen) clothing and treat for hypothermia.

CRIME AND SAFETY

In general, Ukraine is a safe place to travel, and much safer than most of the neighbouring countries. The anarchy of the 1990s seems to have settled down to a semblance of law and order; however, when riches are flaunted in the midst of poverty, there will be crime. No matter how hard you may try to belong in Ukraine, you will stick out as a wealthy foreigner and be the desired target for petty criminals.

Muggings, pickpocketing and robbery are the most common threats. Bad things tend to happen in train stations, bus stations, and marketplaces where there are lots of people continuously moving about and cash and belongings are shifting hands. Be especially alert when you are in any of these places. Also, people have been known to have their bags slashed while riding crowded subways or buses.

Capitalism has not been around long enough to divide Kiev into 'good' or 'bad' areas so both potentials exist everywhere. Bear in mind that public places are badly lit and that people are often mugged at night or in dark stairwells. Bring a small torch (flashlight). Using a mock wallet with expired cards and a convincing wad of worthless cash is a wise precaution. Remember that local crime also tends to involve alcohol and money. If you are drinking with people you have just met – be on your guard. People have been robbed when they are drunk, or worse, they have been drugged and then robbed. Don't engage with drunk people who approach you. Instead, simply get away.

Trains are quite safe. People usually only get robbed on trains when they are alone, so travel in groups or else close the door to your compartment with multiple locks. Taxis are also safe, but beware of any suspicious behaviour. If the driver demands you pay up front, get out of the car. If they pull over midway for petrol or to change a tyre, get out of the car and watch them from the roadside. If it feels suspicious, simply walk away. Only pay a taxi driver after you have stepped out of the car and have your bags with you.

Organised crime (the mafia) gets a lot of talk, but is of no real interest to tourists and vice versa. Mobsters in Ukraine fill a very different niche than they do in the West and will not bother you unless you are purposefully trying to undermine their business.

If you are a victim of a crime, think before you act. If you are staying in an upmarket hotel or are travelling with a tour agency, report it there first. They will have the proper relationship with the authorities. If your passport has been stolen or the crime is of a serious nature, be sure to make a report at your embassy. The slang term for the police is *musor* ('rubbish') which reflects the reputation of Ukrainian law enforcement. Use your own judgement about filing a police report. Travellers have reported good and bad experiences with the police who may or may not be corrupt. In Kiev, law enforcement is a tad more respectable, so depending on the seriousness of the crime, the police can probably help.

Overall, use common sense. Don't walk alone down dark streets in the middle of the night. In the day, walk confidently as if you know where you are going. If you need to check a map, step out of the public eye, or sit down in a café. Don't thumb through huge wads of cash and don't draw attention to yourself through rude and boisterous behaviour. Also, think situations through before you go so that you have a plan in mind, for example, what would you do if someone tries to mug you?

Scams and swindles

Ukrainians freely admit that they don't trust their own countrymen, a general fear which contributes to nationwide tension. Remember that Ukraine is a very poor country with high unemployment, so that foreign tourists with hard cash in hand are the sought-for prey of conmen. Swindles can take many forms. Offering services for cash, or demanding special fees is common, and there has been an increase of staged scenarios to attract your attention and then take your money without your being aware. The latest scheme involves someone finding a large wad of money within your view and then forcing you into confidences or using sleight of hand to take or switch real money for fake. Ignore anyone who approaches you with a plan or blocks you from others' view. Extortion and intimidation are often used to get money from foreigners. Use your logic and just say no. There is no legitimate reason to open your wallet for anyone, unless there's a real threat of violence.

Crime and safety

Visitors are often shocked by the Ukrainian belief that if a crime has been done to you, it is your fault for not preventing it. Be streetwise. For example, Ukrainians will never simply open a door without asking '*kto tam?*' and checking who's there, even in a hotel. You may find that people seem to always be asking you the time or requesting a cigarette. This is a way for them to confirm your status as a foreigner by your look of incomprehension or heavily accented response. Their curiosity may be innocent, but it is acceptable to ignore the question and continue walking, as that's what Ukrainians do. Avoid fortune-tellers who always leave with much more money than you intended them to have.

Internet scams are rife. When making travel arrangements with any Ukrainian company, check their website to see when it was last updated or call them, and refrain from wiring money or sending credit card details. Many 'dating' agencies are high-profile set-ups and romantic meetings often turn into big scams. Realise that you are taking a large risk by getting involved with any of these organisations.

Having been warned, know that Ukrainians have a frightfully honest nature and are above all very kind and hospitable. People in the market will refuse to sell you something that isn't fresh, compliments are sincere and sarcasm non-existent. Don't let unnecessary fear lead to a rejection of everyday Ukrainian hospitality.

Women travellers

On the surface, Ukraine's many decades of communism erased sexism to the point that women doing anything on their own – including travel – is the norm. Females in

Kiev may find that they feel more vulnerable as a foreigner than as a woman. It would also not be facetious to say that a certain solidarity exists among women in Ukraine so that you should feel protected when other women are around. The most obvious risk for women would be travelling alone on overnight trains, where even in first class you may be sharing a compartment with an unknown traveller. Nine times out of ten, you will befriend the stranger and it will be a great experience, but the odd smarmy passenger is not unheard of. You always have the option of buying all the tickets for an entire compartment, which is still a fairly cheap way to travel if slightly lonely. Otherwise, there is safety in numbers, and travelling in a four-person *coupé* will increase your odds of someone else looking out for you. If you find that you are expected to share a train compartment with three men and they all give you the creeps, simply ask the conductor (almost always a woman) to change your place. You will find however, that most men follow train etiquette, allowing women privacy to change clothing and offering the lower berths for sleeping.

Overall, follow your intuition and take the same precautions you would in your own country. Don't walk alone in dark secluded streets. Think ahead and have a contingency plan for ways out of various situations (eg: alternative means of transportation, alternative accommodation). Professional taxis (with signs and phone numbers listed) are normally safe for women. Let others know where you will be travelling and if you are planning on going out at night, tell them when you hope to be back.

Ukraine's dating protocol is mysterious and changing, although some things are fairly obvious. Acting helpless and flirtatious will attract men who will expect more than you may be prepared to give. Accepting drinks from strangers is always a bad idea, as is going back to their apartments. Telling a persistent man that you are Orthodox Christian (*Ya Verushaya*) will get him off your back.

Racial minorities

Racism is another unfortunate aspect of Ukraine, although cities like Kiev and Odessa appear to be rather multi-cultural. In Ukraine, racist mindsets are linked to the general animosity of the poor against the rich as some find it hard to grasp that someone of a different race earns more and lives better than they do. If you are not the same colour as they are, you may suffer double the attitude, but rarely aggression. Expect to be stared at a lot and periodically stopped by the police for passport checks.

WHAT TO TAKE

It is difficult to pack light for Ukraine, where a wide range of situations demands different things, however Ukraine is not so barren these days. In Kiev you can find most consumer goods, so leave the contingency items at home and bring extra money. Some things you can't get in Ukraine are: (good) toilet paper, a Swiss army knife (with screwdriver head – you'll use it), powdered milk if you like milk in your tea or coffee, good nail clippers, hand sanitiser or packaged wipes. You'll use a small torch (flashlight) more than you expect – for unlit stairwells and when the electricity goes off. You can buy all your toiletries in Kiev, including designer razor blades and Clinique products, so don't despair if you've forgotten something. Contact lens solution is just hitting the big shops in Kiev, but is not always easy to find, so bring it all with you. If you are travelling during the coldest part of winter, you may find your contacts (especially hard ones) have a hard time staying in and you'll wish you had your glasses. If you normally wear glasses, bring an extra pair. Many people also find they need sunglasses in summer. Bring a small first-aid kit with anti-gas, anti-diarrhoea pills such as Imodium-D, aspirin, syringes, bandages, Neosporin (or other antiseptic cream) and tweezers. Instead of the pre-packaged travel sewing kits, make your own: bring one spool of dark thread (blue or black), a pack of needles and a fair number of buttons (it is uncanny how they fall off in Ukraine). You may also want to bring a small Russian or Ukrainian dictionary. Also, Ukrainians love business cards and use them passionately. If you have one, bring lots.

Luggage

The smarter your luggage, the more people will have their eye on you. Having beat-up bags makes you a less competitive victim of theft, but then fashionable Kiev could be the exception to the rule. A hard-sided suitcase with wheels is best as large soft-sided bags can be (and have been) slashed open. Much depends on the nature of your trip, be it an organised tour or if you are on your own. If taking the road independently, pack light and inconspicuously. Dark duffle-bags, simple backpacks, or a small, wheeled suitcase are best. The giant, brightly coloured backpacks you see all over western Europe are still too loud for Ukraine and you will only draw attention to yourself. The exception would be a planned hiking trip outside the city. Army/navy surplus stores always sell a good variety of heavy canvas bags, and their colour scheme will help you blend in better in Ukraine. Padlocking bags is also a good idea. When touring during the day, refrain from using a bum bag (fanny pack) or fancy camera bag. Instead, use a large purse or secure backpack. To be truly inconspicuous, carry your belongings (and camera) inside a simple plastic shopping bag like you see all the Ukrainians using. It's all you need and a thief won't think to grab it.

TOILETS

Pack at least one roll of toilet paper with you for the trip. Ukrainian toilet paper is a tribute to recycling with rough chips of pulp still visible (and tangible). Nine times out of ten there will be no paper in your toilet stall so saving paper napkins from restaurants in your pocket is a worthwhile precaution. When in search of a toilet, think like a socialist city planner (train and bus stations, large public parks, city squares). Only newer restaurants feature public toilets. The letter (M) is the Gents and (Ж) is the Ladies. Most public toilets are of the stand or squat variety with raised porcelain

Clothing

You are judged by what you wear in Kiev, and Ukrainians will wear their very best clothes and shoes in public no matter how intense their poverty. The Western impulse to dress down when on the road comes as a shock, since Ukrainians assume all Westerners are rich and therefore should be travelling with designer labels and diamond bracelets. To the other unnecessary extreme, many travellers are loaded down with pre-conceived images of a desolate land and pack for Ukraine as if they were going camping. Comfort should be your main aim, but men should bring at least one pair of nice trousers and a button-down shirt with collar, and women should have one 'semi-nice' outfit (ie: skirt and blouse or

footsteps. The cost ranges from 30 to 70 kopecks so always keep a single hrivna ready to pay the attendant. Ask for *bumaha* (paper) if you see that the attendant has some and be prepared to fork out some kopecks for the privilege. Each wagon on a train has its own toilet at the end of the car, although it is better to use them closer to the beginning of your journey while the floor is still dry. Long bus rides will stop at least once every two hours for a break. If you tend to be fussy about clean toilets, Kiev features over a dozen McDonalds restaurants which almost always guarantee a hygienic experience.

What to take

dress). You will be surprised how a change of clothes will bring you increased respect when needed.

Bring comfortable and sturdy walking shoes, but avoid flashy white trainers which are coveted merchandise. Sturdy clothes are best for daytime activities. Even if it's normally not your style, bring a pair of loose-fitting pyjamas to wear on overnight trains, or a T-shirt and running pants. You will be more comfortable and it's *de rigueur*. Keep in mind that you can buy any kind of clothing in Kiev, so, rather than plan for every fashion contingency, just bring more cash.

Kiev can on occasion get very hot in the summer (+30°C) and people's clothes come off. Women tend to dress skimpily and a lot of men will work in the fields wearing nothing but their underwear. Travellers in public are still expected to keep covered, except for beaches and parks. In other seasons, you will be amazed at how women in high heels never fall on the ice and how men keep mud off their trouser legs, two feats that set the Ukrainians apart.

Winter wear

Ukrainian winters are bitterly cold, with temperatures down to −30°C plus severe wind chill. If you are travelling from November to March, pack warm clothes. Kiev's streets are never cleared when it snows so that thick ice forms on all roads and pavements which later turns to grey slush and gooey mud in the spring. A pair of sturdy, insulated, waterproof boots will prevent you from being cold, wet, dirty and miserable. A hat is also vital – bring something warm that covers your ears, like a woollen beanie. Ukraine knows its weather best, so a lot of travellers purchase their hat after they've arrived. You may have your stance about fur, but the classic Russian *shapka* is still the preferred head covering in winter, and it makes a lot of sense in the cold and wind. If you do choose to buy one, go with rabbit, mink or Astrakhan wool – all made from farmed animals.

Several layers will keep you warm inside and out (proper indoor heating has only just been introduced). A wool sweater is nice and warm unless it gets wet (hang it outside to dry, let it freeze and then beat out the ice crystals). Cotton dries quicker indoors. Wear a thick and heavy coat or parka that is extra long (and preferably water-resistant). Bring at least one pair of long underwear during the coldest part of the year and wear long thermal socks that come up to your knees. Some women also find wearing thick tights beneath trousers works well to keep out the cold. To keep out the wind, wear a long scarf that you can wrap several times around your neck.

ELECTRICITY

AC is 220 volts and outlets fit the same plugs used in continental Europe. Unless you are staying in very posh hotels (four and five stars which have their own power systems), make sure to unplug appliances that you are not using. Frequent electrical surges can destroy your television, iron, or hair dryer (which is why most appliances will not be plugged in when you first enter your room). The electrical outlets on trains are for small razors only. Frequencies are also different (50 hertz), so in certain cases you will require an adapter as well as a converter. Keep in mind that certain electrical

Electricity

appliances will cost much less in Ukraine than in your home country, so for an extended period it may be worth buying it there rather than lugging over your own appliances and adapters.

MONEY

Ukraine is still a cash economy, but credit and debit cards are making headway as banks stabilise, particularly in Kiev. Travellers' cheques are often more pain than their security warrants in Ukraine, although some banks and most luxury hotels in Kiev will accept them. Diversifying is the best method of carrying your money: bring a fair amount in cash, use a debit card for withdrawing more cash, and bring a credit card to pay for hotels, meals in nice restaurants and any other large expenses. Visa, MasterCard, American Express, Maestro and Cirrus are widely accepted in Kiev – other cards are still too foreign. When paying with plastic, be patient. Sometimes (rarely in Kiev) you may even need to show the attendant how to process a credit-card transaction. Credit-card fraud is a known problem in Ukraine, so be conservative in your payments and hold on to all receipts as a precaution. It is best to reserve your credit card for big transactions with reputable businesses. Instead, use debit cards to draw cash from machines (and keep your statements). This gives you the best exchange rate and limits the amount of money you are carrying on your person at any one time. When using a cashpoint, you often are given a choice of taking out hrivna, dollars, or euros. Generally, international banking in Ukraine is trustworthy and secure.

Cash means US dollars or EU euros. British pounds are usually accepted by banks only and will not give you a competitive exchange rate. Go to the bank in your home country and ask for crisp, mint condition bills printed after 1995 as Ukrainian moneychangers often refuse a bill printed earlier and those showing any sign of wear. Foreign citizens are allowed to enter Ukraine with up to US$1,000 cash (travellers' cheques included). If you have more, you must technically fill out a special declaration form. These days it is not necessary to carry that much and you only increase your chances of being robbed. US$300–500 is about the right amount. Wearing a hidden moneybelt is wise, but don't keep all your cash, cheques or cards in one place. Spread them on your person and in your luggage and don't forget where you've put it all. Stuffing bills into shoes or socks is a bad idea as they often tear or get sweaty. Smart travellers will always carry an emergency stash of a US$100 bill or euro equivalent. If you do have old or damaged money, some large banks will take it, but for a lower rate.

When needed, money transfers are convenient. Western Union has been in Ukraine for over ten years and now has literally hundreds of offices all over the country. Call 8 800 500 1000 from anywhere in Ukraine to find the closest point. The main office is in Kiev: Proreznaya 15; tel/fax: 044 228 1780; email: office@westernunion.org.ua; web: www.westernunion.org.ua or www.westernunion.com.

Currency

The hrivna (UAH) was chosen as the new currency because the soft 'h'/hard rolled 'r' diphthong can only be pronounced by the most nationally astute Ukrainians.

Money

Hrivna bills come in denominations of 1, 2, 5, 10, 20, 50 and 100. One-hundred-kopeck coins are the very cute coins that jingle in your pocket; 100 kopecks make one hrivna. Inflation has stabilised to the point that for the past year (2003) the US dollar has been worth about 5.3 hrivna and the Euro worth slightly more. In hotels and more expensive shops, prices are often listed as **y.e.** (standard equivalent) which is Ukraine's politically correct term for the US dollar.

Exchange booths are ubiquitous in Kiev, recognisable for the daily exchange rate chalked in next to the various flag symbols. It is illegal, unwise and unnecessary to change money anywhere else. Gone are the days when foreigners could pay for things in small US bills: people prefer hrivna (or euros!). Even though everyone deals in hrivna, there seems to be a perpetual lack of small change in the city. Always carry a fair stash of 1,2 and 5 hrivna notes for buses, toilets and entrance fees (taxis normally have change). The couple of hundred hrivna you are carrying in your pocket may not seem much to you, but it is a monthly salary for some. It's a good idea to keep your bills in a roll, or folded in your pocket: larger denominations on the inside and smaller on the outside. This system prevents you from accidentally pulling out a huge bill when you're buying something on the street (save the big bills for big purchases). Kopecks often seem a nuisance, especially when you consider their worth; shop attendants will sometimes round up to the nearest hrivna. It is also a good idea to keep at least 50 kopecks, just in case; when you need the toilet, it's better to have some coins in your pocket than to rummage through your bills trying to determine if that's a 1, 10 or 100 hrivna note.

How much?

This is a question only you can answer as only you know your spending habits and the level of comfort you demand. Kiev is not as inexpensive as the rest of the country, but still generally cheaper than western Europe. Remember that what is considered luxury in Kiev may not be luxury in your home country, but you will have to pay a much higher price for some items as they are luxuries in Ukraine (eg: eating lobster). Kiev has quickly transcended being a 'cheap city' and now flaunts an expensive lifestyle that locals can rarely afford.

The tried and tested rule for travelling cheap is living like the locals live. In Kiev, you can skimp by on US$20 a day (or less), by choosing the cheapest hotel rooms (without individual plumbing and in the farthest corners of the city), buying food in markets, eating in cafeterias, and travelling on trains. Roughing it in Kiev can still be

BRIBERY

Paying someone a little extra to make sure something gets done was a past way of life when a collapsed legal framework offered no guarantees. Things have changed a lot in a very little time and now most fees come with receipts. Some bribery still exists, but the practice should not be encouraged by foreigners. These days, a sly slip of American cash rarely solves any problems, but it will draw undue attention.

Money

luxurious to an extent – de-luxe pedicures or haircuts in regular salons are cheap, first-class train tickets are relatively inexpensive for foreigners, the subway costs pennies, museums cost very little, and box seats in the opera cost less than US$5.

Most independent adult travellers I've met (who don't speak any of the language) budget around US$50 a day, but if you want to be comfortable, plan for at least US$100 a day.

Accommodation and extra services (taxis, interpreters) will eat up most of your budget, as many hotels charge per person and a lot of 'tourist' services intentionally overcharge foreigners. Ukraine's tourist industry now caters to foreigners with US$100- and US$200-a-day budgets and you can easily spend that much per day just on a so-so hotel in Kiev. Travelling by chauffeured car and personal guides will increase the price tag further.

Organised tours usually charge US$400–500 a week and include hotel accommodation, meals, transport and guide. If you're part of an organised tour that is taking care of most of these costs, US$50 a day is more than enough.

Tipping

Tipping is not a traditional practice, but slowly making headway with the market economy. In sit-down restaurants, a service charge of 10% will be included in your bill. Otherwise, if you like your service, 15% is the unwritten rule. Taxi prices are usually negotiated beforehand, so a tip might be defeating the purpose of your bargaining. You might find that you have a hard time convincing some people to accept a tip as they don't see why they should accept extra cash for just doing their job. Explain that it is *na chai*, which is the Russian/Ukrainian expression 'for tea' from the old days when servants were given a little extra to spend on meals. Anything up to 5 hrivna is enough. Tipping with US dollars is simply gauche, unless you are in a five-star hotel.

BUSINESS

Business hours are normally 09.00 to 18.00 with a lunch break between 13.00 and 14.00. That said, you'll find many places are open until very late, and many food shops, hotels and stations are open 24 hours. Museums and other tourist spots usually have one or two 'days off' when they are closed, which could be any day of the week. Check before you go somewhere.

Economic specialists and the general media discuss Ukraine's economic 'transition' to capitalism, a term which may apply to changing government institutions, but has little relevance to Ukrainians themselves. Ukrainians have been doing 'business' forever – in fact, Kiev started as a place for business over 1,500 years ago. Kievan Rus acted as an important international trade centre, and it was the success and riches of Kiev that attracted the countless invasions that would lead to the city's downfall. Sure, the last 70 years of Communism have stifled some instinct for free enterprise, but as a walk down Khreschatyk today can attest, Ukraine has fallen right back into the material world with aplomb.

Foreign business is especially interested in this 'emerging market' of 50 million Ukrainians, thirsty for new goods. And yet, the returns on several waves of investment have often been cut short. International businessmen complain regularly that there is little respect for contracts and agreements in Ukraine, payments are frequently delayed for long periods of time, and coping with corruption is burdensome. All these things are probably true, for there does exist an unscrupulous element in the country that has made a lot of money through poor business practices. This bunch is, however, facing minority status as the rest of the country seeks to become fully engaged with the West.

Self-help tapes, home-taught MBA courses, and 'how-to-become-a-millionaire' books are all bestsellers in Ukraine. Dressing for business is a fashion statement that even non-businesspeople strive to emulate. The polyglot younger generation now mocks the stereotypical unsavvy, clumsy mobster businessman. Change is imminent. If you are going to Kiev to do business, you should feel optimistic and adventurous.

As with many cultures, rushing right into business dealings is uncouth for Ukrainians, even after paying homage to pre-required small talk. A natural course of affairs is to build a symbolic trust, most often through a meal or some entertainment. Ukrainians especially like to ply their partners with alcohol and food for hours and keep business talk to a minimum. Punctilious businesspersons from the West can find this highly annoying, especially if it goes on for a few days. Deals are usually finalised with a vodka toast.

Business cards are vital to business survival, and the sign of international business chic is to present cards with Ukrainian on one side, English on the other. Print some before your trip.

SANCTIONED SUPERSTITIONS

- Never shake hands through a doorway. Doing so is a sign of insincerity, misfortune and ill will to the other person.
- Never cross paths with or move ahead of a funeral procession (buses will wait until they pass). Doing so means you are searching for death.
- Whistling indoors means all your money will fly out the window.
- When you see a baby, do not fawn over the child, look at the baby directly in the eye or tell the parent how cute and precious the baby is. It is bad luck – the child may get sick and you may inadvertently pass on the evil eye.
- Never give an even number of flowers – it symbolises death.
- To avoid jinxing yourself when tempting providence, spit over your left shoulder.
- Sit down before leaving on a long journey. Rushing off brings bad luck on the road.

CULTURAL DOS AND DON'TS
Interacting with Ukrainians

Kiev is the most diverse city in Ukraine and comes with all types, so generalising the population's behaviour would prove a false exercise. If you come looking to connect with old-world East European yokels, you will be disappointed. Instead, people in Kiev tend to be highly educated and pragmatic, and their interactions with foreigners reflect that same blend of curiosity and frankness. Overall, Ukrainians are incredibly hospitable and generally understand that foreigners are not always privy to their cultural idiosyncrasies. These quirks are a lot more fun to figure out on your own, but here are a few tips:

Greet others and introduce yourself as you would anywhere else in the world. If you are a man, do not shake a woman's hand unless it is offered to you. Ukrainians love business cards and will pull them out at any time. Bring some if you have them. When entering someone's home, take off your shoes near the entrance. Normally you will be offered slippers to wear. If you have been invited as a guest, bringing a small gift or flowers is customary.

Turning down a drink is considered a very rude gesture and for some carries the same weight as refusing to shake hands. If you are a non-drinker or just want to hold back, a determined *nyet* will hardly do the trick. Stating religious or health reasons is met with more understanding and causes less offence. No matter how hardcore one's habits, don't ever expect to keep up with a Ukrainian drink for drink. I have yet to meet a non-Ukrainian who can.

At birthday parties, weddings, anniversaries, holidays and generally most gatherings Ukrainians will make poetic toasts to one another and in particular those who are to be honoured. As a foreign guest, toasts will be made to you, and you are expected to toast in return. A mere 'thank you' or 'cheers' just won't do. Be vociferous and flowery, ending with very specific wishes of goodwill (eg: 'that our most wise and beautiful host discovers secret happiness and fortune throughout the next year'). In a bar, with friends, or if you're feeling shy, you can simply toast with *'Budmo!'*

Before you eat, say *'Smachnoho!'* (like *'bon appétit'*) to the others at the table. As a guest, you will be fed and fed and fed. If you completely empty your plate or bowl, it will be refilled. If you leave too much on your plate, your host will say you don't like his/her cooking and they will be offended. Either way, you can't win.

The Soviet era created a society that was anything but service-oriented. Dealing with certain concierges, waiters, hotel clerks and ticket sellers can be a taxing experience, especially if you are used to a culture of Western customer service. Being ignored or shouted at can get frustrating. Sometimes it takes making a small fuss to get the attention of the person on the other side of the glass. Being polite but persistent is the best policy.

Standing in a queue (line) also gets little respect in Ukraine. You may find that after waiting 20 minutes, someone will cut in front of you. Be assertive and try to come across as confident. Always be prepared with your request. If you get to a window and are still fumbling for money or a ticket, then someone else has the right to push you aside and take your place, and they will. When a bus, tram or subway train appears, queues disappear and everyone pushes and shoves to get on. If you try to be your version of polite, you may never get on. Learn to throw your body into it and say *izvinitye* (excuse me) or *probachteh* (in Ukrainian).

Poverty

The people of Ukraine suffered tremendously during the economic crash and social ills of the early post-perestroika years. In less than ten years after independence, Ukraine's population declined by six million through massive emigration, a swift rise in the death rate and a dramatic drop in the birth rate. Begging is looked down upon culturally, but people still do it, although much less than in other poor countries. On the other hand, a small percentage of Ukrainian society has become extremely wealthy, especially the *byznesmeny* who got rich quick from privatisation 'deals'. These 'New Russians' are the subject of countless jokes that mock their lack of taste and values. A real middle class is emerging in Ukraine – especially in Kiev – but overall, people are still quite poor and spend most of their time acquiring the basic needs of life. Coming to terms with dire poverty is something travellers must do all over the world, but in Ukraine, the real puzzlement stems from witnessing poverty among such an educated and technologically advanced people. Sticking to the touristy sections of Kiev may give an impression that 'all is well' in the country – as the capital and beneficiary of most government spending, Kiev is in fact much better off than the rest of the country: unemployment is lower and salaries are much higher. That does not excuse the fact that a majority of the population lives on very little and that day-to-day survival is a struggle for most. Know that your presence in the country is already a sign of progression. Spend your money wisely, but make sure to spend it. Encouraging small private enterprise through patronage is one of the best ways to 'give something back' during your trip to Kiev.

Gifts

There is no need to lug an extra suitcase of provisions to hand out to Ukraine's poverty-stricken. You can buy all the basics in the country and a lot more. Gift-giving in Ukraine is sentimental and highly symbolic so don't feel compelled to make an overtly significant contribution. Plus, a lot of Ukrainians believe all foreigners are millionaires, so any irregular display of your financial prowess may bring you uncomfortable demands for sizeable loans or secret explanations of far-fetched business proposals. Token gifts showing appreciation are fine. If you are invited over for dinner, bring a box of chocolates, flowers (odd number) or a bottle of something. Creative and personal gifts will please even more: English books, nifty kitchen gadgets, and any luxury items that hold some merit when from another country (perfume, sports team paraphernalia etc).

GIVING SOMETHING BACK

Travelling is always a two-way experience, where visitor and visited make all sorts of exchanges, both intended and subconscious. As you take in all that Kiev offers, consider how your presence affects this city and what you can do to help during your stay. Just being in Kiev and spending money at local businesses is a positive move, even if you are simply buying sunflower seeds from a *babushka*, but the responsible traveller will see other opportunities to give something back in return for the experience s/he has had in Kiev.

Remember as well that the stories you tell of your travels, and the way you

THE STREET CHILDREN OF KIEV

Homeless, abandoned and orphaned children have become a tragedy throughout the former Soviet Union. Normal social safety nets have disappeared, and with the difficult economy and increased social ills, hundreds of thousands of orphaned and abandoned children have ended up on the streets of Moscow, St Petersburg and Kiev. Exact estimates in Kiev vary so widely it is hard to know the real extent of the problem, but it is safe to say that the suffering of Kiev's street children is extensive, and during the night children with no place to go will roam the streets of the city, sleep in the sewers, and beg for food. Several different churches and organisations work directly to feed, clothe and sometimes house street children. **New Beginnings** is a UK-based organisation that runs a home and a feeding programme for street children in Kiev. For information on how you can help directly, contact Pat Wright, MBE; Vineyard Cottage, 45 Appleby Road, Kendal, Cumbria LA9 6ES, England; tel: +44 (0)1539 727158; email: pat.w@mail.ru. She can tell you where they'll need you in Kiev or how to help out once you've returned to the UK.

Planning

describe Kiev to others after your trip, help to establish how the rest of the world perceives Kiev. Before you say something negative or discouraging, think about all the terrible stereotypes your own country gets pegged with because of some unruly tourist who showed disrespect towards the local culture.

This book includes a few ideas where you can contribute during your travels in Kiev. I am always looking for new service opportunities to pass on to fellow travellers, so I ask that you please contact me with your experiences and new suggestions on giving something back while travelling in Kiev.

Local charities in Kiev

The following organisations will gladly accept your help:

Care and Relief for the Young (CRY) Sovereign Place, Upper Northam Close, Hedge End, Southampton SO30 4BB; tel: +44 (0)1489 788 300; fax: +44 (0)1489 790 750; email: ukoffice@cry.org.uk; web: www.cry.org.uk. This is a UK-based charity that partners with several projects in Kiev. Try to contact them in advance of your trip.

Kiev Special School for Blind Children No 5 Vyshgorodska 35, Kiev 252074; tel: 044 430 0118; fax: 044 430 0032. This school is the leading educational institution in Ukraine and is always grateful for any kind of assistance. The school was founded in 1884 by the Russian Tsar and is located on the corner of Vyshgorodska and Pravdy, in the far Vynohradar (northwest) region of the city. Visit the school when you're in Kiev or ask them how you can be of assistance.

Kiev YMCA, 105, 26 A, Gmyri St, 253140 Kiev; tel/fax: 044 73 0524; email: ymcakyiv@ambernet.kiev.ua. The YMCA functions worldwide, but the one in Kiev has several long-term projects that always require an extra hand. Stop by and find out how to get involved.

A point to note is that most churches and museums receive very little cash from the government for upkeep. Leaving small donations in the box by the door (marked HA PEMOHT XPAMA) is for keeping the gold polished, the floors clean, and the artwork bright. Contributing to Kiev's churches (even with a couple of kopecks) makes the city a little nicer.

Metro sign

Practicalities

3

BANKS

So many banks have popped up around Kiev that you will have no problem getting cash or finding out your bank balance in hrivna. There are also banking facilities at the central post office, and most middle- to upmarket hotels will have an ATM in the lobby. Finding a place to change money is even easier than finding a bank. Just look for the signs with American, Russian and European flags, with corresponding currency rates chalked in. Currency exchange booths are normally open from 09.00 to 21.00, some later. Banking hours in Ukraine normally run from 09.00 to 16.00.

Listing all of Kiev's banks would be like listing all of its fire hydrants. You shouldn't have any problem finding one if you're in Podil, the centre or Pechersk. Things are tougher in more residential areas (although Kievans search for the local McDonalds which always has an ATM). Look for official-looking signs that read Банк (Bank), and better yet, look for bank doors or bank machines with symbols that correspond to the one on your cards (eg: Visa, MasterCard, Cirrus). Ukrainians shopping for expensive goods rarely carry their cash with them, which is why most shopping centres and nice shops now have an ATM machine. Small bank branches are also located inside many of the nicer shopping centres. For the traveller's more sophisticated banking needs, here are a few leads:

Citibank Dymytrova 16г; tel: 044 490 1000 [2 C3]. South side, by metro station Respublikansky Stadion.

Diamantbank Kontraktova Ploscha 10A; tel: 044 490 8383 [1 C3]. In Podil, at the bottom of Andriyivsky Uzviz.

Nadra Khmelnytskovo 4; tel: 044 462 0001 [2 C2]. In the centre, off Khreschatyk, next to ЦУМ.

Parex Bank Striletska 16; tel: 044 244 6715 [1 C4]. Behind St Sophia's Cathedral.

Raiffeisenbank Mykhayilivska 2; tel: 044 490 0526 [2 D1]. The north side of the Maidan Nezalezhnosti.

Western Union Prorizna 15; tel: 044 228 1780 [2 D1]. In the city centre, a block up from Khreschatyk.

MEDIA AND COMMUNICATIONS
Newspapers and magazines

The *Kyiv Post* (www.kpnews.com) is not just the ex-pat weekly, but a rare bit of free press offering reliable insight into what's really going on in Kiev, in English. The newspaper is available free in most upmarket hotels and restaurants or for sale at any news stand. The other English newspaper is the pro-government *Kyiv Weekly*, also widely distributed, but much less informative. *Welcome to Ukraine* magazine is a unique English-language travel magazine with well-written stories and artistic photography focusing entirely on Ukrainian destinations and local history. The high-quality publication is sold in most bookshops in Kiev. *Panorama* is Ukraine International Airlines' bilingual (Ukrainian and English) in-flight magazine published monthly with a back section on visiting Kiev. If you fly to Kiev on a UIA flight, you'll get one – if not, they are sometimes available in bookshops and at nicer hotels. **The Ukrainian** is a progressive, Kiev-based business magazine that addresses current affairs and the Ukrainian business climate. **What's On** (www.whatson-kiev.com) is a colourful English-language weekly similar to *Time Out* magazines in London and New York, detailing restaurants, nightlife and entertainment, as well as special events for that week. You can find some foreign-language newspapers (*International Herald Tribune*, *The Guardian*, *Wall Street Journal*, etc) in Kiev, and most big-name glossy magazines in English-language bookshops. Russian and Ukrainian newspapers spin every bit of news and non-news from the far right to the far left and in between.

Telephones

Ukraine's country code is 380 (although the zero is normally included with the city code). Some public pay phones still take 50-kopeck pieces, but mostly accept UTEL cards that can be purchased at any post office. These are only worth using for domestic calls in Kiev and throughout the rest of Ukraine. Most hotels will let you make international phone calls from your room, but tend to charge a fair amount (at least US$2 a minute to Britain, US$1 to USA and Canada). Most post offices will also have international phone booths, where you pay a deposit, make a phone call at regular rates and then retrieve your balance. Some international phone-cards are now sold in Kiev which halves the cost.

To call within Ukraine, dial 8 (for long-distance), then the city code (i.e. 044 for Kiev) and then the number. In this book, all phone numbers are listed with Kiev's city code for calling from outside the city. When in Kiev, drop the 044 and just dial the last seven digits. When calling internationally from Ukraine, dial 8, wait for the tone, then dial 10, followed by country code, city code and so on. Sometimes it takes a few tries. If you find you just need to make a quick international phone call and have no access, go to the central post office right off the Maidan Nezalezhnosti. There are lots of international phone booths there where you can pay and make calls.

Foreign-language operators are also available in Kiev. Dial 8, wait for the tone, and then dial:

191 French	192 English	193 German
194 Ukrainian/Russian	195 German	

If you have a European mobile phone that lets you roam, it will probably work in Ukraine. When calling outside Ukraine, you'll have to dial + followed by the country code and then the number. For long stays and to cut costs, consider buying a pay-as-you-go Ukrainian chip, which can be purchased at any number of mobile phone stores (Kyivstar and UMC are both on the Maidan Nezalezhnosti). This option is good for making calls in Kiev and the rest of Ukraine, but becomes fairly pricey when calling abroad.

Practicalities

Internet

Ukraine is more internet-savvy than some Western nations and you'll have no problem getting access in the computer clubs, internet cafés and hotels of Kiev. Cyrillic letters are printed beneath the Latin letters of the QWERTY keyboard, and you can change the typing language by clicking the prompt at the bottom right-hand corner of the screen.

The email and websites listed throughout this book were checked at the time of writing, but you may find that it takes a while to get an e-response from the other side. Be patient, as communicating in English is not a given.

More and more hotels in Kiev are sporting 'business centres' that cater to business travellers. Normally there are two to three computers with internet access, a copy and fax machine and small office spaces to work. Some are great and very useful, others are slow, inefficient and pricey. If you want to cut down on costs, go to an internet café, which is never more than US$2 an hour. Cyber cafés are not lacking in Kiev and the English-language signs will point the way. Prices hover around US$1 to $2 an hour. The downside (or upside) is that some cafés are filled with young kids glued to the screen, noisily blowing up helicopters and killing digital enemies with mouse-powered karate kicks. On the flip side, cyber cafés have much faster internet connections, the younger staff normally speak English well, and they are great at getting you started. If you're panicked and disoriented but need email badly, go to the Central Post Office (the entrance on the Maidan Nezalezhnosti) and go up to the second floor, where there is a real café with lots of internet connections. Otherwise, here are a few centrally located cafés:

Bunker Artyoma 11A; tel: 044 212 4860 [1 B4]
Cyber Café Prorizna 21; tel: 044 228 0548 [2 C1]
M16 Pechersky Uzviz 3; tel: 044 235 3840 [2 E3]
Orki Khmelnytskovo 29/2; tel: 044 228 1187 [2 C2]
Orbita Khreschatyk 29, 2nd floor; tel: 044 234 1693 [2 D2]
Pentagon Khreschatyk 15; tel: 044 228 2182 [2 D2]

Post

Traditionally, the *Poshta* was for paying electricity bills and receiving pensions. Travellers can get confused by the dozens of queues and windows. If you want to buy stamps to mail a letter, find the window with all the colourful envelopes and cards. Always send letters *Avia* (airmail). Traditionally, letters were addressed in an opposite manner to European post (1st line: post code, city; 2nd line: street address; 3rd line: surname, name), but now Ukraine is changing over to the standard sender's address in the upper-left corner and the receiver in the middle. Note that postcards can be sent as open cards only within Ukraine and that if you are sending them internationally you must put them inside a red-and-blue striped airmail envelope. Receiving letters in Ukraine by *poste restante* has become a less secure option in recent years. If you are going to be in the country for a while,

Practicalities

getting a post office box is cheap and reliable, otherwise, better to use email on your travels. Letters from Ukraine to Europe take around ten days to arrive and to North America expect at least two weeks.

Kiev's huge **Central Post Office** on the Maidan Nezalezhnosti (Khreschatyk 22) is open from 08.00 to 21.00 every day, closing on Sunday at 19.00. Besides buying stamps and mailing things, there is an internet café and a number of international phone booths that charge about US$0.60 a minute for calls to North America and US$1 to western Europe. You can also fax things here, and it is one of the few places to buy postcards, although sadly, no-one has had the enterprising vision of making quality photographic prints of Kiev. (There are great alternatives though, such as Happy Red Army Day cards.) Mail letters in the little yellow boxes with dark blue writing marked ПОШТА that hang from the sides of buildings and outside post offices. There are 232 post offices in Kiev (a statistic to please Soviet sensibilities), and each is named as it is numbered. Naturally, Kievans are still more likely to know 'their' post office by its number. Ask the concierge at the hotel where you're staying, or ask a stranger on the street *'de poshta?'*.

Centre
Post Office No 19 Hrushevskovo 5; tel: 044 293 2896
Post Office No 53 Artyoma 59; tel: 044 211 3091
Post Office No 225 Mayakovskovo 45; tel: 044 515 6636
Post Office No 40 Vasylkivska 7/7; tel: 044 263 8093

Media and communications

West
Post Office No 57 Peremohy 57; tel: 044 446 5289

Left Bank
Left bank (Livoberezhno) Lunacharskovo 16/4; tel: 044 517 3529

Podil
Post Office No 33 Saksahanskovo 48; tel: 044 220 6416

Parcels
DHL has offices all over Ukraine; in Kiev, Vasylkivska 1; tel: 044 264 7200. FedEx works through the local Elin, Inc; Kiev, Kikvidze 44; tel: 044 495 2020; fax: 044 495 2022; email: fedex@elin.kiev.ua. Inside Ukraine, you can send parcels on trains or buses, and it is a lot more secure than it sounds, if you have someone picking it up at the receiving station. Bring your package to a window at the station, with the destination clearly marked.

FOREIGN EMBASSIES IN KIEV
Australian Consulate Komynterna 18, Apt 11; tel: 044 235 7586; fax: 044 346 4223; web: www.embassy.gov.au/ua.html
Belarus Sichnevovo Povstannya 6; tel: 044 290 0201; fax: 044 290 3413; web: www.belembassy.org.ua

Belgium Leontovicha 4; tel: 044 238 2600; fax: 044 238 2602; web:
www.diplomatie.be/kiev/

Canada Yaroslaviv Val 31; tel: 044 464 1144; fax: 044 464 0598; web: www.kyiv.gc.ca

Czech Republic Yaroslaviv Val 34A; tel: 044 212 0431; fax: 044 229 7469; web:
www.czechembassy.org

France Reytarska 39; tel: 044 228 8728; fax: 044 229 0870; web: www.ambafrance.kiev.ua

Germany Khmelnytskovo 25; tel: 044 247 6800; fax: 044 247 6818; web:
www.german-embassy.kiev.ua

Hungary Reytarska 33; tel: 044 238 6381; fax: 044 212 2090; web: www.konzulatus.uz.ua

Israel Lesi Ukrayinky 34; tel: 044 239 6979; fax: 044 294 9748

Italy Yaroslaviv Val 32B; tel: 044 230 3100; fax: 044 230 3103; web: www.ambital.kiev.ua

Japan Muzeny 4 Suite 700; tel: 044 490 5500; fax: 044 490 5502; web:
www.ua.emb-japan.go.jp

Moldova Sichnevoho Povstannya 6; tel/fax: 044 290 7722

Poland Yaroslaviv Val 12; tel: 044 230 0700; fax: 044 464 1336; web: www.polska.com.ua

Romania Kotsyubynskovo Mikhayla 8; tel: 044 234 5261; fax: 044 235 2025

Russia Povitroflotsky 27; tel: 044 244 0963; fax: 044 246 3469; web:
www.embrus.org.ua

Slovakia Yaroslaviv Val 34; tel: 044 212 0310; fax: 044 212 3271

Turkey Arsenalna 18; tel: 044 294 9964; fax: 044 295 6423

UK Desiakynna 9; tel: 044 490 3660; fax: 044 490 3662; web: www.britemb-ukraine.net

USA Kotsyubynski 10; tel/fax: 044 490 4000; web: www.usinfo.usemb.kiev.ua

HOSPITALS

Try not to go to hospital if you can help it. We've all heard horror stories, and a few of them are still true, about Ukrainian hospitals although in general, staff are conscientious and knowledgeable, and work with a desire to help anyone who walks through their doors. The **Central Hospital** in Kiev is based at Berdychivska 1; tel: 044 244 6647. If you do need emergency treatment, here are a few recommended, Western-standard hospitals that are open 24 hours:

American Medical Center Berdychivska 1; tel: 044 490 7600; email: kiev@amcenters.com; web: www.amcenters.com. The best in Kiev for now.
Boris Clinic Velyka Vasylkivska 55A; tel: 044 238 0000; email: Med_Boris@ukr.net; web: www.boris.kiev.ua
Medikom Kondratyuka 8; tel: 044 432 8888; fax: 044 234 0303; web: www.medikom.kiev.ua. One of Ukraine's first private clinics; 24-hour first-aid.
Ukrainian-German Clinic Chervonoarmiyska 67/7; tel: 044 220 5572; email: info@unk.kiev.ua; web: www.unk.kiev.ua

PHARMACIES

Finding medicine in Kiev is as easy as finding food. Look for the sign Аптека (*Aptyeka*) or the tried and true international colour scheme of white and green. If you are in the city centre, you can go into any of the major underground shopping centres (Globus, Metrograd, Kvadrat) and find easy access to over-the-counter service.

Chance Khreschatyk 15; tel: 044 228 3249
Europharm Khmelnytskovo 40/25; tel: 044 234 2988
Pharma Kyiv Artyoma 32/38; tel: 044 219 4035

VO Pharmacies:
Podil
Verkhny Val 48; tel: 044 463 7028

Centre
Khreschatyk 22; tel: 044 229 2434

Left Bank
Raisy Okipnoy 2; tel: 044 516 2177

Pechersk
Bankova 11; tel: 044 255 7758
Klovsky Uzviz 13A; tel: 044 254 0555

TOUR OPERATORS

Be wary of companies that advertise themselves as 'travel agencies' which are often covers for shady operations that help Ukrainians get out of the country. Instead, search for operators specialising in *priyom* (incoming) tourism. The following are the largest and most secure of Ukraine's larger tour operators with a reputation for professionalism:

Albion Chervonoarmiyska 26, Kiev; tel: 044 461 9746; email: info@albion.com.ua; web: www.albion.com.ua. Bus tours to Crimea combined with Lviv and Kiev.

Intourist Bohdana Khmelnytskovo 26B, Kiev; tel: 044 229 8458

Kiev Travel and Excursion Bureau Velyka Zhytomyrska 17; tel: 044 229 1923

Mandrivnyk Poshtova Ploscha 3, Kiev; tel: 044 463 7604; email: mandrivnyk@adam.kiev.ua; web: www.mandrivnyk.com.ua. Cruises and basic city visits.

Meest-Tour Shevchenka 23, Lviv; tel: 0322 728 710; email: office@meest-tour.com; web: www.meest-tour.com. Trekking in the Carpathians and Crimea; adventure tourism.

New Logic Mikhayilivska 6A, Kiev; tel: 044 462 0462; email: incoming@newlogic.kiev.ua; web: www.newlogic.com.ua. Best for young independent travellers.

Olymp Travel Khreschatyk 21, Kiev; tel: 044 228 1650; email: welcome@olymp-travel.kiev.ua; web: www.olymp-travel.kiev.ua. A nationwide company offering comprehensive 'theme' tours.

SAM Ivana Franka 40B, Kiev; tel/fax: 044 238 6959; email: raskin@samcomp.kiev.ua; web: www.sam.com. The largest and most established in the country.

Sputnik Pushkinskaya 9, #21, Kiev; tel: 044 228 0938; fax: 044 464 1358; email: income@sputnik.kiev.ua; web: www.sputnik.kiev.ua. Longer excursions and diverse tours combined with Russia trips.

Ukrzovnishintour Khmelnytskovo 26, Kiev; tel: 044 229 8464; email: uit@uit.kiev.ua; web: www.uit.com.ua. Travel for business and leisure.

UNA Travel Agency Dovzhenko 1, #16A, Kiev; tel: 044 241 7502; fax: 044 490 9178; email: una@una.kiev.ua; web: www.una.kiev.ua. Eco-tourism and adventure tours.

RELIGIOUS SERVICES

Kiev's religious traditions form such a vital part of the city's legacy that a Sunday service in one of the older Orthodox cathedrals is definitely in order. The following can help if you're looking for your own community:

Anglican
Church of Christ Lyuteranska 22; tel: 044 293 7458; English service at 15.00 on Sundays.

Buddhist
Kiev Buddhist Centre Budivelnykiv 39, Apt 11; tel: 044 559 9421

Catholic
St Alexander's Cathedral Kostelna 17; 044 229 7309; Sundays 09.00, 18.00 (English); 07.30, 13.00 (Polish); 10.00, 19.00 (Ukrainian).

Jewish
Central Synagogue Shota Rustaveli 13; tel: 044 235 0069; Hebrew service at 10.00 and 20.00 on Saturdays.
Podil Synagogue Schekavytska 29; tel: 044 416 1383; Saturdays 09.00 and 19.00 (Russian).

LDS (Mormon)
Pushkinska 2-4/7; tel: 044 461 9019; services in English, Ukrainian and Russian.

Muslim
Vasylenka 15; tel: 044 490 9900; service Fridays from 12.00.

Ukrainian Orthodox

St Vladimir's Cathedral Shevchenka 20; tel: 044 225 0362; daily 08.00, 17.00; Sundays 07.00, 10.00, 17.00.

St Mikhayil's of the Golden Domes Monastery Tryokhosvyatytelska 6; tel: 044 228 6646; daily 07.15, 08.30, 17.00.

Church of the Assumption, Kievo-Pecherska Lavra 21 Sichnevoho Povstannya; tel: 044 290 1508; Sundays 09.00 and 18.00 (Moscow Patriarchate).

Ukrainian Greek Catholic (Uniate)

St Michael's Church Parkova Doroha 1; tel: 044 514 9185; Sundays 08.30, 10.00 and 17.00.

THE *BANYA*

Ancestral tradition and a lack of hot water helped to make public bathing a favoured pastime in Ukraine and a cultural institution. A sauna is a dry sweat-bath of the Finnish variety, usually accompanied by a small pool of freezing water for intermittent dips followed by much yelping. The Russian *banya* is more traditional in Ukraine, and resembles a Turkish bath. As the whole ritual usually takes place in the nude, men and women visit separately. A stone oven in the *parilka* generates incredibly hot steam and people stand or lie down on the varied levels. Once your body is running with sweat, bunches of lime, birch or oak branches (depending on what effect you want) are used to whip and beat you until the green gel of broken leaves, bark and dead skin cells stands out against your red back. Traditionally you are supposed to scream for more (*yescho!*) until you almost pass out. Stepping out of the *parilka*, you should immediately immerse yourself in cold water, rest a bit, and then go back for more. Going to the *banya* also includes taking a series of showers at various temperatures, scrubbing yourself with soap, getting a massage, shaving, drinking lots of fluids and engaging in vigorous conversation with the lads (or the girls). The experience is very communal, not least for the fact that people must partner up to beat each other. You emerge feeling clean inside and out, revived and ready to take on anything. In winter, regular visits to the *banya* will prevent catching colds.

Entrance normally costs less than US$5, although private rentals cost much more. The experience is meant to last several long hours, if not the whole day. You'll be given a white sheet as a wrap, and you can buy *veniki* (branches) there. Nearly all of Kiev's hotels will have a sauna, which is part of the stay, while in some cases, you can rent it out by the hour. For the real experience though, ask around for a traditional *banya*. For many Ukrainians, it's still a weekly tradition. Here's a few in Kiev:

Solomenskye Bany (Solomon's Baths); Urytskovo 38; tel: 044 244 0198. Communal and historic.

Troitskye Bany (Trinity Baths); Chervonoarmyiska 66; tel: 044 227 4068. Private and luxurious.

Tsentralnye Torgovye Bany (Central Trade Baths); Malaya Zhytomyrskaya 3A; tel: 044 228 0102. Huge and famous.

The *banya*

4 Local Transport

Communism granted Ukraine an exceptional system for moving lots of people around quickly and as the Soviet Union's third city, Kiev has benefited from an impressive transportation infrastructure. Decades of wear and tear have slowed things down a bit, but this will always be the best way to go from A to B in this city. The average Ukrainian travels only by public transport and you'll be amazed at the number of bodies that can be squeezed into a single carriage. Things can get very cramped during rush hour (07.00–10.00, 16.00–19.00) so keep your purse or backpack against your chest and breathe slowly. Before a stop, individuals inch their way to the door, asking each person in their way if they are getting off. If someone taps you on the shoulder and mutters something, move out of the way or else nod if you are getting off. At times you will have no choice and be ejected by sheer inertia. Learn to be pushy and fight your way on and off transport.

METRO

Construction of the Kiev metro was begun only after World War II, in 1949, and many of the oldest stations (on the red line) exhibit classic examples of socialist realist design, some of which are remarkably beautiful. Busts of communist leaders, Lenin's more inspiring quotes engraved in the marble walls, and the impressive androgynous statuary of the post-war memorial boom are all bound to make Kiev's metro a tourist attraction in itself. Because Kiev is built on the highest sides of the

Dnepr's ravine, many metro stations are dug extremely deep underground, and this may be the longest (and fastest) escalator ride you've ever been on. During the five minutes it takes to descend, everyone stands and stares at everyone else before zooming off into different directions. I feel truly sorry for the many foreign visitors to Kiev who never witness the slowly shifting masses coddled in fur coats (in winter), and the boundless bundles of vegetables, gardening tools and people that move beneath the city in summer. You haven't seen Kiev unless you've been underground.

Forty-one subway stations are divided into three separate lines, coloured blue, green and red, laid out in classic Soviet style (crossed in three locations forming a central triangle). Remember that these routes were designed to transport people from outer residential communities to work – so the metro is not always the assumed way to go from one tourist attraction to another, however, with Kiev traffic being Kiev traffic, it tends to be the quickest way to get around the city.

The metro runs from 05.30 until midnight every day with constant and frequent trains all day long, becoming sparser in the very late evening. During rush hour (from 07.00–10.00 and 16.00–19.00), things get very tight and pushy. Move with the flow of people and don't be afraid to shove. Politeness never got anyone very far on the Kiev metro and at times this is the only way you'll ever get on. Keep bags and wallets close at hand and be alert. For now, one ride on the metro costs 50 kopecks, including transfers. The orange metal machines in the entryway of the stations take 1 and 2 hrivna notes and give you plastic tokens in return, or just wait

Metro

in the queue and buy them from the cashier. For longer stays you can purchase unlimited travel on a monthly card – for around US$5, or a half-month card for half the cost after the 15th of any month.

Finding your way underground is yet another incentive to learn Cyrillic, although in recent months, some trains have begun posting maps subtitled with Latin transliterations. It always helps to take a good look at a map and think out your journey before descending. In the actual tunnels, arrows show the direction the train travels as well as the remaining stations on that line. When transferring from one station to another, read the signs, ask, or in some cases, simply follow the crowd climbing the stairs from the middle of the platform rather than moving to the ends of the hall.

See the Kiev metro map in the colour section at the back of the book.

TAXIS

Riding in Kiev's traffic cures atheism – pavements can become an extra lane, or lanes will suddenly change direction. U-turns across four lanes of oncoming traffic, reversing speedily around uphill turns and zipping in front of trams are just a few of the daredevil stunts that Kiev's cabbies have perfected. In addition, Kiev's taxi drivers are picky about who they pick up – if traffic is bad they'll tell you by refusing to go, although occasionally money talks.

Having said all that, taxis are generally easy to find and use. Meters have only recently been introduced and are still not the norm. Keep in mind that throughout

Ukraine taxi drivers have a well-earned reputation as minor-league conmen, so it pays to be savvy. Remember that they drive like this all day long for the money, and some will double the price when they encounter a foreigner. Using hotel-registered cabs and private companies promises a secure and trustworthy experience for a higher price, although Kiev has become cosmopolitan enough that everyone seems to be equally overcharged. It never pays to be too paranoid about getting ripped off, but still – bargaining for taxis is part of the drill.

Dialling 058 on any phone will give you a voice that can get you a cab – but flagging one down is quicker and more negotiable. If you have the choice, go for the little guy – meaning the beat-up *Lada* and *Zhigulii* with self-positioned taxi signs. These are entrepreneurial taxi drivers who must still pay off a higher hand for the privilege to be working. They cost less than the larger taxi companies and tend to be of more honest character. There is no such thing as a free ride in Ukraine, and hitching in Kiev means getting picked up by a civilian and offering a gift of cash to be carried to your desired destination. This scenario works much better if you speak the language. Talking to the driver during the ride (or even trying to) can teach you more about Kiev than most tour guides.

For a no-nonsense (but less fun) ride, you can call one of Kiev's private companies:

Art Tel: 044 229 8543
Avtosvit Tel: 044 234 4444
EuroTaxi Tel: 044 246 1036

Taxis

Radio Taxi Tel: 044 249 6249
Taxi Blues Tel: 044 296 4243
Ukrprominvest Tel: 044 574 0574

With any taxi, always agree on a price before sitting in the car and don't get talked into paying more. Taxi prices change by the minute, but US$3–4 is normal for two or three people travelling a good distance inside the city, and trips inside the centre should only cost around US$2. If you are planning on taking a taxi on a long trip outside the city, the general rule around Kiev is 2UAH to 4UAH per kilometre. Often the driver will offer to wait, or else you will have asked him to make the return journey. He will charge you extra for the wait so make sure you have both agreed on the price beforehand.

TROLLEYS, TRAMS AND BUSES

The *tramvai* and trolleybus are eastern Europe's best institution for moving short distances through town, and tend to service Kiev's residential neighbourhoods. Tram and trolley routes are usually depicted on some city maps, albeit very badly. Local advice, pure trial and error, and adventurous intuition all make trustworthy references, but logic has most lines following large boulevards and prospects with connections to large markets and metro stations. As a general rule, trams are very useful for getting around Podil, and the same goes for trolleys in Pechersk and buses on the left bank. Signs mark the stops.

People are usually packed on too tightly for you to just walk on and pay. The best method is to hold a one hrivna note in your hand as if you are ready to buy a ticket. The conductor will come and sell you one for between 40 and 60 kopecks. Otherwise, people pass money hand over hand all the way to the driver, and the change is passed all the way back. A ticket is ripped or hole-punched to show that it's been used. Hold on to it in case of random checks by the controllers. If you are carrying heavy luggage, you may be expected to pay extra. It is safer to buy one ticket per bag and avoid the likes of big city controllers who enjoy fining foreigners.

Following years of complete apathy, Kiev's trams and trolleybuses now feature vigorous ticket controllers that seem to be making up for all the lost time. If you are a foreigner, they will be especially keen to check your ticket and fine you for something or other. Make an effort to buy a ticket (50 kopecks) from the driver upon boarding, or keep some change out for a ticket seller. In addition, buy a ticket for every large suitcase you may be carrying. Nodding your head and saying you don't speak Russian won't help the situation. A *straf* (fine) costs around US$2 and you'll wish that you'd simply taken a taxi.

MARSHRUTKA

Marshrutka taxis are both public and private minibuses that run maze-like routes through the city delivering people where they need to go. The thousands of these Mercedes vans in Kiev reflect a quick response to increased demand for quick and reliable transportation in such a big city. *Marshrutka* use regular bus stops, but you can also flag them down anywhere you see them. Number and route are usually posted in the window, but always check with the driver by stating your destination and waiting for a *da* or *nyet*. In Kiev, costs run from 1UAH to 3UAH, and once you get the hang of it, this is the cheapest and fastest way to move above ground. There are over 400 official *marshrutka* routes through Kiev and not one of them goes in a straight line. A major central pick-up stop is in front of Universitet station (and all other metro stations), as well as in front of the Kievo-Pecherska Lava, although you can really flag down a *marshrutka* anywhere. If you can't read the signs in the windscreen telling the destinations, simply ask. Fellow passengers tend to be very helpful as well. Routes tend to hit all the metro stations they pass, so hopping on will usually assure you get to the underground network. *Marshrutka* can also get crowded and your view may be blocked. Ask someone next to you to let you know when to get off or just call out *na ostanovkye!* ('next stop!').

CAR

There are not enough pages in this book to list the reasons why you should not want to drive in Ukraine, and yet thousands still do it. Touring Ukraine behind the wheel is more stressful than it is adventurous, and paranoia about your car getting stolen or wrecked will quickly replace the joy of being able to roam freely around the capital city. For the few who still dare to drive, consider the following:

If you are driving your own car, have every possible bit of paperwork and registration with you when you're behind the wheel, especially your customs declaration form. A valid international driver's licence is required, a very solid anti-theft device (eg: steering-wheel lock) is mandatory, and a car alarm is highly recommended. Foreign cars are known targets, especially outside the city. You'll notice that people park (and drive) almost anywhere, including the pavements. Try to park in secure or guarded car parks and avoid driving between cities after dark as this is when most car-jackings occur.

Ukraine's roads are abominable and the streets of Kiev particularly bumpy. Often there are more holes than there is road and it is common to get stuck in slow motion to save wrecking the shock absorbers. Cobblestones and a hilly cityscape don't help the process. Every season has its perils: deep sticky mud in spring, ice in winter and dust and pebbles in summer. Cracked windscreens are very common. Auto facilities are legion inside Kiev, and petrol stops, roadside-stop cafés and motels are becoming more regular in rural areas (but only accept cash). International road signs apply and most Ukrainian bookshops sell good quality road atlases, some with Roman spellings. By far the best driving atlas for Kiev is the ringed notebook-style 'Atlas Kyiv' published by Kartografia, Inc (web: www.ukrmap.com.ua).

Kiev's traffic is downright painful due to a dramatic increase in private car-ownership, bizarre street layouts, and frequent political celebrations that shut down huge portions of the city. In a *probki* (traffic jam), you'll walk the length of Khreschatyk quicker than your car will drive it.

Highway roadblocks are also a favoured pastime of the Ukrainian police (aka 'auto-inspection officers'). Drivers in the other lane will flash their front beams to

Car

warn you of an upcoming roadblock and to slow down. A patrol will signal you to pull over by holding out a black-and-white stick. If you do get pulled over at a roadblock, the best strategy is shrugging your shoulders and speaking only in English. Usually this gets you waved on. If not, be co-operative in showing them the requested documents and don't try anything silly like bribing them.

Car rental

Kiev is leading the way for Ukraine's new private car-rental industry, and most upmarket hotels can offer some sort of car-hire services. Until very recently, driving on your own in Kiev (especially in a rental car) was widely perceived as foolhardy, although plenty of ex-pats drive to and from work every day. International car hire companies with reliable insurance policies facilitate the practice although prices are two to three times higher than what you would expect at home (this is not including the additional, higher than average priced insurance). Professional auto thieves target rental cars so take every precaution for security. Some car-hire companies are:

Avis Hospitalna 4; tel: 044 490 7333; email: avis@avis.kiev.ua; web: www.avis.com.ua
Europcar Gorkovo 48A; tel: 044 238 2691; email: ua@europcar.relc.com; web: www.europcar.com
Hertz Muzeiny 4; tel: 044 296 7614; email: hertzua@i.kiev.ua; web: www.hertz.com.ua

A pleasant option for the hard-core sightseeing tourist is to hire a car with driver for the day. By paying a base fee, you can be taken to where you want to go, and it saves time looking for several drivers throughout the day. Car rental companies, travel agencies and almost all hotels can arrange such transportation. Costs can range from US$50–100 a day.

Here are a few companies that offer driver services for vans and small cars:

A Car Rental Pushkinska 8, #15; tel: 044 229 7092
AutoService Gagarina 8A; tel: 044 579 5774
Driver Havro 20; tel: 044 418 8840
Navigator Khmelnytskoho 16B; tel: 044 235 6188

AIRPORT TRANSFERS IN KIEV
Borispol Airport Бориспіль

Communist logic dictated that a city's international airport should be built incredibly far away, and Borispol is no exception – located 40km away from the city centre. Luckily, transferring between the airport and the city has become much easier. Expect to pay up to US$25 for a taxi from the airport into the city, while for some reason, the journey from Kiev to the airport costs half the price. Catching a bus is just as easy and much less expensive. The **Polit** airport bus travels regularly from Peremohy Square in the centre of Kiev to Borispol and back, leaving every 15 minutes between 05.00 and 23.15; tel: 044 296 7367, cost US$2. The journey takes about one hour. The private bus company **Autolux** (Kiev, V. Chistyakovskaya 30; tel: 044 536 0055; email: info@autolux.ua; web: www.autolux.ua) makes a connection between Borispol and Kiev's Central Bus Station for each of its transit journeys. This is the most comfortable option and takes only 35 minutes. Other regular buses serve both airports from the Central Bus Station at Moskovskaya Square.

Zhulyany Airport Жуляни

Zhulyany airport is only 7km southeast of the city centre and therefore more convenient. To travel into the city on public transport, take either trolleybus #9 or #213, or else have a more bearable ride on *marshrutka* #568 which goes to Prospekt Shevchenka. If you have sizeable luggage, a taxi would seem the best bet (around US$5–7). Transferring between Zhulyany and Borispol is not too difficult as there are buses every 90 minutes or so from 07.00 to 22.00, or a taxi between the two airports should cost around US$30. The phone number at Zhulyany airport is 044 242 2308.

BY RAIL

Kiev's train station is actually two stations joined by a causeway crossing all the tracks and platforms. Vokzalna metro station is the closest public transportation access. The closest main entrance is the 'Central' station; the other side is the 'South' station. If you have a talented taxi driver who knows the trains, he will drop you off at the side closest to your train, otherwise, it's a matter of walking over the long causeway terminal to your platform. An impressive renovation has turned Kiev's station into the most modern and user-friendly station in Ukraine, and visitors will be grateful for the English signs and listings.

There are over 100 ticket counters in Kiev's main station, all for different purposes. Counters number 41 and 42 (2nd floor of the South station; open 07.30–20.00) are designated to sell to foreigners and the attendants speak limited English. You can still buy tickets elsewhere, but it is to your advantage to use these attendants since they are more flexible, have special access to better seats and give foreigners priority on full trains. The other ticket office in central Kiev is located at Prospekt Shevchenka 38/40. Dialling 005 on any Kiev phone will put you through to the train station, but if you don't speak Russian, the lady on the other end is not much help. Most Kiev hotels will have agents who can also book tickets for you.

There is a left-luggage area in the basement of Kiev's South Station. Pay your money to the nice old woman and you'll get two tokens – one that locks the locker and another to open it later. Set your own combination on the inside (and write it down somewhere), drop in the token, and shut it firmly while it's buzzing. To open, set the outside combination to match, drop in the token and carefully yank it open. You are allowed to leave luggage for 24 hours before it's cleaned out. The lockers are safe and well-guarded and using them can give you some peace of mind. This helps if you want to check out of a hotel and spend the day around Kiev before boarding a night train to somewhere else.

Getting a taxi from the train station can be overpriced. If you are trying to save money, take the metro one stop to the station Universitet and you'll be able to catch a cab there for much less.

By rail

All train tracks lead to Kiev, making it the easiest destination in Ukraine to reach and the easiest place to leave. In fact, even if you don't want to come to Kiev, you may have to stop over in order to get somewhere else.

On any given day, you can get a train to anywhere and come to Kiev from anywhere. Whether or not there are any spaces is the catch – especially during holiday seasons. The earliest you can buy tickets is one month before you travel, but many people wait until a few days before or the morning of travel. You should also check times and length of journey, since this can vary a great deal. Trains to Crimea either go to Sevastopol (2 daily; 18 hours) or Simferopol (4 daily; 16 hours). There are also plenty of trains to Lviv (5 daily; 11 hours) and Odessa (5 daily; 11 hours). Travel to and from Kharkiv (5 daily; 5 or 9 hours) has recently become easier with the advent of Ukraine's first luxury train, the *Capital Express*, which makes two daily connections with stops in Poltava and Mirgorod and gets to Kharkiv in five hours. There is only one daily train to and from Donetsk (12 hours), and one to Dnepropetrovsk (8 hours), although many other trains pass through Dnepropretrovsk on their way to Kiev. The train's departure platform number is posted in English and Ukrainian 30 minutes before departure.

International routes to and from Kiev are numerous and inexpensive. Russian destinations are usually listed as domestic routes, with 14 daily connections to Moscow (14 hours) and just one to St Petersburg (via Chernihiv; 24 hours). A few cars leave from Kiev every other day to be connected to Ukraine's Trans-Siberian Railway all the way to Vladivostok (via Kharkiv; 7 days). Other trains come and go from Minsk (twice daily, via Chernihiv; 12 hours) and Kishinev (twice daily; 14 hours) while train schedules to Riga (24 hours) and Vilnius (18 hours) constantly change. The most popular international routes are between Kiev and Warsaw (1 daily; 20 hours; US$50), Berlin (1 daily; 24 hours; US$100) and Prague (1 daily; 34 hours; US$120).

BY BUS

Like the train, you can catch a bus from anywhere and get to Kiev and vice versa, but you must ask yourself if this is the best way to meet your particular travel goals. Schedules change daily on the smaller lines, so if you like to have set plans beforehand, you will be limited to the new private companies.

Bus routes spread out in a radial pattern from Kiev, divided into five directions: Zhytomyr, Chernihiv, Uman, Cherkassy and Poltava. The Central Bus Station (3 Moskovskaya Square; tel: 044 265 0430) is best reached by travelling to Lybidska metro station and then taking a bus (#4 and #11), taxi, or walking to the next junction. Western destinations leave from Dachna Terminal (Peremohy 142; tel: 044 444 1503); eastern destinations leave from Darnytsya Terminal (near the metro station Darnytsya; Gagarina 1; tel: 044 559 4618). Northern destinations leave from Polissya Terminal (Shevchenka Square; tel: 044 430 3554) and southern destinations depart either from Podil Terminal (Nyzhny 15A; tel: 044 417 3215) or Pivdenna Terminal (Glushkova 3; tel: 044 263 4004). If in doubt, go to the Central Bus Station where many long-haul routes still originate. Bus tickets can also be purchased at the central bus office; Lesi Ukrayinki 14; tel: 044 225 2066.

KIEV BY BOAT

Taking the funicular or the metro to the station Poshtova Ploscha brings you next to the **River Terminal**; tel: 044 416 1268 [1 D3]. Luxury boat tours and cruises originate and end here, many of which travel all the way down the Dnepr to Crimea. There are also basic passenger services available to other Dnepr towns and short boat tours of Kiev, as well as short transits to some of the islands and beaches (in summer). Ice covers the Dnepr for about three months of the year, and the river terminal is only in full swing from May until October. Schedules change all the time, so either check out the terminal (River Port Excursion Bureau; Poshtova Ploscha 3; tel: 044 416 1229), or else contact one of the tour agencies that organise river tours (eg: SAM, Mandrivnyk).

Regular buses are cheap, slow and bumpy. The most popular routes go to Zhytomyr (3 hours) and Pochayiv (12 hours). Shorter routes also visit the tourist sights just outside Kiev, such as Kaniv and Pereyaslav. A few private bus companies run out of Kiev's Central Bus Station that travel as fast as or faster than the train, are very comfortable and charge about the same amount as the train. **Autolux** has the most widespread service, with buses to and from Lviv (10 hours), Yalta (17 hours), Odessa (8 hours), Kharkiv (7 hours), Zaporizhzhya (9 hours) and every city in between. Besides their office at the station, their central office is at Chistyakovskaya 30; tel: 044 536 0055; email: info@autolux.ua; web: www.autolux.ua. **Gyunsel** (Novopolevaya 2; tel: 044 488 8801/ 044 265 0378; email: office@gunsel.com.ua) has good connections between Kiev and the East (Kharkiv, Dnepropetrovsk and Donetsk) as well as the Carpathians.

International bus routes to and from Kiev include Paris, London, Rome, Antwerp, Athens, Prague and the Baltic capitals. For now, the best international coach company in Ukraine is **Lviv Inturtrans**; Reitarska 37/401; tel: 044 212 3340. As a non-Ukrainian, make sure you know the route of travel and have made prior arrangements (ie: transit visas) for the countries you'll be passing through. Taking a bus to Kiev from another country is only worth it if you are really trying to save money on the international journey, otherwise, just cross the border and then take a train to Kiev. Remember that inside Ukraine, if the trip is over six hours by bus, consider the train as a more comfortable option, albeit slower.

5 Accommodation

If only the rest of Ukraine's economy had made the same swift conversion that Kiev's hotels have recently experienced! In less than five years, the capital's illusions of grandeur have helped churn out a pile of very swish hotels that smell of new money and new paint. The high-reaching standard is slightly problematic, since every hotel wants a piece of the luxury market and subsequently prices its rooms as such – whether or not its facilities are actually upmarket. Even though few hotels merit the price, offering US$100-a-night rooms has become the ultimate status symbol for Kiev's hoteliers. Such inflation is the curse of capital cities everywhere but in future years, where foreign visitors choose to stay may push supply and demand curves back into synch.

Until recently, Ukraine's hotels were either bawdy hangouts for the Soviet *nomenklatura* or basic dormitories to house the travelling proletariat. In Kiev however, major refurbishing has turned a few crumbling buildings into shiny, high-standard hotels, otherwise, expect hotel standards to be lower than back at home. Most Soviet-era hotels are in the midst of staggered reconstruction. The push to make everything *Evro* (European) standard has generated higher prices and some saccharine décor, while often overlooking the essentials. Awareness of the following will help:

Plumbing is not a Ukrainian forte, and enquiries about water can incite a frank display of optimism ('No, we don't have hot water, but we *do* have cold water!'). In most luxury hotels, there will always be hot water, but in middle-range and budget hotels, be sure to check, even if it means visiting the room and turning on the tap. Countrywide, hot water is usually turned off sometime in late spring and then it comes back on in October. During the winter months, most hotels will post hot-water schedules in the lobby (usually early morning and late evening). 'European' showers are often perceived to be more upper-class than bathtubs, and so remodelled rooms will often only have showers. Budget rooms also sometimes have a 'shower' which is a drain on the bathroom floor and a hose coming out of the wall. *Lux* rooms will have both.

The concept of double beds is fairly elusive. Normally, a 'double' room means twin beds. You'll have to make a special request for 'a single bed for two people', and even then, this is usually two single beds joined together. The very nicest hotels will have real king- and queen-size beds, but this is still very much a new thing. Traditional Ukrainian bedding consists of a two-sided sheet covering a thick woollen blanket, much like a duvet, and most pillows are filled with goose down. During colder months, you can always find extra blankets stuffed in the cupboard.

Central heating and air conditioning has also just made its debut in Ukraine, and many hotels will advertise that their best rooms have *konditsioner*. If travelling in winter among the humblest of hotels, you can stay warm by stripping the bedclothes and mattress off the frame and making your bed next to the heater on the floor.

Accommodation

Ukrainian rooms are traditionally classified as *odnomestny* (single; *one place*), *dvukhmestny* (double; *two places*), *pol-lux* (junior suite) and *lux* (suite). Suites can be much nicer, or simply more complex, with multiple rooms, multiple TV sets and multiple toilets, but, for value-for-money, it is sometimes better to get a *lux* or *pol-lux* in an average hotel then to get the double room in a more expensive hotel. This may have something to do with the fact that Ukrainians rarely stay in a hotel for functional reasons, but usually hold parties in larger suites.

SECURITY

Middle-range and luxury hotels always have a security guard posted at the entrance or near the lift to prevent non-residents from entering. Hotel management also provides a secure safe, and some upmarket rooms will also have their own safes. Leaving things in your room is normally fine – the cleaners will dust underneath the wad of bills you left on the night table and put them right back as they were. The real threat is from people from outside the hotel who know you are staying there. Stash valuables away in different places in your room. Always lock the door behind you when you enter the room. If someone knocks, ask who it is *(kto tam?)* and if it is not a sweet old lady with cleaning supplies, then don't open.

PAYMENT

Making a reservation (*bronirovaniye*) in Soviet-age hotels usually means contacting the hotel ahead of time and paying a non-refundable fee equal to half the price of the room upon arrival. As yet there is no norm for pricing in Kiev: some hotels charge per person, others charge per room. Aside from in newer, luxury hotels, all amenities are considered extras and will be added to your bill: telephone, refrigerator, television. Hotels usually specify if breakfast is included in the price (which it normally is). Even though laws and protocol have changed, some of the older hotels will still charge foreigners at least twice as much as Ukrainians for the same room, although the practice is fading away as some Ukrainians become much wealthier than foreigners. Some lower-standard hotels will charge you in advance for the whole duration of your stay. When you check in, try to communicate clearly so that you are sure that you and the receptionist understand the arrangement.

CLASSIFICATION

Establishing a fixed system for grading Kiev's hotels is impossible since price, quality and service vary so much from place to place (even floor to floor). Ukraine's star-rating system should also be ignored since it is inconsistent and irrelevant. Never trust outside appearances: the hotel entrance may sport a gold-emblazoned 'Reception' sign (in English) over smiling uniformed staff, while two floors up the rooms lack hot water. Meanwhile, the dingy grey concrete block down the road may turn out to have comfortable luxury rooms. For the sake of consistency, this book classifies hotels by room price. There is some correlation to standard, but not always. As a general rule, always have a look at the room before you take it.

Luxury

Most of Ukraine's poshest hotels have only been open two or three years and range from an élite corporate standard to very opulent palaces that would easily rank as five-star in the West. Anything upwards of US$100 a night is considered luxury, but in Kiev, you'll find the value of US$100 highly variable. Ukrainians expect all foreigners to stay only in luxury hotels, but the rooms don't feel very Ukrainian. All luxury hotels have their own private source for hot water and electricity, usually feature very nice restaurants (with staff who speak some English), and accept major credit cards.

Middle-range

The nebulous in-between means anything that is neither an obvious luxury hotel nor of the lowly Soviet variety. Prices range from US$50 up to US$100, and this is where tour groups usually stay. Most middle-range hotels are in flux, meaning some rooms have been remodelled, many have not, instilling a two-tiered pricing structure for 'standard' rooms of lower quality, and the better 'comfort' rooms. Middle-range hotel rooms will have their own bathroom that usually features hot water and since most of these were former Inturist hotels, they offer convenient services for travellers.

Budget

Finding a really cheap night's stay in Kiev is becoming more of a nightmare since foreign travellers are perceived as wealthy and spendthrift. The few remaining discount hotels often illogically charge foreigners the same Ukrainian price but in dollars. This is still inexpensive, but with the push to modernise, wealthier markets are taking over. Kiev's budget hotels mainly consist of the old Soviet hotels that have not been bought up by business developers, but be prepared to spend US$20 to $40 for a very basic room – not a lot by Western standards, but higher than what you'd pay in Ukraine's provinces for the same.

If you are trying to stretch your money in Kiev, consider the following:

- Try staying further outside the city, especially on the left bank. You can still get into the centre on the metro and prices drop significantly if you are on the other side of the river.
- A lot of middle-range hotels also have cheap rooms, which are simply not yet remodelled. The rooms are not always advertised to foreigners, so it is always worth checking. These tend to be nicer rooms but cost less than the budget hotels' 'nice rooms'.
- You can knock a fair amount off the room price by differentiating between a room with *udobstv* (conveniences) or *bez udobstv* (without conveniences). Getting a room with sink only and no toilet or shower means sharing a communal facility in the hall for which you normally pay 3UAH to 5UAH each time for a hot shower.
- For US$20 to $30, you can rent a one-room apartment with kitchen and bathroom near a subway station just outside the centre. This is a much more comfortable option than some of Kiev's dingier hotels.

RENTING APARTMENTS

One option for a reasonably priced stay in Kiev is renting a private apartment, and may be worthwhile if you are planning on staying for more than a week. Traditionally, the square in front of the central train station is busy with female agents who either advertise their own apartments or arrange rentals for a range of accommodation. Recognise them by their call: *kvartira* (apartment) or *komnata* (room). For now, the going rate in Kiev is about US$20 a day for a semi-decent one-room apartment with double bed, kitchen and bathroom. If making arrangements on your own, ask the price, see the apartment, and then make a deal and get the keys. Arrange beforehand if you will pay up-front or pay per day. Use caution, since prices will already be jacked up a bit and this is a black-market trade where foreigners can be targeted for swindles.

Much better to go the legal route and use one of Kiev's many apartment rental agencies. A good company can do all the hard work for you and meet you at the airport with keys in hand. This is rarely the cheapest option, but it is much less expensive than hotels, while the housing situation is often much nicer and more secure. Expect to pay around US$50 a night for a clean, centrally located apartment. The following accept credit cards and can arrange secure and comfortable apartments for around US$500 to $600 a month:

Albion 9 Lesi Ukrayinki; tel/fax: 044 295 9860; email: albion@ukrpost.net; web: www.albion-hotel.kiev.ua

Avanti Apartment Services Tel/fax: 044 247 0558; email: hotel@avanti.kiev.ua; web: www.avanti.kiev.ua

Absolut Tsvetayevoyi 10/87, office #17; tel/fax: 044 530 1310; email: hotel@hotelservice.kiev.ua; web: www.hotelservice.kiev.ua.

Predslava Gorkovo 100, Apt 30; tel/fax: 044 268 6283; email: predslava@nbi.com.ua; web: www.predslava.com.ua

Sherbourne Apartments Sichnevy Provulok 9; tel: 044 490 9693; fax: 044 295 8832; email: reservations@sherbornehotel.com.ua; web: www.sherbornehotel.com.ua

Visit Hospitalna 2, Apt 42; tel/fax: 044 235 3668; email: visit@visit.kiev.ua; web: www.visit.kiev.ua

RAILWAY STATIONS

Every train station in Ukraine used to have its own small hotel where late-night arrivals could sleep on until the next day or stay the night before a long journey. The nicest of these is in Kiev's South Train Station (*Pivdenny Vokzal*) [2 A2] – at the more modern end of the main rail terminal on the 4th floor – just follow the signs with the bed on it. Everything is sparkling new, and the rooms are heated in winter, cooled in summer. None of the rooms is en suite, but the bathrooms are new and clean with continuous hot water. US$18 a night per person, breakfast included.

HOTELS

Hotels are categorised by price range and then location, then listed in order of recommendation.

Luxury

Every hotel in Kiev considers itself as 'lyuks' and advertises that way. If you want the tops, stay in the Premier Palace, otherwise, the smaller luxury hotels in Podil make a very acceptable alternative to some of the giant hotels in the centre, which differ little from one another.

Centre

Premier Palace Shevchenka 5–7; tel: 044 244 1200; fax: 044 229 8772; email: info@premier-palace.com; web: www.premier-palace.com [2 C2]

Kiev's most impressive hotel also offers the most comfortable night's rest in the city, with every luxury provided. Growing bigger and better by the year, the Premier Palace is the only true five-star hotel in Kiev, with a beautiful interior and high-quality service. Rising up from the crossroads of Kiev's most impressive boulevards, few superlatives need be spared on this hotel. Elegant, high-ceilinged rooms are tastefully decorated and rival most upmarket European hotels, and an excellent health club and competent business centre complete the atmosphere of luxury and relaxation. Business travellers, NGO workers, and diplomats reluctant to visit Ukraine find solace in these walls and the courage to explore the city. The classy mood is reinforced by the hotel's Latin creed reminding visitors that their 'name says it all'. The Palace's panoramic restaurant 'Imperia' on the eighth floor offers a pleasant setting for top-quality meals and a fantastic view of Kiev by day and by night. Rooms start at US$420 a night.

Dnipro Hotel Khreschatyk 1/2; 044 229 8450; fax: 044 229 8213; email: reservation@dniprhotel.kiev.ua; web: www.dniprohotel.kiev.ua [1 D4]
Once upon a time, this was the only hotel foreign visitors were allowed to stay in, meaning the Dnipro has a slight advantage in working with group tours and taking care of all travel arrangements. Attempted grandeur makes it a pleasant enough hotel to stay in, but it is difficult to mask the Soviet construction, meaning rooms tend to be very small, except for the few larger and more expensive suites. The division between superior and standard rooms further complicates pricing. Single superiors cost US$135, a double, queen-size room costs US$205; suites are US$300. Only double superior or higher standard have baths, otherwise, all rooms are equipped with showers. Standard (meaning Soviet) rooms are about US$40 cheaper, but if money is a concern, there are cheaper and better rooms elsewhere. Although the Dnipro presents itself as Kiev's other luxury hotel, there is no real comparison. Two advantages are the Dnipro's advantageous location at the end of Khreschatyk, and the very entertaining restaurant run by a highly ambitious Ukrainian chef.

Hotel Rus Hospitalna 4; tel: 044 294 3020; fax: 044 220 4396; email: reservation@hotelrus.kiev.ua; web: www.hotelrus.kiev.ua [2 D3]
Considered upmarket in Kiev, the Rus is a giant hotel tower with hundreds of clean and orderly rooms, used frequently for conferences and group tours. Visitors will probably find

Hotels

that the service and standards are just about average compared to back home, but staff are very professional, and are especially good at dealing with high-maintenance groups. The location is somewhat central, although there is no public transportation close by, leaving you at the mercy of the hotel's taxi service. Prices are per room, meaning singles and doubles cost US$120, while the much more spacious suites are US$150.

President Hotel Kyivsky Hospitalna 12; tel: 044 220 4144; fax: 044 220 4568; email: book@ukrhotel.com; web: www.ukrhotel.com [2 D3]
Sister to Hotel Rus (and just across the street), the Kyivsky is another towering high-rise chock-full of respectable rooms. The pool and fitness centre make it a little more special, as does their nightly cabaret. US$140 for a single and US$170 for a double.

Lybid Peremohy 1; tel: 044 236 0063; fax: 044 236 6336; email: info@hotellybid.com.ua; web: www.hotellybid.com.ua [2 A1]
Within walking distance of Kiev's main railway station and St Vladimir's Cathedral, Lybid's location is fairly convenient and very conducive to getting around the rest of the city. Besides being incredibly tourist-friendly, the Lybid's sensibly stylish rooms are modern and comfy. Singles are US$100, doubles are US$120, suites cost US$150.

Hotel Sonya Volodymyrska 77; tel/fax: 044 228 5878; email: info@hotelsonya.kiev.ua; web: www.hotelsonya.kiev.ua [2 C3]
Comprising eight, well-furnished apartments in a fantastic location, this 'alternative hotel' is a great option for families with small children. Rooms are comfortable and the service

amiable. Prices range from US\$70 for a basic single to US\$150 for the first class suite – much better value than most hotel rooms for the same price.

Pechersk

Natsionalny Lypska 5; tel: 044 291 8888; fax: 044 291 8997; email: natsionalny@ukrsat.com; web: www.natsionalny.kiev.ua [2 E2]
Located within walking distance of the Verkhovna Rada, the Natsionalny is the official hotel for government delegations and guests of the state, so getting a room is not always easy, depending on what's happening in parliament. Located in one of Kiev's older and more personal neighbourhoods, these are some of the best rooms in the city. Singles are US\$175, the amazing junior-suites cost US\$230, and suites US\$280.

Podil

Vozdvyzhensky Vozdvyzhenska 60; tel: 044 531 9900; fax: 044 531 9931 [1 C3]
Small and quiet, this endearing hotel is tucked away just off Andriyvsky Uzviz, making it the perfect hotel for first-time visitors to Kiev, allowing one to stay in central Kiev, but hidden away from the central rush. Vozdvyzhensky is also the rare Ukrainian hotel where you actually get what you pay for. Professional management and big, brand-new, fully-equipped bathrooms put this hotel a step ahead of the rest so that the luxury is not just the price. A double room (with king-size bed) is US\$180; large suites cost US\$290, but there are a few 'tourist class' rooms that are much cheaper (around US\$70) in their Andreyevsky wing. Personal attention to guests is everyday policy.

Hotels

Domus Yaroslavska 19; tel: 044 490 9008; fax: 044 462 5145; email: postmaster@domus-hotel.kiev.ua; web: www.domus-hotel.kiev.ua [1 C2]

Located in the heart of Kiev's historic Podil neighbourhood, the pale-pink Domus hotel is thoroughly quaint and favoured by businessmen. The comfy beds and tactful renovation deserve mention, as does their dapper Italian restaurant. Singles/doubles cost US$140/$190, suites are US$270 a night.

Hotel Impressa Sahaidachnovo 21; tel: 044 239 2939; email: impressa@happydays.kiev.ua; web: www.impressa.com.ua [1 C3]

On one of the main streets in Podil, the Impressa offers a more intimate alternative to larger hotels, with fewer than 20 rooms, all of which are luxurious in a disco-like way, but more importantly – clean. The Impressa also has one of the hotter casinos in Kiev. Singles cost US$140, the junior suites are US$200, and suites are US$290.

Middle-range

These middle-range hotels cover a varied quality spectrum so make sure to always see the room first. Price dictates little of the quality, since many of these 'middle-range' hotels are in transition, moving up from their Soviet past to the desired luxury hotel market. At the time of writing, all of these middle-range hotels accept credit cards, but if making prior reservations, you should always check. Staying farther out from central Kiev can knock 30 to 40 bucks per night off your hotel rate, but remember to take transportation into consideration as some of the following are located in Kiev's left bank, sometimes near a metro station.

Centre (Maidan Nezalezhnosti)

Hotel Kozatsky 1/3 Mykhailivska; tel: 044 229 4925; fax: 044 229 2709; email: kozatsky@ukrnet.net; web: www.kozatsky.kiyv.ua [1 C4]
There is no better location than the Kozatsky, looking out above the action on the Maidan Nezalezhnosti. Most rooms for foreigners (*lux*) cost US$100 a night although there are some decent rooms for around US$75. Unless you really want to be on the square, your money would buy better quality somewhere else. The Kozatsky is owned and operated by Ukraine's Ministry of Defence, so your neighbours will always be interesting.

Ukrayina Instituska 4; tel: 044 229 0347; fax: 044 229 1353 [2 D1]
Towering opposite the Maidan Nezalezhnosti, the 'Ukraine' is the most visually prominent hotel in Kiev, so if it's a view you're looking for, here it is. Rooms are comfortable and pretty fairly priced, considering the location. Singles are US$70–100; doubles cost US$100–120.

Centre

Hotel Kiev Hrushevskovo 26/1; tel: 044 253 0155; fax: 044 253 6432; email: kievhtl@ukrtel.com; web: www.hotelkiev.com.ua [2 E2]
Located directly across from the *rada* (parliament), president's house, and the Marinsky

Hotels

Palace, Hotel Kiev is operated by the presidential administration and often used by government employees. The structure and atmosphere is not unlike most renovated Soviet buildings, but at the time of writing Hotel Kiev is the best deal for budget accommodation in terms of location, price, and standards (there is hot water). Singles are US$75, doubles are US$100.

Express Shevchenka 38/40; tel: 044 239 8995; fax: 044 239 8947; email: hotel@railwayukr.com; web: www.railwayukr.com [2 B2]
A spectrum of economy rooms to lavish suites means the Express doesn't really fit in any one category. The hotel charges per person in the room, so standard singles/doubles are US$20/$30, while the nicer rooms cost US$50/$60 up to US$100 for 'suites'. From the outside things look dismal, but a massive remodelling has really turned things around on the interior. The ground floor is also the central office for booking rail tickets and the train station is a short walk down the boulevard.

Left Bank (Livoberezhna)
Adria Raisy Okypnoi 2; tel: 044 516 2459; fax: 044 517 8933; email: reservations@eurohotel.com.ua; web: www.eurohotel.com.ua [3 K1]
A Polish–Ukrainian joint venture, the Adria offers the same quality and comfort as any of Kiev's upmarket hotels, but is located further from the centre. This 'Euro-hotel' is the private 'luxury' wing of the giant Turist complex. Rooms cost US$90–$100.

Turist Raisy Okypnoi 2; tel: 044 517 8832; fax: 044 517 6243; email: hotel-tourist@uprotel.net.ua; web: www.hotel-tourist.kiev.ua [3 K1]
Officially Kiev's largest hotel (next to the Adria), this 27-storey building is not unlike the millions of Soviet apartments that house most of Eurasia today, although slightly better inside. The left bank location may seem dissuasive, but the Livoberezhna metro station is literally next door, the river and Hydropark are close by, and after all, this is true, residential Kiev. The regular budget rooms cost US$45–55 per person, whereas the remodelled rooms cost upwards of US$90.

Bratislava Malyshka 1; tel: 044 559 6920; fax: 044 559 7788; email: Bratislava@ukrti.com.ua; web: www.bratislava.com.ua [Kiev D2]
Rooms are quite modern, all with showers and new bathrooms. With singles US$40–50 and doubles US$60–90, this is probably the best deal on the left bank. Darnitsya is the closest metro station.

Pechersk
Salyut Sichnevoho Povstannia 11A; tel/fax: 044 290 6130 [3 F2]
Like a reject piece of the *Star Wars* set that got dropped in one of Kiev's more beautiful neighbourhoods, the Salyut's main attractions include (ironically) the Caves Monastery, just down the street, and its flashy casino lights. The cylindrical construction does offer a myriad of views. Single rooms with double beds go for US$90, double suites with two beds cost US$130.

South

Sport Chernoarmiyska 55A; tel: 044 220 0252; fax: 044 220 0257 [2 C3]
Another towering Soviet high-rise with decent rooms, known for its casino below. Singles cost US$55, doubles are US$75, and there are also a few suites for US$100 and up. The location is also not too bad, just south of the centre and right next to the Respublikansky Stadion metro station.

Myr Holosiyivsky 70; tel/fax: 044 264 9646 [4 B3]
On the far south side of the city, hotel 'Peace' is yet another Soviet-style high-rise, but not a bad deal for the money you spend. Singles are US$60, and doubles and junior suites are US$80. Rooms tend to be small, and not everything has been remodelled, giving a quaint USSR-feel to some of the less-expensive rooms. This is a good hotel if you are arriving in Kiev by bus, as the Central Bus Station is just up the street.

Budget

If you really are trying to save money in Kiev, shop around. Some of the bigger, luxury hotels will have some cheap rooms that are simply not remodelled and therefore not advertised to foreigners (check out the Dnipro and Vozdvyzhensky). Renting apartments will also save you money, especially if you are travelling with others. If you are travelling on your own and really don't want to spend cash, try the rooms at the railway station, or the St Petersburg.

Centre

Alexandria Peremohy 62A; tel: 044 455 6362; fax: 044 446 2128; email:
hotel@alexandria.com.ua; web: www.alexandria.com.ua [Kiev A2]
'Middle-range' in terms of quality, the Alexandria gets slotted in the budget section simply
because it's such a good deal for couples or small groups of travellers. The hotel charges per
room for a single and for the apartments, and per person for doubles and triples, meaning
three people could stay here for around US$25 per person. First-class singles (with double
bed) cost US$60, and doubles are US$40 per person. The large apartments are also not a
bad deal for groups, costing around US$100 a night for up to four people. Cash only.

St Petersburg Shevchenka 4; tel: 044 229 7364; fax: 044 229 7472; email:
s-peter@i.kiev.ua [2 C2]
Across from the Premier Palace, the St Petersburg has seen better days, but the old building
means rooms are spacious and hallways creaky. Rooms cost US$10–40 depending on the
extras you want with your room, and everything is extra, especially any form of plumbing. A
double with toilet costs US$26. If you are used to travelling in hostels, enjoy intimate mixing
with curious neighbours and just want to be in central Kiev, this is the place.

Left Bank (Livoberezhna)

Slavutych Entuziastiv 1; tel: 044 555 3859p fax: 044 555 5637 [3 J3]
The hotel has both standard (old) rooms and new (refurbished) rooms, indicating a two-tiered
price structure. The old rooms rent for US$18–30, while everything else is around US$50.

Hotels

One must decide if the cost of the cab ride offsets the money saved for a somewhat mediocre hotel. The left-bank location is no treat in terms of access, but from this side there are some great views of the Pechersky Lavra and all of Kiev. The closest metro is Livoberezhna.

South

Druzhba Druzhby Narodiv 5; tel: 044 268 3406 [4 E2]

A good find for budget travellers, hotel 'Friendship' is located right next to Lybidska metro station and offers typical no-nonsense rooms for fair prices. The Druzhba is what travelling in the rest of Ukraine is like all the time, providing a healthy dose of reality and local interaction. Singles are US$25, doubles are US$38 and suites are US$47.

West

Prolisok Peremohy 139 tel: 044 294 3020; fax: 044 220 4396 [Kiev A2]

Kiev's main 'motel', the Prolisok is located on the far-western outskirts of the city, and it can take from 30 to 45 minutes to drive into the centre. If you're already driving to Kiev, this is a logical stop off the main road. Rooms and the little cottages are attractive and low-priced. Singles are US$48 and doubles are US$58.

Park Hotel Tsyurupynska 2; tel: 044 422 0344; fax: 044 422 0355; web: www.park-hotel.kiev.ua [Kiev A2]

Aptly named for its location in Nyvky Park, this small, unpretentious hotel is within walking distance of Nyvky metro station. Rooms are well kept, and the staff very personable, making

Accommodation

this more of a bed-and-breakfast-type place. Singles are US$35, 'business-class' doubles US$45, junior suites US$65, and suites cost up to US$100. The higher-priced rooms can be ideal for families and groups.

6 Eating and Drinking

DRINK

Drink is synonymous with alcohol in a country where vodka is the national pastime and a cultural rite. All holidays, birthdays, weddings (and funerals) are celebrated with *horilka* (vodka). Business dealings are done over a vodka toast, and new friends are made to feel welcome with '100 grams'. In the dead of winter, a stiff swallow at breakfast time keeps workers warm as they set off into the cold, but only when followed by frequent doses throughout the day. Without a doubt, vodka is imbibed in alarming quantities in Ukraine. Hetman is the most refined brand, but there are more brands of vodka than there are first names in Ukraine, and vodka takes up the most shelf space in food shops. *Samogon* is a homemade vodka brew and each family has its own special method for distilling it. Only drink *samogon* if it is offered to you in someone's home or in a restaurant. The stuff sold in the open-air market is not regulated and is often laced with lethal ingredients (like anti-freeze) to increase its volume and potency. *Pyvo* (beer) is the most widespread 'soft' drink, with varying strengths of alcohol content (up to 12%). Chernihiv, Obolon and Rogan are the most beloved Ukrainian brands. Foreigners take differently to Ukrainian wine, but if wine-tasting is your thing, there are a few Crimean and Tavrian wines with reputation, in particular those from Massandra. Georgian and Moldavian wines are next in popularity and *Sovietsky* champagne is uncorked at the slightest allusion to festivity. Most upmarket restaurants will serve French wine, but very dry Georgian wine is the most widely available.

The national non-alcoholic beverage is *kvas*, made from old black bread and sugar. It has a malted flavour and tastes best cold and home made. Ukrainians also bottle *kompot*, a light drink made from their homegrown fruit and boiled water. Cherry is the best. *Uzvar* is another very traditional drink, made of smoked fruit and definitely an acquired taste. A very wide selection of juice (pear, peach, plum, grape etc) is available in restaurants, kiosks and shops.

Mineral water is always available, and it is a good idea to become acquainted with the Ukrainian springs and choose one you like. Evian and Volvic are sold in the fancier marketplaces, but locals will insist you benefit from the healing qualities of their own mineral water. Ukrainian brands tend to be a bit saltier than you may be used to. Mirhorod and Truskavets are the best-known. If you want less mineral taste and no fizz, ask for Bon Akva Negazova.

Coffee (*kava* in Ukrainian, *kofye* in Russian) will be on offer even in the humblest of circumstances. *Chai* (tea) is revered in Ukraine almost as much as it is in England, and is usually served with lemon and sugar. Having milk with your tea is a foreign concept and may be treated as an impossible request; bring your own milk powder if it is important. Herbal teas (*chai iz trav*) make a nice hot drink. Chamomile (*romashki*) and mint (*myata*) are widely available. Ukrainians like to collect *lipa* from the flowering lime trees after which the month of July is named. In homes, homemade jam or natural honey is served with tea to be stirred into the cup or else eaten plain by the spoonful.

Drink

FOOD

Ukrainian cuisine is such an honest expression of the land itself that a traditional meal can teach you more about Ukraine than any guided tour in a museum. The richness of natural ingredients comes from centuries of growing things in fertile soil and an intimate relationship with the woods and steppe. Poverty, shortages and political turmoil kept store-bought goods from being used in recipes. The heavy workload of the peasant lifestyle with the added stress of severe winters and repeated famine meant food's main function was to fill empty bellies and keep bodies warm. This it does.

Borscht is the mainstay of the Ukrainian table and is probably the number one connotation foreigners make with Ukraine. It is not simply 'beet soup' as it tends to be known, but rather an important staple made with anything that grows in Ukraine. The bouillon base is boiled with meat or vegetable stock, and then the various ingredients are slowly added one by one to bring out each flavour. Cabbage, potatoes, onions and dill are a must, and the beet is added to give colour. Everything else is thrown in at the discretion of the cook. A good bowl of borscht will be more vegetables than liquid and have a tangy aftertaste. The proven rule is that your spoon won't sink when placed in the centre of the bowl. As the ultimate comfort food, borscht is boiled in massive proportions in Ukrainian homes and served for breakfast, lunch and dinner. It always tastes better after a day in the pot. In restaurants, the soup will usually come with soft buns called *pampoushki* to dip into garlic sauce, or else black bread and *smetana*, a rich and flavourful cream.

Varenniki are large stuffed dumplings and considered *the* national dish of Ukraine. Generally, they are filled with potatoes and smothered in fried onions and *smetana*. They can also be filled with meat or farmer's cheese, and in spring, they are stuffed with cherries, apples or strawberries and served for dessert. *Holubtsi* is another traditional dish of meat and rice rolled up in cabbage leaves and covered with a creamy tomato sauce. Technically from Siberia, *pelmeny* are meat-filled ravioli.

Meat is still treated as a luxury even though most people can afford it now. The traditional Ukrainian recipe is to stew it in little clay pots with potatoes, mushrooms and black pepper. Pork dishes are the most popular. *Balyk* is smoked pork tenderloin with very little fat, while *salo* is pure smoked pork fat carved right off a pig's back. Ukrainians love the stuff and there are many jokes about how wonderful it is. (When a beautiful woman lands on his desert island, a stranded Russian calls to a stranded Ukrainian on another island telling him to come quickly, the thing he wants has just arrived. The Ukrainian jumps into the sea and swims furiously gasping, '*Salo, salo!*') The lard is usually cut in thick slices and served as a snack with bread or whole raw garlic cloves. Sausage tends to be very fatty and usually eaten cold with bread.

Chicken Kiev is a legitimate Ukrainian dish but ordered only by foreigners. Fish abounds on restaurant menus, but skip anything from Ukraine's polluted rivers. Also, even though it's on nearly every menu in Kiev, steer clear of *osetrina* (sturgeon) or black caviar. Admittedly, both dishes taste delicious, but sturgeon is an endangered species, and both of these Russian delicacies kill its chances for survival.

Food

(Red caviar is from salmon and is OK to eat.) Sardines and anchovies on toast are popular party fare.

What food you will eat depends largely on the time of year you are travelling, although shiny imported produce is quickly becoming the norm for the new élite. Generally, market tables are laden with fresh fruits and vegetables – sweet peppers, cucumbers and every form of squash imaginable. All summer long, Ukrainians work in their country plots and then preserve the food for the barren winter months. These bottles of fruit, relishes and pickles spruce up the potatoes and soured cabbage. If you don't pucker up when you bite into a Ukrainian pickle, then it isn't Ukrainian. Fistfuls of salt, home-grown garlic and hot peppers give the piquancy. Ukrainians also take their mushroom and berry collecting seriously, using them in all kinds of traditional dishes (mushrooms sold in the market are safe and tasty). In Kiev of course, little depends on the season and much more on what kind of restaurant you will be frequenting.

Vegetarians need not fear as abstaining from meat has been a necessity for Ukrainians during lean years, and is also a religious practice for faithful Orthodox believers fasting for Lent and other holy days. Keep in mind that eating and serving meat of some sort is perceived as a sign of status, while lack of meat at a dinner table is a reluctant admittance to poverty. If you do turn down meat offered by a host, make sure to sincerely compliment another part of the meal. Traditional vegetarian staples include *deruny* (potato pancakes), buckwheat *kasha* and various vegetable stews and soups. *Mlyntsi*, or *blyni* in Russian, are pancakes, sold like

BREAD ХЛІБ

Bread *is* life in Ukraine, and you'll find it an important staple on your travels, by itself or else with cheese, *smetana* or sausage. Buy bread in the morning as all bakeries are sold out by early afternoon. *Baton* are the short white loaves that resemble oval French bread, except much heavier. You can also find sourdough (square loaves) and all kinds of braided varieties for festivals. The traditional Ukrainian loaf is black bread (*chorni khlib*), made with buckwheat and rye flour and tasting slightly of vinegar. As a rule, one round loaf should weigh exactly one kilo. Black bread was the main staple of peasant diets far into the 20th century (and again during the last stretch of national poverty). The rallying cry and slogan of the first Russian Revolution was 'Bread, Peace and Land' and the central role of wheat in Ukraine means that bread has always been a symbol of food, independence and wealth. Ukrainian tradition welcomes guests of honour in a ceremony of 'bread and salt' where a decorated loaf and a small bowl of salt are presented on an embroidered cloth. Originally, guests were meant to break off a piece, dip it in the salt, eat and nod. Nowadays, the loaf is usually spared for a later meal, so simply nod or bow in recognition of the ceremony.

Food

crêpes in outdoor stands with either jam or savoury meat and cheese. If you want truly good Ukrainian cuisine, do what you can to be invited into someone's home for a meal. No restaurants can imitate the cooking of a Ukrainian *babushka*.

Street food

Food sold on the street is usually safe and very tasty (if it's steaming or smells fresh, it won't come back to haunt you). *Babuskhi* are always selling hot *pirozhki* filled with potatoes, seasoned cabbage or meat and you'll soon recognise their universal call and learn to buy a few of these stuffed buns for the road. Modern street cuisine reflects the 'friendship of the nations' or multi-culturalism of Soviet days. Originally from Crimea and the Caucasus, *chebureki* pastries are stuffed with spicy meat and onions but their nourishing value comes from the heavy grease left on your fingers. In restaurants and homes you'll taste *plov,* a rice and mutton dish from Central Asia and *adzhika*, a spicy Georgian sauce made of herbs and tiny peppers served with meat or potatoes.

It is a sin to travel without food in Ukraine and people you've just met may pack elaborate hampers for the next leg of your journey, even if it's only just a two-hour bus ride. Train and bus stations sell more and more sweets and alcohol and fewer staples, but a stop at any food shop (*gastronom* or *produkty*) can stock you for a journey. Fresh fruit, yoghurt, cheese, sausage, rolls, juice and water make good reserves for train trips. For long hikes, Ukrainians normally pack canned goods, chocolate, bread and bottled water.

Thank goodness the fall of the Soviet economy did not end Ukraine's faithful sweet production. The brightly wrapped sweets are sold in bulk on the street, in shops, and even from restaurant menus. Try *byelochka* (chipmunk) – a delicious hazelnut cream chocolate, or the crunchy *metior* – little balls of nuts and honey covered with black chocolate. Kiev's sweet shops are easily recognisable from the street: large glass windows and bright piles of coloured foil-covered sweets. Ukrainians also eat ice-cream year round, and it is sold and eaten on the streets even on the most frigid of January days (if it doesn't melt in your mouth, chew it).

If you're in the town centre and want to buy some fresh fruit, or just normal groceries to make your own meal, go to Bessarabsky Rynok (at the end of Khreschatyk) or the Tsentralny Gastronom (on the corner of Khreschatyk and Khmelnytskovo) – a very convenient food shop at a very convenient location.

Restaurants and cafés

Eating out is still considered a luxury for most Ukrainians, with cosmopolitan Kiev being the exception to that rule. Even so, you may find that you are one of the very few patrons in an upmarket restaurant or that the only other guests are there for a wedding, birthday or business deal.

Kiev has more restaurants per capita than any other Ukrainian city, a feat inspired both by the city's general demand for nice places to eat and an entrepreneurial explosion that introduced a lot of gaudy décor (like mermaid waitresses or motorcycles hanging from the ceiling). Kiev's eating establishments often seek an

Food

exotic approach and follow scattered trends – for a while, Mexican restaurants were popping up everywhere, while the next big thing seems to be sushi. Be warned that eating out in Kiev often comes loaded with gimmicks and theme-park- like exotica. Pizza- and fast-food joints have also made a vigorous stand in the capital.

Naturally, when visiting Ukraine, you should want to sample Ukrainian food. A number of restoration Ukrainian folk-restaurants offer a good range to choose from in Kiev, and if you are part of an organised tour, you are most likely to visit at least one, if not several. Still, some travellers find that eating *varenniki* every night becomes tiresome. This is often the case elsewhere, but in Kiev there really is no excuse for restaurant burnout. Learn about what you are eating and shop around. Kiev's Ukrainian restaurants may look similar in décor, but their menus tend to express a richer diversity.

Kiev's upmarket restaurants will have a bilingual or separate English menu, and so it is always worth asking for one, even in a small café. Otherwise, never let difficulty in reading the menu be a deterrent. Ask what something is, sound it out or take a stab in the dark. Many restaurant menus will appear fairly inexpensive at first glance, which they are. Eating out in Ukraine is normally ridiculously cheap, but in Kiev, food prices can be comparable to other European countries. These days, you can get anything in Kiev, from exquisite French gourmet cuisine on crystal to Ukrainian fast food served in plastic. Kiev's burgeoning corporate culture has also made *'byzness lanch'* an institution for all respectable eateries. A full lunch will cost from US$5 to $8 and match the traveller's appetite and pocket. A general rule in

Kiev (but not in the rest of the country) is that if a restaurant has seats to sit down in, they most likely have a menu in English and will accept credit cards.

The budget-conscious can still eat elaborate dinners for practically nothing, however, the accepted restaurant tactic is for bills to add up quickly. Menus usually state the price of a food per 100 grams – you pay separately for any extras, and everything is extra. Also, you may often find that the menu is several dozen pages long, but when you start ordering you may be told that everything you want is unavailable. In such a case, find out what the kitchen is prepared to make or ask about the house specialities (*firmeny blyuda*).

The best way to judge a restaurant is by the price of a bowl of borscht, a universal common denominator in Ukraine. US$1–2 should be standard. Anything more than US$4 means the restaurant is pretentious and if it costs below one dollar, the general food standard may be lower than your stomach can handle.

There exists no traditional concept of breakfast and Ukrainians eat much the same food in the morning as they do for lunch and dinner. Hotels generally offer a 'Swedish table' in the spirit of a *smorgasbord* with smoked meats or sausage, cheese, bread, coffee and tea. Some better hotels also offer fresh fruit, cereals, yoghurt and omelettes. Cafés in the city are only just beginning to offer continental-style coffee and croissants. (If you're out on your own, fresh rolls from a bakery make a fine walking breakfast.)

Official cab drivers will know the majority of the restaurants listed in this book, so getting there comes down to hailing a taxi. If not, simply ask on the street or

Food

use the map. Remember that Kiev is one of the largest cities in these parts, so that eating out may not prove too different from other major European capitals. So, be sure to enjoy Kiev's culinary landscape for what it is: an experiment of possibilities.

RESTAURANTS

Kiev's restaurants are also open quite late, and some never close. Many will take reservations beforehand, which is a good idea if you want a luxury restaurant in the evening.

Luxury

US$30 and up:

Ukrainian

Empire Shevchenka 5-7/29, 8th floor; tel: 044 244 1235 [2 C2]
On the top floor of the Premier Palace hotel, the Empire puts out a refined version of Ukrainian and European cuisine with one of the best panoramic views of the city. Open to guests and non-guests of the hotel, the food is simply exquisite. Anywhere from US$20 to US$60.

Tsarskoe Selo Sichnevoho Povstannya 42/1; tel: 044 573 9775 [2 G4]
Located right between the Pechersky Lavra and the giant motherland statue, this complex of Ukrainian huts goes all out to create the ultimate Ukrainian theme-dining experience. Meat

is grilled on a brick fireplace, and waiters keep your glass filled with authentic *uzvar*, *kvas* and vodka. A fun place by day, things turn jazzy and boisterous at night. Around US$30 a head.

Lypsky Osobnyak Lypska 15; tel: 044 254 0090 [2 E2]
If you're in search of 'real Ukrainian food' but think it's all peasant fare, sit back and be impressed. True, Ukraine's tradition of haute cuisine has been stifled by decades of famine and oppression, but Kiev's finest restaurant counters history by delivering the natural comfort food of Ukraine with an exquisite native style that blends the baroque with the creative. Beautiful 19th-century interior, first-class service and an incredible wine collection.

Za Dvuma Zaitsiamy Andriyivsky Uzviz 34; tel: 044 416 3516 [1 C3]
'The Two Hares' features a rare rendition of old Slavonic cuisine and a welcome twist to the everyday Ukrainian fare. US$40 a head.

International
L'Amour Naberezhno-Khreschatytskaya 17/18; tel: 044 451 5080 [1 D3]
A quaint French cottage, propped next to the Dnepr, serving stylish French cuisine prepared lovingly by a talented gourmet chef. The grilled tuna is *magnifique*. US$20–30.

Concord Pushkinskaya 42/4 8th floor; tel: 044 229 5512 [2 C2]
A glamorous interior, the Concord features unique French–Asian fusion cooking. Expect to pay US$40 a head.

Restaurants

Da Vinci Fish Club Volodymyrska 12; tel: 044 490 3434 [2 C1]
Despite an appalling name, the fish club enjoys an established Kiev following. Seafood reigns supreme, but there's plenty of authentic Italian fare and Venetian décor. US$30 a head.

Dnipro Khreschatyk 1/2, 2nd floor; tel: 044 254 6790 [1 D4]
Inside one of Kiev's biggest hotels, the Dnipro features a proud chef who's eager to take Ukrainian cooking to a new level. Not a bad choice, if you enjoy long and sumptuous meals. Without drinks, meals US$30–50.

Haiffa Kostyantynivska 57; tel: 044 417 2512 1 C2]
In the far north of Podil, this Jewish restaurant not only serves Israeli cuisine, but several favourites from the Ukrainian–Jewish tradition. Around US$30 a head.

Le Grand Café Muzeiny 4; tel: 044 228 7208; web: www.legrandcafe.kiev.ua [2 D1]
Both pricey and elitist, this French-style café is Kiev's flashiest hangout, dressed in *fin-de-siècle* Parisian décor and offering dramatic highbrow dishes. The menu explores some interesting Ukrainian–French hybrids (like *vareniki* with foie gras) while the drinks are more sturdy and conventional – the pastry cart is highly recommended. Come with heavy pockets.

Marché Chervonoarmiyska 13; tel: 044 451 4050 [2 C2]
The French grandeur gets laid on thick, but the *provençal*-style cooking, exquisite French

cheeses and diverse wine list transcend the sunny surroundings. A very popular venue in Kiev for the time being. Plan on US$40 a head.

Pena Yaroslaviv Val 30/18; tel: 044 234 1701 [1 B4]
Elitist and super pricey, Pena caters to those with a hankering for impossible dishes. This is the most likely restaurant responsible for introducing the word 'fusion' into Kiev's culinary lexicon. Fresh Japanese fish (flown-in daily) and exotic veggies in teeny salads. Plan on spending US$60 for your meal.

San Tori Sahaydachnoho 41; tel: 044 462 4994 [1 C3]
Kiev's most perfect Asian food: delicate sushi, incredibly fresh fruit, and first-class setting. On one of Podil's central squares, the masterful combination of Thai and Japanese will outlast current fads. US$50 per person minimum.

Tampopo Saksahanskovo 55; tel: 044 244 4420 [2 B3]
Kiev is still going crazy over the discovery of sushi, and this dainty restaurant features a sushi conveyor belt that continues to wow Ukrainians. Good if you have Ukrainian friends or clients. US$40 a head, at least.

Middle range
US$10–30

Restaurants

Ukrainian

Hunter (Myslyvets) Saksahanskovo 147/5; tel: 044 236 3735 [2 A1]
A wild mountain theme is reinforced by lots of fur and dried plants hanging from the walls.
Food is Carpathian-style, specialising in wild birds and game. Around US$30.

Khutorok Naberezhno-Khreschatytska (Pier No 1); tel: 044 463 7019 [1 B3]
Occupying a giant wooden riverboat still afloat on the Dnepr, this old-time Ukrainian
restaurant makes for a very fun lunch or dinner. Burning hearths and a live folk band add to
the rustic country style, and the food is hearty and delicious. Around US$20 a head.

Kozachok Kyrovogradska 118; tel: 044 250 9352
Traditional Ukrainian cabin-style restaurant/pub with singing Cossacks that serve all the
Ukrainian basics and dozens of different vodkas. Open round the clock. US$15 a head.

Kozak Mamai Prorizna 4; tel: 044 228 4273 [2 D1]
Ukraine's Cossack past is relived in a series of decorated rooms just off Khreschatyk,
but the Ukrainian food is exceptional and the atmosphere more peaceful than would be
expected if the uniformed waiters really were Cossacks. Expect to spend around
US$20.

Nobu Shota Rustavelli 12; tel: 044 246 7734 [2 C3]
Minimalist sushi joint and Asian drinks bar. US$20 a head.

Pechersky Dvorik Krepestnoi Pereulok 6; tel: 044 253 2667 [2 E2]
Representing a late-19th-century Kiev salon, the well-lit and open space of the Dvorik offers
a relaxed atmosphere and a creative menu. Food is mainly Russian/Ukrainian, with a few
recipes borrowed from the earliest Slavic chronicles. One block down from Hotel Kyiv;
main dishes are US$5–10.

Pervak Rohnidynska 2; tel: 044 235 0952 [2 C2]
Artistic and slightly over the top, Pervak is a testament to Kiev finding its own happily
eclectic style. Traditional Russian favourites and fancy little dishes served with tribute to
Kiev's style before the revolution. US$15 a meal.

Schekavytsya Kostyantinivska 46/52; tel: 044 417 1472 [By Petrikva Metro]
US$20 per person for dinner.

Taras Park Shevchenko; tel: 044 235 2132 [2 B2]
Right in the park (by Universitet metro station), Taras has an advantage over other country-
style restaurants, for the fact that the little wooden hut is surrounded by trees and greenery.
Food is pretty typical Ukrainian; around US$15 per person.

USSR Sichnevoho Povstannia 42/1; tel: 044 290 3066 [3 G4]
Rightfully next to Kiev's most Soviet monuments, CCCP is a delightful take on the Soviet
era, and the jovial cuisine only adds to the atmosphere of goodtime nostalgia. Enjoy
specialities from each of the former Soviet republics. US$20 for dinner.

Restaurants

International

Alazani Chervonoarmiyska 55A; tel: 044 205 4467 [2 C3]
One of Kiev's Georgian greats, especially if you have a Georgian love for good food and wine. Around US$20.

Antalya Fedorova 10; tel: 044 220 6157 [2 C3]
Refined Turkish food outside Kiev's centre. Under US$20 a meal.

Asakhi Saksahanskovo 1r; tel: 044 244 2237 [2 C3]
Authentic Japanese food prepared by a real Japanese chef. Lots of sushi and sashimi and plenty to drink. US$20 per person.

Capucin Chervonoarmiyska 81; tel: 044 531 1378 [2 C3]
Gregariously French cuisine served with medieval flair. US$20 a head.

Caravan Klovsky Uzviz 10; 044 290 9577 [2 E3]
Uzbekistan's unique culinary tradition hallmarked the most exotic cuisine during the Soviet era. Caravan highlights Central Asia's diverse cuisine with dumplings, grilled meat, *plov* (aromatic Pilau rice dishes), kebabs and spicy vegetables. US$15 for a meal.

Fellini Gorodetskovo 5; 044 229 5462 [2 D2]
Obviously named after the famed Italian film director, Fellini's b&w movie stills cover the

walls of this upmarket, all-day, all-night supper club. Cooking blends French and Italian elements. US$25 a head.

Lun Van Khmelnytskovo 26; tel: 044 229 8191 [2 C1]
One of Kiev's earliest Chinese restaurants, now serving classy Asian food (including some Japanese specialities). A royal atmosphere with a well-designed interior and dedicated chef. US$25 a head.

Mandarin Naberezhno Khreschatytskaya (Pier No 6): tel: 044 459 0877 [1 D3]
Asian fusion served on a Han Dynasty-style riverboat on the Dnepr. Great Chinese and Japanese food. Around US$25 per person.

Marokana Lesi Ukrayinky 24; tel: 044 254 4999 [2 E4]
A post-modern blend of international cuisine served with oriental mystique (lavish silk pillows and poofy cushions) aimed at Kiev's more fashionable set. Around US$25 per person.

Mimino Spasska 10A; tel: 044 417 3545 [1 C2]
Georgian food is fantastic, and if you're uninitiated, this is the right place to start. One of Kiev's very best restaurants, this cosy venue (complete with crackling fireplace) is right in the heart of Podil. Around US$20 per person.

Pantagruel Lysenka 1; tel: 044 229 7301 [2 C1]
Italian gourmet restaurant, with blissful pasta dishes and a famous wine list. US$20 a head.

Peschera Tarasovska 10A; tel: 044 244 3372 [2 B3]
Another great Kiev gimmick: hearty food served by cavemen in caves. Everyone orders the
steak cooked on a hot stone for their first visit. US$20 a head.

Poseidon Naberezhnoe Shosse and Navodnytsky; tel: 044 254 2137 [1 D3]
Built in a riverboat on the Dnepr, this restaurant specialises in fresh fish with elaborate
sauces. Plush, secluded surroundings make things feel a little more upmarket and intimate,
even though meals run under US$20.

Sam's Steak House Zhylyanskaya 37; tel: 044 227 2000 [2 B3]
There is some novelty in watching Kiev imitate a quaint American restaurant. When that
wears off, there's steak and wine. US$15–20.

Soho Artyoma 82; tel: 044 244 7351 [1 A4]
Kiev's secret desire to be New York City. If you like red wine with a giant T-bone, this is the
place. US$25 a plate.

Steak House Chokolovsky 16A; tel: 044 241 0597 [4 A2]
A name that says it all: big steaks and lots of meat. Besides pork, fish, chicken and lamb,
there's a big salad bar and rich desserts. US$20 a head.

Svitlytsya Andreyevsky Spusk 13B; tel: 044 416 3186 [1 C3]
This rustic French café and crêperie is right off Kiev's major tourist street and serves wonderful meat fondues, delicious crêpes and light meals for generally low prices. A full meal will cost around US$12.

Tequila House Spasska 8A; tel: 044 417 0358 [1 C2]
Did you really come all the way to Kiev for a poor imitation of Tex-Mex? If you really love tequila, then come and try one of the dozens of varieties served. Otherwise, leave the locals to enjoy the novelty of guacamole and tortillas. US$20 a meal.

Vostok Naberezhno-Khreschatytska; tel: 044 416 5375 [1 D2]
A tribute to eastern exoticism, this Chinese restaurant stands out from the rest for its sense of style and authenticity. Diverse chefs from various regions of China serve up unique and unfamiliar dishes. If you order fish, you'll be asked to pick it out of their small pond before it wriggles off to the kitchen. Main dishes cost US$10–20.

War and Peace Chervonoarmiyska 23B; tel: 044 234 6976 [1 C2]
Not only does this restaurant pay tribute to Tolstoy's novel, the menu pays tribute to each cuisine of the warring sides. Around US$20 for dinner.

011 Ilinska 18; tel: 044 416 0001 [1 D3]
Tasty Yugoslav cuisine served in an ambient hall or out on the covered terrace (011 is the telephone code for Belgrade). Medium prices.

Restaurants

Budget
Average US$10 and below

Ukrainian
Budmo! Mykhailivska 22A; tel: 044 229 6193 [1 C4]
A brand-new spot for Kiev, 'Cheers' is located on one of Kiev's busier streets and strikes a happy medium between prim European café and old Ukrainian tavern. Bound to be a classic.

Elanda Mezhyhirska 22; tel: 044 416 1977 [1 C2]
A Ukrainian restaurant of the old-school variety: ultra-glamorous and 'European'-style cuisine. This is what eating out in the rest of the country is like.

Kobzar Khreschatyk 25; tel: 044 234 0935 [2 D2]
Intimate and lively Ukrainian restaurant that has fun the Ukrainian way. Cosy tables and cosy food.

Kruhla Vezha Shorsa 44; tel: 044 294 6537 [2 E4]
Right next to the Pecherska metro, dig in to tasty Ukrainian food like the Ukrainians eat. Cute, authentic and real.

Kyivska Perepichka Khmelnytskovo 3 [2 D2]
Without shame or modesty, I confess that this is the author's favourite place to eat in Kiev and it is the only food stand to have remained open for the entire decade since

Eating and drinking

independence. The *perepichka* is a quintessentially Kiev snack similar to a sausage roll; hot dogs are covered in *pirozhki* pastry and then deep-fried (of course!). The hot, hand-held treat costs about US$0.30 and you'll find it impossible to eat just one.

Pid Osokom Mikhayilovska 20 [1 C4]
This small café caters mainly to the Ukrainian business set during lunch hours, seating people together on long wooden benches. It can get crowded because it is so popular, however the aromatic food is worth it. Authentic and inexpensive Ukrainian cuisine is served hot by a matronly staff.

U Seny I Gogy Shosta Rustaveli 4; tel: 044 234 0692 [2 D2]
Urban restaurant near the Central Synagogue, serving simple Ukrainian fare for low-ish prices.

International
Chateau de Fleur Khreschatyk 24; tel: 044 228 7800 [D 2D]
Looking on to Kiev's main drag, this is not a French restaurant, but more of a modern cafeteria serving soup, salad, pancakes etc. Known for the view of the street from above; under US$15.

Gavroche Mezhyhirska 3/7; tel: 044 416 5524 [1 C2]
This hole in the wall in Podil did not have to try too hard to look like a hole in the wall from the set of *Les Misérables*. Hearty French fare but good-natured enough to be Ukrainian.

Restaurants

Great Wall Kostiantynivska 2A; tel: 044 230 6027 [1 B2]
No-frills Chinese food that's fit for the pickiest, most culturally insensitive tourist out there.

Himalaya Khreschatyk 23; tel: 044 462 0437 [2 D2]
Kiev's main Indian restaurant for the time being. The location on Khreschatyk is convenient and visible, the atmosphere pleasant enough, and the chef is really Indian. Fixed lunches cost around US$8.

Makabi Kosher Rustavelli 15; tel: 044 235 9437 [2 C3]
'Kosher food for kosher prices' – so says the slogan. Located next to Kiev's central synagogue, authentic Israeli fare, grilled meats and delicious vegetarian food attract both Jew and Gentile. Meals go as low as US$4.

Mangal Pankivksa 11; tel: 044 244 1990 [2 B2]
A hearty and feelgood kind of place, this open restaurant grills fish, poultry and beef over an open fire. US$8 buys a very good-sized meal.

Non-Stop Prospekt Peremohy 6; tel: 044 216 4073 [Kiev A2]
As the name implies, this bar and grill is open 24 hours, offering a broad vegetarian menu, fantastic barbecue, and lots of drinks. Prices range from kopecks up to US$15.

Uno Pizza Volodymyrska 40/2; tel: 044 228 4362 [2 C1]
Real Italian pizza for about US$7. Next door to one of Kiev's loudest Irish pubs.

Yakitoria Lesy Ukrayinky 42; tel: 044 295 8161 [2 E4]
Kiev's early introduction of Japanese cooking – the antithesis to Ukrainian food. US$10 a meal.

CAFÉS
This is a pretty wide range of what constitutes 'café' culture in Kiev, although there are plenty of unknown basement cafés throughout the city that rarely get listed and will promise a more 'Kievan' experience. Most of the following take plastic:

Aquarelle Hospitalna 12; tel: 044 220 4144; fax: 044 220 4568 [2 D3]
Elite piano bar inside the President Hotel Kyivsky. Listen to the lounge piano while twirling fancy Italian food on your fork. US$40 a head.

Charme Khmelnytskovo 50; tel: 044 224 9065 [2 B1]
This tiny underground café and bar presents a much more honest picture of Kiev's café life. A good refuge on rainy days and snowy evenings, here the food is straightforward, with a range of Ukrainian beers on tap. (Inexpensive, warm meals.)

Cafés

Chayny Club Mezhyhirska 22; tel: 044 416 1877 [1 C2]
Kiev's ultimate tea house, serving dozens and dozens of different, global teas and all the cakes and sandwiches you need to go with it. Inexpensive.

Le Cosmopolite Volodymyrska 47; tel: 044 228 7278 [2 C2]
Jazzy continental bar that serves Belgian beer and all that tastes good with it: French *fondue*, German sausages and heavy bread. Also serves a full vegetarian menu. US$30 a head.

Coupole Sichnevoho Povstannya, 27B; tel: 044 290 6650; fax: 044 254 5763 [3 F3]
An intimate circular café near the Caves Monastery, Coupole serves 'original meals for loyal prices'. Good for quiet, leisurely lunches and dinners. Entrées from US$8.

Deja Vue Khmelnytskovo 30; tel: 044 235 9802 [2 C1]
Although it bills itself as a restaurant, this underground café goes way beyond its peculiar Chinese/European menu. Imagine motorcycles on the walls, stolen street signs and Soviet memorabilia, with great live music (talented local bands) every night. If it's midnight and you need tea, cake and a sad song, this is the place. US$20 for a meal.

Dno Peremohy 45; tel: 044 456 4505 [Kiev A2]
Popular with Kiev's younger set, this tribute to the Beatles recreates the psychedelia of The Yellow Submarine and is aptly named 'bottom' in Russian. The food is unique, hip and Slavic,

meaning it mixes well with alcohol. The 'beat café' is very close to Shulyavksa metro station, if you're young and want to meet locals your age … Meals for US$10–15.

Dva Gusya Khmelnytskovo 46B; tel: 044 221 1231 [2 C2]
'Two Geese'. A simple, pub-like atmosphere right in the centre of Kiev. Good for a quick, mid-sightseeing lunch.

Dveri Reitarska 13; tel: 044 229 5168 [1 C4]
Open bar and urban café not far from the Golden Gate that's fast becoming a Kiev regular.

Fruktopia Shevchenka 2; tel: 044 235 8347 [1 C2]
Billed as a 'fashion café', this colourful downtown venue serves fresh, inexpensive meals that challenge the grey of the streets.

Marquise de Chocolat Prorizna 4; tel: 044 235 4546 [1 D2]
This dessert café has already made its name in Kiev with an advertisement of a woman covered in melted chocolate. Besides all things dark and delicious, the menu offers colourful cocktails and a range of stylish coffee.

Massandra Naberezhno-Khreschatytska 19/21; tel: 044 416 0440 [1 D2]
Ukraine's most famous wine is served with custom-made dishes meant to bring out the best of this Crimean favourite.

Cafés

Nira Khreschatyk 13; tel: 044 229 7962 [2 D2]
A groovy green coffee shop with high ceilings, small tables and only the necessary frills.
Serves pancakes of all sorts.

Passazh Khreschatyk 15; tel: 044 229 1209 [2 D2]
Viennese-style coffee house and pastry shop that serves delicate cream cakes, hefty
patisseries and delectable truffles. By far the best place on Khreschatyk for teatime
(follow under the archway to get there).

Time Out Gorkovo 50; tel: 044 248 7390; email: timeout@timeout.com.ua [2 C3]
Nothing too different from back home: European and American food served with gusto
24 hours a day. Around US$10.

The Wall (Stina) Bessarabska Ploscha 2; tel: 044 235 8045; next to Bessarabsky Rynok [2 B2]
The heavy influence of Pink Floyd, East Berlin and old-school rock offers a foggy glimpse at
the former angst of Soviet Ukraine's once youthful generations now happily feasting on a
bizarre Mexican/Ukrainian menu.

BARS
Art Club 44 Khreschatyk 44; tel: 044 229 4137 [2 C2]
A pretty hip place in Kiev of late, the '44' serves five-buck cocktails from an ultra-long bar
and provides *the* venue for all of Kiev's most rocking bands.

Belle Vue Saksahanskovo 7; tel: 044 220 8780 [2 C3]
Belgian beer bar, serving some food.

Double Bass Kostyantynivska 34; tel: 044 467 6018 [1 B2]
Live jazz and live blues played late into the night; the chef who works this creatively
decorated 'bar' happens to go in for the gourmet – not a bad choice for a late night repast.
Good vibes, good music, and considerate staff offer a low-key night out.

English Pub Raisy Okypnoyi 2; tel: 044 552 5091 [3 K1]
Part of the out-of-control funfair that is Hotel Turist's Joss nightclub; come and enjoy
Ukraine's take on how the English have fun: lots of beer, pub games, big-screen footie, and
live music.

Golden Gate Volodymyrska 40/2; tel: 044 235 5188 [2 C1]
Kiev's other Irish pub that differs little from any other Irish pub anywhere else in the world.
Draught beer and plenty of whiskey.

Korona Club Rohnidynska 4; tel: 044 220 0216 [2 D2]
With a zany interior that features the East European hybrid of bar/restaurant/casino, the
'club' reflects the outlandish tastes of Kiev's early mafia set, but feels most comfortable
when you go there to drink. Corona is served as well.

Bars

Lounge Bar Muzeyny 4; tel: 044 228 7208 [2 D1]
Just as the name implies, the lounge is a place for kicking back and having a cocktail. As part of the Grand Café complex, élite attitudes soar as high as the prices, letting you feel suave.

Mambo Druzhby Narodiv 5; tel: 044 252 8224 [3 F4]
Spanish and Latin American bar/restaurant with live music, creative drinks, and spicy food to go with it.

A TASTE OF KIEV

True, globalisation being globalisation, you can find anything to eat in Kiev, so if you want to spend your time in Ukraine dipping sashimi into wasabi, then please go right ahead. However, for the geographical purists out there, Kiev offers certain delicacies not found elsewhere. Pushing these dainties past your palate is bound to heighten your experience:

- *Salo* – pure, smoked pork fat, often served with raw garlic; Ukrainian 'sushi' or 'Snickers'. (Tastes like pork fat.)
- *Kyivska perepichka* – a Kiev-only speciality (See *Budget restaurants; Ukrainian*.)

Moda Bar Naberezhno-Khreschatytska, Pier #6; tel: 044 416 7388 [1 D3]
Known for outlandish parties, daily fashion shows and bartenders who perform dazzling tricks to brain-shattering techno music. Open all night every night, located on a Dnepr river boat.

O'Brien's Mikhaylovska 17A; tel: 044 229 1584 [1 C4]
Knowing it wasn't a part of the global community until its capital sported an Irish pub, Kiev quickly adopted O'Brien's as its own. If you like hearing English all around you, come and watch sports here.

- Poppyseed buns – sold in bakeries and for breakfast in some hotels. Brush your teeth well afterwards.
- Ukrainian pickles – not just cucumbers, but tomatoes, peppers and anything else that grows in Ukraine and can be bottled.
- *Kyivsky tort* – layered cake with walnuts and hazelnuts and filled with sugary buttercream. You can find these only in Kiev, but not in restaurants. Check bakeries and *gastronom* or go to the railway station, where they're sold like souvenirs in pink boxes.
- Red caviar on fresh black bread with butter (buy your own at Bessarabsky Rynok).

Bars

Pilsner Pushkinska 20; tel: 044 225 2101 [2 C2]
A Czech beer hall in Kiev that serves Czech beer and Czech food. Comfy and casual.

Sapphire Bar Shevchenka 5-7; tel: 044 244 1262 [2 C2]
On the 2nd floor of the Premier Palace hotel, the bar is sophisticated and the drinks overpriced, but you can watch BBC World and the fashion channel while eavesdropping on the latest business gossip.

111 Peremohy 1; tel: 044 221 7741 [Kiev A2]
Kiev's most original cocktails served all day, all night with a steady stream of entertainment kept lively by a super-energetic staff. Located inside the Lybid Hotel.

VEGETARIANS

Kiev boasts more vegetarian-friendly restaurants than your average East European city, although that's not saying much. With advanced capitalism comes increased options, and most Ukrainian restaurants will now serve a few vegetarian (but somewhat skimpy) entrées. Simply state your dietary preference to the waiter/waitress (*vegeteryanyets* with a hard g) and keep in mind that to many Ukrainians, vegetarianism is a state of Ukrainian Orthodox believers who are abstaining from red meat, and not fish or poultry. If you are a strict vegetarian or vegan, there are a few things to look out for: the base for borscht is often made with meat, but smarter restaurants will have a purely vegetarian version on offer.

Varenniki are usually filled with vegetarian ingredients (potatoes, cabbage or cheese) and *deruny* (potato pancakes) are meat-free, but heavy on the starch. For good vegetarian restaurants and vegan options try Mimino (Georgian), Non-Stop, Himalaya and Le Cosmopolite. Also try the Kosher establishments (Haiffa and Makabi Kosher), which are at least 50% vegetarian, or other ethnic restaurants (like Caravan).

Vegetarians

7 Entertainment and Nightlife

THEATRE

Ukrainians love a good drama, so it should come as no surprise that Kiev's world of theatre thrived through World Wars, repressive regimes and total poverty. The capital's recent cultural renaissance was led in large part by Kiev's unofficial acting guilds, and it is on the stage that the real drama of Ukraine's present cultural experimentation unfolds with passion.

Regardless of the language spoken, watching a play in Kiev puts you face-to-face with the city you aim to discover. If it's classic theatre, then enjoy, or follow along in English for there is something about watching Chekhov performed in the country where he wrote. Part of the fun is watching all the families and young children who come dressed up for an affordable night out. Ukrainians of all ages enjoy even the most serious plays and to be seen at the theatre is a true sign of one's cultural prestige.

You can find theatre listings in *What's On* (www.whatson-kiev.com), at the various theatres themselves, or in any of the theatre booths that sell tickets in the city centre. Also try the booths at Khreschatyk 13 and 21; tel: 044 228 7642.

Actor Theatre Velyka Zhytomyrska 40; tel: 044 219 1048 [1 B3]
Some of the latest in Russian and Ukrainian playwriting, along with lesser known classics.

Bravo Drama Theatre Honchara Olesya 79; tel: 044 216 4022 [2 A1]
Highbrow drama and stark romanticism by Ukraine's leading professionals.

Drama and Comedy Theatre Brovarsky 25; tel: 044 517 1955 [Kiev D2]
On the left bank, specialising in dark comedies that only Ukrainians could get away with.

Lesya Ukrayinka Russian Drama Theatre Khmelnytskovo 5B; tel: 044 224 4223 [2 C2]
Kiev's renowned Russian-language playhouse.

Ivan Franko National Drama Theatre Ivana Franka 3; tel: 044 229 5991 [2 D2]
Diverse and innovative Ukrainian-language performances.

Kiev Youth Theatre Prorizna 17; tel: 044 235 4218 [2 C1]
European classics produced by the capital's young and creative.

Kolesa Theatre Andreyevsky Spusk 8; tel: 044 416 0422 [1 C3]
Small avant-garde playhouse that already has an established following in Kiev. The upstairs theatre produces more well-known pieces (eg: Henry James, Ionesco, Flaubert) while the lower floor is a working café with interactive theatre every night of the week. Somehow or other, patrons will get roped into the performance art and vaudeville.

Theatre

Podil Drama Theatre Kontraktova Ploscha 4; tel: 044 416 5489 [1 C3]
World famous and very entertaining, doing everything from adapted Shakespeare to poetic
Ukrainian pieces.

Suzirya Theatre Yaroslaviv Val 14B; tel: 044 212 4188 [1 C4]
The experimental and traditional mixed right before your very eyes.

OPERA AND BALLET

The true Kiev experience should include a show at the **National Opera and
Ballet** (Volodymyrska 50; tel: 044 224 7165 [2 C1]). Not only is the building a
valuable historic monument to Kiev, Ukraine and the Russian Revolution, its
architecture amazes (inside and out), and the shows are truly entertaining. The
longstanding traditions of the Russian and Ukrainian ballet have not faltered and
many a traveller who thinks ballet is not his/her 'thing' gains a new fascination with
dance. Kiev's Opera is just as invigorating, and most theatres will rotate a very large
repertoire over the course of the season. There is something every night (starting
at 19.00), and often a different matinee show as well (starting at 12.00). Tickets sell
for US$3–20 for a range of classics like *Swan Lake* and *Rigoletto*. The shows are
always outstanding. To complete the experience, eat red caviar toast during the
intermission, bring flowers for the ballerinas and shout 'bravo' louder than anyone
else. Monthly listings are posted outside the opera house, and tickets can be
purchased in the small booth (through the door) on the left side of the main

entrance on Volodymyrska. Take special care to avoid ticket touts in this spot. Good seats cost around US$5, a private box will cost around US$10. If you don't mind paying more, most hotels can arrange to get you tickets to the opera.

MUSIC

Classical music abounds in Kiev by night; the trick is finding out what's on and when. What was once an easy and inexpensive form of entertainment is now following the way of the West and becoming exclusive and expensive. Ask around when you arrive; you can often find symphony concerts with available tickets at the **National Opera** (see above). Otherwise, try the **National Philharmonic (**Volodymyrska Uzviz 2; tel: 044 229 6251/044 228 1697 [1 D4]). Featuring one of the country's most beautiful architectural interiors, the Philharmonic provides Kiev with stunning classical and folk performances almost every night. Like many churches during the Soviet era, St Nikolai's was transformed into the respectable **House of Organ and Chamber Music** (Chervonoarmiyska 75; tel: 044 268 3186 [2 C4]) 'Organ Hall'. The respectability continues with circumspect performances of chamber music and powerful organ recitals. The **National Conservatory** (Arkhitektora Horodetskovo; tel: 044 229 0792 [2 D2]) also makes good with its broad European classical repertoire. For something slightly more lively, try the **Palats Ukrayina** (Chervonoarmiyska 103). Pop stars from the former USSR like to show their stuff at the *palats,* or you might be lucky and catch an evening with one of the burned-out stars from the West. For Kiev's best and brightest live rock bands, try **Soho** (Artyoma 82; tel: 044 244 7351).

Music

CINEMA

In Kiev, cinemas are nearly always showing American films that are badly dubbed into Ukrainian or Russian, with the very rare exception of a Russian film that isn't, and some subtitled movies. Prices can be as low as US$2 to get in, and up to US$10. Check out Kiev's *What's On* to get an update on what's playing and when (www.whatson-kiev.com). More important than the film and definitely unique are the big Soviet-style movie houses throughout Kiev. This was culture built for the masses before Hollywood came along, and can still be enjoyed as such.

Butterfly Moskovsky 6; tel: 044 531 3977 [2 E2]
Kino Palats Institutska 1; tel: 044 228 7223 [2 D1]
Kinopanorama Shota Rustavelli 19; tel: 044 227 3041 [2 C2]
Kyiv Chervonoarmiyska 19; tel: 044 221 0881 [2 C3]
Kyivska Rus Artyoma 93; tel: 044 251 6051 [1 A3]
Ukraina Horodetskovo 5; tel: 044 229 6301 [2 D2]
Zhovten Kostyantynivska 26; tel: 044 251 6095 [1 B2]

NIGHTCLUBS

Kiev's new *diskoteky* scene has erupted in a crazy race to outdo one another in lavishness, colour, exoticism and gimmickry. Until things settle down, visitors can enjoy the human circus up close and personal. A lot of popular clubs advertise to foreigners only, as foreigners are the only ones that can afford the drinks there. In

KIEV FOR KIDS (AND ADULTS)

Kiev's got plenty of home-grown alternatives to the 'dinner-and-show' remedy to a travellers' evening. A classic form of local entertainment is the Kiev **Circus** (*Tsyrk*) (Peremohy 2; tel: 044 216 3856 [Kiev A2]). You don't need to speak the language to enjoy the animals, sequins and death-defying feats. Call ahead to get tickets, buy them from the theatre ticket booths, or from the people standing next to the circus posters in the subway. Your hotel concierge should be able to hook you up as well.

Kiev dearly loves its several puppet theatres, which provided kiddie entertainment during the Soviet era, and continue to serve as a revered art form for all ages throughout Ukraine. Try the **Marionette Theatre** in Podil (Sahaydachnovo 29/3; tel: 044 417 3058 [1 C3]). The theatre is known for its artistic puppet renditions of classic Ukrainian fairy-tales. The **Kyiv State Puppet Theatre** (40-richia Zhovtnya 22; tel: 044 265 4183 [4 C3]) is more traditional with giant-sized puppets and cool lighting. For a little more rhythm and energy, try the **Children's Musical Theatre** (Mezhyhirska 2; tel: 044 416 4280 [1 C2]) with lively song and dance numbers.

addition, Russian mafia culture (or lack of it) has introduced a whole new series of casinos and tawdry nightlife in Kiev, which in recent years has crept slowly towards

Nightclubs

a more sophisticated level. Striptease has become the mistaken trademark of a 'classy' restaurant or club, and you might be surprised by the entertainment at what seems to be a billiards bar or a dance club. (Most of these dancers are under-employed ballerinas – go to the ballet instead!)

Caribbean Club Kominterna 4; tel: 044 244 4290 [2 B2]
The awkwardness of Latin American dancing, music, food and festivals in Kiev is probably why this place is so popular with ex-pats.

Dino Khreschatyk 12; tel: 044 228 1852 [2 D1]
A fun dance club that's all about prehistoric times. A fair mix of Ukrainians and locals.

Freedom Frunze 134; tel: 044 468 4068 [Kiev A1]
If you weren't a foreigner, you wouldn't get in. Kiev's mafiosi and beautiful people gather for dancing, gambling and ogling. Come with a lot of cash.

Fusion Artyoma 82; tel: 044 244 5668 [1 A3]
A showy new club for Kiev with a steady following of young, hip professionals. A bit more of what you'd find back home.

Joss Raisy Okypnoyi 2; tel: 044 516 8674 [3 K1]
Kiev's left bank extravaganza; you'll see this place advertised all over the city. Nightly cabaret shows dazzle tourists and the Ukrainian business crowd.

Opium Saksahanskovo 1г; tel: 044 205 5393; web: www.opiumdance.com.ua [2 C3]
Kiev's hippest hard-core dance club bringing the rave scene to Podil with freshly spun house music by 'renowned' DJs. Youngish local crowds.

The River Palace Naberezhnoe Shosse/Dnepr Bridge; tel: 044 490 6695 [1 D3]
It doesn't get much better than this: real live disco music from the disco years sung out on a refurbished Soviet riverboat. Plus, there's a supper club and casino.

Tato Fashion Club Perovskoy 6/11; tel: 044 456 1782 [Kiev A2]
A dance club that parades the models all night long and then puts them out on the floor to dance. All ages and nationalities.

CASINOS
Most of Kiev's dozens of casinos never close, and most other entertainment venues (nightclubs, dance clubs and bars) are often connected to casinos. In addition, nearly every hotel will run their very own in-house casino or be located very close to one.

Casino 21st Century Saksahanskovo 51; tel: 044 220 1703 [2 C3]
Specialising in poker, prize-drawing, and late-night shows.

Imperial Casino Saksahanskovo 1г; tel: 044 244 3957 [2 C3]
Pink lights, gold pillars, blondes and roulette.

Metro Jackpot Mechnikova 14; tel: 044 234 7934 [2 E3]
Slots, slots and more slots. Advertised as 'honest gaming'. Hmmm.

Mirald Chervonoarmiyska 15; tel: 044 234 8385 [2 C2]
Where the foreigners come to gamble. Poker and blackjack.

Split Club Prorizna 8; tel: 044 536 1717
Glitzy casino with high stakes and strip club.

Entertainment and nightlife

Shopping

Capitalism has conquered Kiev without an ounce of shame, but making cold purchases in Kiev is still not completely devoid of local culture. The Ukrainian way is to make deals and exchanges, but they still do it after their own fashion. Dressy shop attendants are frightfully honest if an item of clothing doesn't look so good on you, and they will let you know by their facial expression or a sharp tongue. Grannies selling cakes on the street will refuse to let you take the ones you're pointing at, quickly refilling your bag with the freshest variety. In Kiev, shopping reflects a person-to-person relationship between the buyer and seller. Being choosy reflects good taste on your part, and interacting pleasantly with shopkeepers (especially as a foreigner) shows good manners.

Traditional shops in Kiev normally open at 10.00 and close at 20.00, with a one-hour lunch break sometime during the day (13.00 to 14.00, or 14.00 to 15.00). More and more shops are staying open until very late. You can buy anything in Kiev, which is quite a statement since only a few years ago there was quite literally nothing in Ukrainian shops. Posh shopping centres now grace the streets and underground passages (*kvadrat*) of Kiev where foreigners and successful Kievans are meant to buy things like crocodile-skin handbags and US$2,000 shoes. At the other end of the shopping spectrum are grannies who sell shoelaces, apples and sunflower seeds on the street. During the early transition years, the commerce that was not conducted on the street corner was based in temporary metal kiosks, which you still see in Kiev's residential neighbourhoods. Everything that's for sale will be hung in the window so you only have to point and pay. You can still buy magazines, drinks and snacks in kiosks, but most have been phased out in favour of normal walk-in shops with merchandise on the shelves.

To get a good idea of the Soviet-cum-capitalist shift, check out the old Soviet state department store ЦУМ (the acronym for Central Universal Shop); Khmelnytskovo 2; tel: 044 224 9505 [2 D2]. Not long ago the store offered everything the USSR produced, but of late, the elite five-storey building has gained the same local respect as Harrods of London. In fact, Khreschatyk is looking more and more like any high street with mobile phone dealers, swish clothes shops and Nike and Reebok outlet stores. The formerly dingy metro station passages have all been transformed into sparkling luxury and high-tech shops that sell perfume, teeny bathing suits, diamonds and laptops. Here are a few starters for your Western-equivalent shopping experience:

Globus Shopping Complex Maidan Nezalezhnosti 4; tel: 044 238 5938 [2 D1]
The largest of Kiev's 'malls' occupies the space beneath the Maidan Nezalezhnosti, offering two floors of wealth and glamour year-round. Just go to the main square and descend into the various stairwells. This space is anything but typical in Ukraine.

Mandarin Plaza Baseina 4; tel: 044 490 5700 [2 D2]
Kiev's latest and poshest multi-level shopping complex, just south of Bessarabska Rynok. The city's wealthier echelons enjoy shopping here.

Metrograd Undergound Shopping Complex Bessarabska Ploscha; tel: 044 247 5665 [2 D2]
Beneath the Bessarabska Rynok and connected by the underground passages on the corner
of Khreschatyk and Shevchenka, and a lot more sensibly priced. This is the best place to
look if you're having a travel emergency. Down here you can buy anything from a white
leather sofa to wool leggings and the *101 Dalmatians* in Ukrainian.

Traditionally, shopping in Ukraine has been an outdoor experience, where clothing
and food are sold on the street for bartered prices. Obviously, this is changing, but
if you're on a tightly chaperoned tour or business trip, you may (sadly) spend time
in Kiev without enjoying a real Ukrainian open-air market. If you do manage to
break away and want to see how a large percentage of Kiev shops, take the metro
to **Kontraktova Ploscha** and have a walk around. All things considered, this is a
pretty typical Kiev *rynok* (market) in action. Farther out, you should check out
Druzhby Narodiv and **Shulyavska,** both longstanding Kiev markets where the
people actually shop, digging through piles of goods shipped from Istanbul or Italy.
If in the end you find the natural sounds and smells of the open-air market too much
to handle, you can find a much less exciting refuge at Kiev's snootiest fashion shop,
the **Grand Gallery (**Khreschatyk 27; tel: 044 235 1318).

SOUVENIRS
With the new rise in tourism comes the advent of mass-produced 'Ukrainian'
goods, many of which are not Ukrainian at all. Everyone thinks first of the *matroshka*

doll, the wooden personage inside another inside another inside… These days, *matroshka* have turned into a comic venture, often painted with the faces of foreign politicians, but traditional dolls are painted with a family's faces and flowery designs (there should always be an odd number). Ukraine's traditional embroidered hand clothes – *narushniki* – should be made of long white linen or cotton with ornate stitching on the ends. Those in the know can tell the difference between machine-spun and authentic hand designs. Red, brown, orange, yellow, black and blue are traditional colours, although some regions vary. Ukrainian folk painting uses ornate bright flowers or fairy-tale themes on a black lacquered surface, usually on a bowl, platter, round jewellery box or wooden eggs. Woodcraft is also genuinely Ukrainian: combs, ornate spoons, pipes, plates and bowls; small clay pots are also very authentic. The black, charcoal-fired variety of Ukrainian pottery is sold more and more in Kiev, and marks the rebirth of an ancient art-form.

Buying fur should be discouraged all round; however if you really must have that Russian fur coat or *shapka* (fur hat) choose wisely as buying fox, beaver, lynx or sable will further deplete endangered species. Ukraine (and Russia's) red and silver fox population is slowly disappearing due to unregulated trapping for the cash foreigners will spend. Know what you are buying; you can always find *shapkas* made of farmed rabbit and mink, or even dog. Traditional Ukrainian jewellery includes amber necklaces, earrings and brooches of all sizes, from the clunky to the petite, as well as strings of red ceramic beads which Ukrainian women wear in abundance as part of the national costume. Nearly all souvenir shops will sell some form of amber.

Avoid getting roped into visiting Ukrainian 'souvenir art galleries', which usually include a vast collection of kitschy canvases: flowers in a vase, naked women or old-time Kievan street scenes that resemble Montmartre. Also, the days of buying *real* Soviet paraphernalia are also finished, although someone might make you a gift of some personal item. On occasion, some individual collectors will sell their wares on the street. The stuff in the markets emblazoned with red stars is made in China. Also to note, and perhaps a tip-off for any future investors, Kiev (and the whole country) lacks any good quality, photographic postcards. Tourist sites will sell some picture postcards, but they're old-fashioned and/or poorly printed.

If you're looking for regular old souvenirs, there tends to be quite a few street vendors on the Maidan Nezalezhnosti who sell music, books, flags and Ukrainian-themed knick-knacks. Most people find all their gifts at the city's most renowned souvenir market on Andriyvsky Uzviz. In summer, the street is packed, but the stuff that's sold out on the street itself is not always very real. Here are a few upmarket souvenir shops that sell authentic, quality gifts:

Gonchary Andreyevsky Spusk 10A; tel: 044 416 1298 [1 C3]
High-quality decorative crafts and ceramics.

Kristina 4 Kostyolna; tel: 044 228 7950 [2 D1]
A more regular Kiev souvenir shop.

Souvenirs

Perlyna Khreschatyk 21; tel: 044 228 1773 [2 D2]
Fine jewellery.

Silk Route Suvorova 4; tel: 044 295 0324 [3 F2]
Elaborate and artistic in Pechersk, selling beautiful things.

Suveniry Khreschatyk 32; tel: 044 235 4134 [2 C2]
Selling classic Ukrainian souvenirs and lots of books.

Ukrainian Folk Art Khreschatyk 27A; tel: 044 228 8332 [2 D2]
A great collection of authentic souvenirs.

ANTIQUES

Kiev most likely harbours the world's most incredible, undiscovered antique collection. Furthermore, most of what's out there is still unavailable, and lastly, the Ukrainian government is not too keen about letting any of it go, even if they don't know what 'it' is. In your dusty hunting, be conservative. Religious icons are traditional and some very beautiful modern examples can be purchased at most churches, however it is illegal to export any antique icons so don't try it. Ukraine enforces very strict laws about keeping national art treasures, historic coins and medals in their country. If you get caught exporting a bunch of Soviet (or earlier) medals in your hand luggage or suitcase, the penalty is financially severe. If you fancy something old and historic, ask if what you're buying is legal. Certified antique shops should provide you with any necessary documentation to accompany your purchase through customs.

Antique Salon Tereschenkivska 19; tel: 044 246 4332 [2 C2]
Antique Centre Andriyivsky Uzviz; tel: 044 416 1237 [1 C3]
Belle Epoque Andriyivsky Uzviz; tel: 044 228 3955 [1 C3]
Chef d'oeuvre Horodetskovo 12; tel: 044 229 6274 [2 D1]
Relikviya Baseina 21; tel: 044 235 9123 [2 D2]

FOOD

In Central Kiev, most food is sold in the *Gastronom* – the equivalent of a supermarket. Often the shop will appear as one large market, but you need to pay different attendants for different items. If you want some basics to take back to the hotel room, or want to stock up on inexpensive but quality vodka, try the **Tsentralny Gastronom** on the corner of Khreschatyk and Khmelnytskovo, or any of the shops like it that occur on practically every other street corner. You'll notice them for the signs ГАСТРОНОМ and the sausages, vodka bottles and bread seen from the window. Food shops are normally open from 09.00 until 21.00.

For a more traditional Ukrainian shopping experience, try the **Bessarabsky Rynok** at the corner of Khreschatyk and Prospekt Shevchenko. What was once Kiev's functioning, Soviet-style market has now turned into an overpriced, élite

Food

food shop, but it's still fun to walk around in. This is the way people have been shopping in Kiev from the beginning, only now the products have changed. All the vegetables and fruit are imported and picture-perfect, as are the flowers and jars of caviar. The name of the market comes from the Bessarabian (Moldavian) merchants who lived and worked in this section of town. Lots of noise and free samples are part of the act.

Everyday open-air street markets are more commonplace by the metro stations further outside the city. The traditional Ukrainian *rynok* (market) should be a part of the travel experience: taste-testing honey or cream on your knuckle, tumbling through melons and sniffing smoked chickens. Don't start bartering for something simply because it's an outdoor market. Fixed pricing is more and more regular in Ukraine and the tag will usually tell you how much it costs. Food is often the exception to that rule, and if you are indecisive, you may be offered a discount, or you can request a deal.

FINE ART

Kiev has always been an artists' town, and with the lifting of (most) censorship, a plethora of private galleries now sell a distinct brand of local talent that falls into every category of known art. If you're keen to buy, or simply appreciate refreshingly new art, go down to Andriyvsky Uzviz (see pages 229–34) and check out the real galleries. The following are recommended for their quality and diverse collections of contemporary Ukrainian artwork:

Gallery 36 Andiyivsky Uzviz 36; tel: 044 228 2985; web: www.Gallery36.org [1 C3]

L-Art Andriyivsky Uzviz 2Б; tel: 044 416 0320; web: www.lartgallery.com [1 C3]

Triptych Andriyivsky Uzviz 34; tel: 044 416 4453 [1 C3]

BOOKS

Books are on sale everywhere in Kiev – in churches, museums, souvenir shops, hotels, regular shops and the street. For a wide variety of books and magazines in Russian, Ukrainian or English, try **Orfey** (see below). Otherwise, the underground shopping complex beneath Bessarabsky Rynok also carries a large collection of almost everything you can think of, in Cyrillic.

Antique books and artistic prints, old maps and photographs are sold at the lower portion of Andriyvsky Uzviz. If you really want to get lost in books, head out to **Petrivka** metro station, where an expansive, open-air book market goes full blast all day, every day.

Baboon Khmelnytskovo 39B; tel: 044 234 1503 [2 C1]
Groovy bookstore and coffee-shop with daily poetry readings.

Bukva Lva Tolstovo 11/61; tel: 044 234 7508 [2 C2]
'The Letter'; open round the clock.

Mystetstvo Khreschatyk 24; tel: 044 228 3668 [2 D2]
Souvenirs and bookshop for all languages.

Books

PIRACY

Shopping thrills come cheaply in Kiev. Admittedly, it's fun to purchase a film on DVD that works in any zone and has not even been released on big screen in your home country. It's even better to update your music collection with ten CDs that cost less than one back home, and I confess that I know the spine-tingling joy of buying US$500 software packages for US$2. Alas, piracy is illegal, even in a country like Ukraine. In fact, Ukraine is fighting desperately for a new reputation minus the corruption and shadiness. Somewhat comically, buying 'licensed' music is now a mark of sophistication among Ukrainians, and Kievans joke about the poor quality of pirated movies. Remember that as long as Ukraine's pirate economy flourishes, legitimate investment will steer clear. Don't be guilty of contributing to one of Ukraine's more unseemly attributes.

Orfey Chervonykh Kozakiv 6; tel: 044 464 4945 [Kiev A1]
Kiev's biggest supplier of English-language books.

Planet Khreschatyk 30; tel: 044 224 0373 [2 C2]
Classic Kiev bookshop, some English-language media.

Syaivo Chervonoarmiyska 6; tel: 044 224 0001 [2 C2]
Another ex-pat favourite.

MUSIC AND MEDIA
CDs, cassette tapes, DVDs and videos are for sale at all metro stations, kiosks, street corners and everywhere else. For good Ukrainian folk music, go and find the big music table at the Maidan Nezalezhnosti, run by a young man named Yaroslav. He's got a huge collection and is good at introducing foreigners to Ukraine's most traditional music. Ask Ukrainians what they recommend. Metro station market places will have music kiosks as well, and the stunning Orthodox chants and singing are sold in almost every church.

Walking Tours

Kiev falls into that convenient category of 'walking city', but its more interesting streets are varied and diverse, and do not always flow into one another. The true rambler will feel total bliss by simply wandering through central Kiev – the back streets and 'unsightly', unrenovated, older sections of the city reveal crumbling architecture and the everyday life of hanging clothes, children playing and grandmothers shopping. Newer parts of the city feature large, Soviet-age concrete high-rises, and more importantly, Soviet-size city blocks. Even the most dedicated urban trekker can get worn out moving on to the next cool little bit of Kiev. If you get tired, stranded, or lost, it's always very easy to flag down a taxi and for US$2 be brought back to the recognisable centre. If you enjoy getting lost in the city, decide first where you want to be lost. Pechersk and Podil are recommended neighbourhoods, since they are compact, notably historic, and serviced by several subway stations.

No doubt about it, the best way to see Kiev's 'sites' is on foot. The following walks can offer some guidance, but bear in mind that travellers will often find greater memories and meaning in the things they were not planning on seeing, rather than the planned agenda.

A WALK THROUGH THE SITES OF KIEV

If you take the time to visit each site on this itinerary, the walk should take you the whole day and you will return to your hotel exhausted and enlightened. If you only have one day, then:

- Start your walk at Universitet metro station, exit and cross the street to **St Vladimir's Cathedral**. (You can't miss the yellow and gold structure.)
- After visiting St Vladimir's, walk down Leontovycha (the side street below the church) to Khmelnystkovo, turn right and walk one block to the Opera House.
- Cross the street and you are in front of **Ukraine's National Opera House**. Buy tickets for an evening performance to experience what's inside.
- Walk up Volodymyrska (north) to the green park where you see the remaining **'Golden Gate' (Zoloti Vorota)** of Kiev's pre-Mongol fortress and a monument to Yaroslav the Wise.
- Continue further down Volodymyrska (two blocks) to the entrance of **St Sophia's Cathedral**, beneath the baroque bell tower. Take some time to wander through the parks and to visit the grave of Prince Yaroslav the Wise, inside the left apse of the cathedral.
- Upon leaving St Sophia's (through the bell tower), go to the middle of Sofiyska Square, where you'll find the **Monument to Bohdan Khmelnytsky,** Cossack liberator of Ukraine from the Poles in the 17th century. Cross the park/thoroughfare to the gold domes rising up from the opposite St Mikhayil's Square. On the way you will pass the monument to Princess Olga, Saints Cyril

and Methodius, and the Apostle Andrew, and near the entrance to St Mikhayil's you see the monument to the victims of the Ukrainian famine. Proceed through the painted gates and enter **St Mikhayil's Monastery of the Golden Domes.** (Historic detour: facing the gates of St Mikhayil's Monastery of the Golden Domes, turn right and walk one block to a small path that runs alongside the outer walls of the monastery. Follow the path – about 300m – to the **statue of St Vladimir** and a great view of the Dnepr.)

- Exit through the same gates and walk towards the stately and rotund white building across St Mikhayil's Square – Ukraine's Ministry of Foreign Affairs. Walk past it and continue one block down Desiatynna, to the floorplan-like ruins of **Desiatynna Church,** Ukraine's **History Museum** and Kiev's ancient linden tree.

- Continue down Desiatynna past the paintings lying in the street to where the path opens up in descent and you see the turquoise and teal-blue **St Andrei's Church.** Follow through your descent down **Andriyivsky Uzviz** (which can take a whole day by itself if you really want to soak everything in). Browse the art galleries, stock up on souvenirs, but be sure to take in the **Bulgakov Museum** and most definitely the **Museum of One Street** at the base of the hill. At the very bottom of Andriyivsky Uzviz, turn left and walk two blocks into the heart of **Podil** at Kontraktova Ploscha. Enjoy dinner in Podil and take the metro back from metro station Kontraktova Ploscha on Spaska, or catch a taxi on the square.

A WALK DOWN KHRESCHATYK

A wonderful way to know Kiev's main street and to get oriented in the city. A disinterested, fast-paced walker could do this all in less than two hours. Others may want to allow a leisurely half-day.

- Start by browsing the stalls at **Bessarabsky Rynok**, the large tan, brick-covered market on the corner of Shevchenka and Khreschatyk.
- Exit onto Khreschatyk (the biggest and busiest street), and walk up (right from Bessarabsky Rynok).
- Pass the many shops to where Khmelnytskovo ends at Khreschatyk. On your right stands one of Kiev's original skyscrapers, resembling the towering, Soviet-style, tiered structures seen throughout Moscow (Khreschatyk 25). Across the street is ЦУМ, the leading, Soviet-age department store in the city.
- Continue up the street and you will pass (on your left side) a giant stone building with Ukrainian flags and normally, a small band of protestors (Kreschatyk 36). This is Kiev's **City Hall**.
- Continue another block and you will pass Kiev's **Central Post Office** (featuring its perfectly Stalinist façade) and enter Kiev's main square, the **Maidan Nezalezhnosti** (Square of Independence). To the right is the towering hotel Ukrayina, and below a central pillar topped with a golden statue of a woman with laurel, Ukraine's **Monument of Independence**. Below, to the right, is the **Monument to the Founders of Kiev**.
- Follow any of the steps underground and cross to the other side, on to the

actual Maidan. Have a good look around the square, and then continue up on the opposite side of the street. Khreschatyk ends in a semi-roundabout, now called 'European Square'. To the left is the cake-like **Ukrainian House**, once the pride of the Ukrainian Communist Party, and now a popular conference and rock concert venue. Cross (underground, as the traffic is busy here) to the **National Philharmonic**.

- Walk down the path to the titanium arch with the two brothers holding hands in union, a monument symbolising the **Friendship of Peoples** between Russia and Ukraine. Either end your walk here, or continue down the park path along the Dnepr.

A WALK ALONG THE DNEPR

A walk that takes you through Kiev's history and holy sites, and lets you experience one of Kiev's great green spaces. If you're visiting in spring this is the place to come. The walk is a little less than 6km in length, but taking in all there is to see, including the Caves Monastery, it can take the whole day to complete. If you want to spend more time looking and less time walking, start the walk at the entrance to the Caves Monastery.

- Start at the titanium archway of the **Friendship of Peoples Monument**.
- Follow the pedestrian path past the **Dinamo Stadium**, home to Kiev's famous football team.
- Continue on the path and through the **City Gardens** with its fountains and

many monuments to famous Ukrainians. Walk around to the front of the blue and white **Marinsky Palace.** The domed building on the left is Ukraine's **Verkhovna Rada** (parliament).

- Continue south through Marinskhy Park and then down the road (about 800m). On your left is **Askold's Grave.** On your right is the **Monument to St Andrew**, the 'First-Called'.
- Veer left and head south, making almost a complete turn on to Ploscha Slavy (Square of Glory). Head south on the path past the obelisk **Monument to the Unknown Soldier** commemorating those who died liberating Kiev from the Nazi invasion. The path will lead to Sichnevovo Povstannya and the walls of the Kievo-Pecherska Lavra.
- Walk to the main gates of the **Kievo-Pecherska Lavra (Caves Monastery).** Tour the upper Lavra and exit at the very bottom. Enter the lower Lavra and tour the caves. After visiting the **Far Caves,** exit the Lavra and continue south, under the walkways and past the bas-relief statues depicting Kiev's experience in World War II, the **Eternal Flame Monument** and on towards the giant titanium statue with the sword, the **Motherland Monument** *(Rodyna Mat).*
- Beneath the statue is Kiev's **Great Patriotic War Museum**, dedicated to Kiev's experience of fighting the German Army in World War II. After visiting the museum, follow the path towards the steep winding staircase that descends the hill towards the cloverleaf highway overpass.
- At the bottom of the hill, cross under Druzhby Narodiv, turn left and continue

LESSER STROLLS

Here are three short walks on specified streets that give a good feel for the city and the diversity of Kiev's neighbourhoods. Each walk gives a general direction, and each presents the inviting detours of a dozen side-streets.

Podil offers historic, residential Kiev as an everyday event, with straight, level streets full of colour and action.

- Start at **Kontraktova Ploscha** (reachable by the metro station of the same name). Cross the square to **Kyiv Mohyla Academy.**
- Walk up (north) Mezhygirska, past the markets, crossing Nyzhny Val and continuing up to Schekavytska. Turn right and walk to the cheery **Podil Synagogue.**

Lypky is just below Khreschatyk, built on a hillside once covered with flowering linden (*lipa*) trees. Now much of the area manifests large government buildings, but during the Russian Empire, and more and more in the present, Kiev's rich and powerful live among these more imaginative palaces.

- Start at **Bessarabsky Rynok**, walk due east and on Kruty Uzviz (uphill and then up the stairs). Go straight until the street ends at Lyuteranska.

- Turn left on to Lyuternska and continue until it meets Bankova. The mansion at Lyuteranska 23 is known as the **House of the Weeping Widow**, because of the stone female visage that 'weeps' at the top of the house.
- Turn right on to Bankova. On your left (Bankova 11) is the giant and austere-looking **Presidential Administration Building**.
- On your left, at Bankova 10 and in stark contrast, is the **Horodetsky House**, built by the Kiev architect Vladyslav Horodetksy in 1903 and covered with fanciful statuary.
- Walk down the steps next to the house across from the President's offices. On your right is the **Ukrainian Drama Theatre**.
- Continue past the square and fountain, descending towards Khreschatyk on Arkhitektora Horodetskovo, named after the architect.

Pushkinska is one of Kiev's more intriguing, but often overlooked side-streets.
- Start at **Ploscha Lva Tolstova** (at the metro station by the same name).
- Walk up Pushkinska for three blocks, cross under the archway.
- Continue on Hrinchenka to the **Maidan Nezalezhnosti**.

southeast. Eventually, a side road will lead off from Naberzhne Shosse, heading slightly uphill into the forest. Continue up the hill and follow the signs to reach **Vydubytsky Monastery** (a little over 2km from the Caves Monastery).

- After going through the churches of Vydubytsky, walk directly west (uphill) through **Kiev's Botanical Gardens.** If you're not tired and want to save some cash, walk all the way up Bastionna to Druzhby Narodiv metro station (a good trek). Otherwise, hail a cab and rest your feet.

Obviously, you can do this whole walk in reverse, starting at the more isolated Vydubytsky and heading north along the Dnepr's shore and ending close to civilisation at Khreschatyk, however, the path in that direction is more or less uphill.

Museums and Sightseeing

SEEING THE CITY

Foreign tourism is still new to Kiev, meaning there is no well-worn circuit for visitors to follow. In some ways, Kiev favours the independent traveller who either picks what s/he wants and goes after it, or simply wanders, questioning what s/he is seeing. If you want someone else to do the work, try a local tourist agency, or go to the railway station (metro station Vokzal) and join one of the bus tours. This chapter is by no means comprehensive of Kiev's sightseeing landscape, but should provide some reference.

The centre

The first place you'll be shown, or the first place you'll find on your own, is Kiev's most central north-south boulevard **Khreschatyk**. The road was one of Kiev's very first and once followed a clear stream flowing into the Dnepr. During World War II, the retreating Soviet Army sabotaged most of the street so that it would blow up after the Nazis had entered the city. The violent welcome was answered by the systematic shooting of tens of thousands of Kiev's citizens. Everything you see today has been rebuilt – people may criticise the pomp of post-war Stalinist architecture, but these monumental structures define Kiev today. The central focal point of the boulevard is the **Maidan Nezalezhnosti** (Independence Square) that seems to be moving in the direction of Times Square in New York or Piccadilly Circus in London with its large-scale electronic advertising and billboards. This used to be the Place of the October Revolution but now features Kiev's largest shopping centre (underground), a chic McDonalds, the central post office, and lots of friendly Ukrainian nationalists selling flags, books, and music. On the opposite side of the street is Kiev's newest **Monument of Independence**, a white and gold pillar erected in 2001 to celebrate the first ten years of freedom from the Soviet Union. Down below, on the left side of the square is another recent bronze sculpture showing the **Founders of Kiev**: Kyi the elder brother, after whom the city is named, Lybid, his sister who was reported to have chosen the spot, and their two younger brothers, Shchek and Khoriv.

Where Khreschatyk begins its descent to the river stands a giant titanium arch over the brawny statues of two 'brothers' – Ukraine and Russia – raising fists in a joined union. Of course, the monument to the **'Friendship of Nations'** is controversial today, but the space has remained, probably for its wonderful view of the river and the city. The park continues south all the way to the Caves Monastery, *Rodyna Mat*, and botanical gardens.

Volodymyrska runs parallel to Khreschatyk and is a special 'backstreet' for Kievans. Central to the boulevard is the **Golden Gate** (Zoloti Vorota), a replica of the last remaining portion of Kiev's original ramparts prior to the Mongol invasion. Kneeling in front of the Gate is a **Monument to Yaroslav the Wise**, who defended Kiev from the Pecheneg invasion of the 11th century and founded St Sophia's Cathedral in thanks (his statue holds a model of the church in his hands).

Further down the street (on the corner of Khmelnytksovo and Volodymyrska) stands the **Ukrainian National Opera** (50 Volodymyrska) – an incredible building from Kiev's fleeting *belle époque*, completed in 1901; Taras Shevchenko's name and bust have been added to this national monument as well. The building's luxurious hall reflects the typical Viennese style for an opera house, and is one of the most well-preserved historic interiors in the city, thanks to its everyday use during the Soviet era. The opera house is also renowned for the 1911 assassination of Pyotr Stolypin, prime minister to Tsar Nikolai II during the first attempt at reforming the St Petersburg government. He was shot point blank during the second intermission of Rimsky-Korsakov's *The Tale of Tsar Saltan*. Nobody has died here since, and it is quite easy to get tickets for any of the shows – the ballet and opera boast an amazing repertoire. Few things in Kiev compare to an evening spent in this building, and for now, tickets to a show are the only way to get inside.

Upper city

At the opposite end of Volodymyrska is Sofiyska Square with the landmark tower of **St Sophia's Cathedral** and the mighty statue of **Bohdan Khmelnytsky,** the Cossack *hetman* who liberated Kiev from the Poles and subsequently handed the country over to the Russians. From here it is an easy walk across the park to Mikhayilovsky Square, and **St Mikhayil's Monastery.** Behind the monastery is Kiev's most fun form of public transportation – the **funicular**, which takes passengers down from the 'upper city' into the lower Podil. Rising behind the

Seeing the city

monastery is Vladimir's Hill, where the famous **Statue of Prince Vladimir** holding a cross still stands above the river as he did in legend when all of Kiev was baptised.

At the end of Volodymyrska and Desyatina are the ruins of Kiev's oldest stone building, the **Desiatynna Church** – first constructed as the Mother of God Church under the rule of Prince Vladimir. 'Desiatynna' means 'tithing' in Russian, and following Kiev's conversion to Christianity, the prince ordered that one-tenth of the city's tribute be granted to the church. Walking among the floorplan-like ruins of the church today, you can witness that for the time, this was a sizeable church. The original church was crushed by the Mongols. (The ancient tree providing the shade for the ruins is a linden that was most likely planted around the 13th century.) Further down from the church, Desiatynna meets the very vibrant and arty street **Andriyivsky Uzviz.**

Official Kiev

The seat of the Ukrainian government is based along the blocks of Hrushevskovo that runs south from Khreschatyk. The street is named after Mikhail Hrushevsky, a renowned Ukrainian academic, who was elected as the first president of independent Ukraine (sadly, his presidency lasted only three months in 1918). At the intersection (now called European Square), you will see the round white **Ukrainian House**, once home to the Ukrainian Communist Party. On the other side, moving up Hrushevskovo is the playing field and **stadium** of Kiev's famous 'Dinamo' football team with a huge following in the West and throughout the former Soviet Union.

Of all Ukraine's government buildings, the rococo **Marinsky Palace** is one of the prettiest, built in 1752 as a royal residence fit for the Russian aristocracy, after they had complained there was nowhere decent to stay in Kiev. Today the blue and white building is used only for the president's private state functions, but in principle tourists may walk the grounds (although at times you will be hurried along by the guards that stand on every corner). Next door to the palace is the **Verkhovna Rada,** the national parliament of Ukraine. All of Ukraine's representatives meet beneath the big rounded glass dome and it is in this building that Ukrainian independence was declared on August 24 1991. Life within the Rada today is as exciting as ever, as Ukraine's *deputaty* (parliamentarians) wage war with one another.

Further down Hrushevskovo, in the park by the river, stand a few key monuments in Kiev's history. The princely duet Askold and Dir were the first of the Varangians (Vikings) to raid Kiev, boasting of their spoils to the northern principality of Novgorod. Jealous, their older brother Helgi plotted, attacked and killed the pair. Askold was buried on this hillside in Kiev, and the small round church was added in 1810. Sadly, Askold's actual grave (and many others in this same place) did not withstand Stalin's wave of destruction, which wiped the area clean in the mid-1930s.

Andriyivsky Uzviz
According to the Bible, Andrew was the first apostle to be called to follow Christ, and according to legend the saint sailed up the Dnepr and landed in this particular spot – prophesying that on these hills a great city would rise up (legend also claims

ANDRIYIVSKY UZVIZ

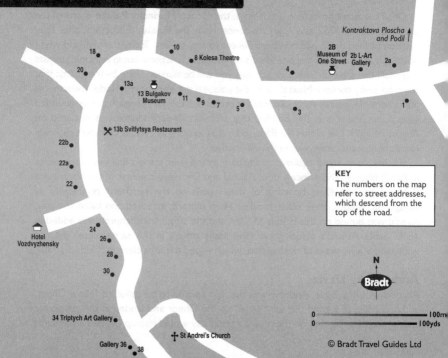

Kontraktova Ploscha and Podil

18
20
13a
13 Bulgakov Museum
10
8 Kolesa Theatre
11 9 7 5
2B Museum of One Street
2b L-Art Gallery
2a
4
3
1

13b Svitlytsya Restaurant

22b
22a
22

24
26
28
30

Hotel Vozdvyzhensky

34 Triptych Art Gallery
Gallery 36   38
St Andrei's Church

KEY
The numbers on the map refer to street addresses, which descend from the top of the road.

N

Bradt

0 ————————— 100m
0 ————————— 100yds

© Bradt Travel Guides Ltd

he landed in Crimea). The saint supposedly climbed this particular hill in Kiev and fixed a cross in the ground – a curved and narrow lane now twists from this spot and follows St Andrew's path down to the Dnepr. After Kiev adopted Christianity, the great pagan idol Perun was tied to a stag and dragged down 'Andrew's descent', beaten with sticks, and shoved into the river.

Today the sea-green and dark-teal-blue **St Andrei's Church** crowns the top of Kiev's favourite street with spindly turrets and a fanciful baroque dome. The unique design is the work of Italian architect Rastrelli who had already built St Petersburg's most famous buildings, the Winter Palace and Tsarskoe Selo. The church in Kiev was his last masterpiece, completed in 1762, after which he was fired by Catherine the Great. The church was turned into a museum of architecture to avoid the wrath of Stalin and remains a museum today. The interior has only just been renovated and is still rather empty, except for the two very interesting paintings of St Andrew and Prince Vladimir; open 10.00–18.00, closed Wednesday; entrance 5UAH.

By the time you get to St Andrei's, someone will have tried to sell you something to remember Kiev by. In the 19th century, Andriyivsky Uzviz was the proud domain of artists and writers and since then, the street has harboured Kiev's more bohemian elements. Today, souvenir markets and so-called art shows run along the entire length of the street and this is where most tourists are directed to buy gifts. Most of the stuff for sale is mass-produced, but it is what most people want: *matroshka* dolls, fake Soviet paraphernalia, machine-stitched Ukrainian embroidery or T-shirts with Lenin making obscene gestures. Further down the street the bits and bobs become more varied with wood carving, home-knit wool, old prints, books and coins. The festive antique and souvenir bazaar is kept alive with the help of musicians, street poets and mime artists. Much of the art consists of rows upon rows of kitschy painting, but there are still a few authentic galleries on the descent. Have a look in **Gallery 36** (Andriyivsky Uzviz 36; tel: 044 228 2985; email: infor@Gallery36.org.ua; web: www.Gallery36.org.ua), a private gallery that features quality work by contemporary Ukrainian artists. Next door, the gallery **Triptych** (Andriyivsky Uzviz 34; tel: 044 229 8385; web: www.triptych-gallery.org) also deserves a serious browse. For more traditional Ukrainian themes and Socialist Realist painting, try the very professional **L-Art** (Andriyivsky Uzviz 2Б; tel: 044 416 0320; web: www.lartgallery.com) at the bottom of the hill.

From the top of the street, you will spot the modest white **Statue of Apostle Andrew**. This marks the beginning of the old residential area, and most of these homes are architectural monuments, including the wooden house at #34, known as 'Noah's Ark' for its wooden exterior and a history of cramming lots of poor starving artists onto its floors. Every building has a story – the seven-storey yellow edifice with one single tower is known as 'Richard's Castle', named after King Richard I in Ivanhoe (#15) by the children who once played on the street. These were once the favoured flats of Kiev's more prestigious artists.

The famous Russian writer Mikhail Bulgakov was born in Kiev, and moved to house #13 with his theologian father at age 15. Here he attended high school and medical school and then worked as a doctor during the revolution. The **Bulgakov**

Museum (Andriyivksy Uzviz 13; tel: 044 416 3188; open 10.00–17.00, closed Wednesday; entrance 5UAH, 12UAH for a guided tour in English) now occupies his home. The ghostly surrealist exhibit incorporates ideas from all of his well-known works, but mainly from his autobiographical first novel *The White Guard*, which recounts his experiences in Kiev during the Russian Civil War. Any object that is not painted white is an original object from the Bulgakov family. Enthusiasts of *The Master and Margarita* may find fewer allusions to this book than might be hoped for, but a general knowledge will help for understanding some of the stranger features in the house. Bulgakov spent most of his writing career in Moscow but published very little in his lifetime due to harsh censorship.

It's not too hard to find food on the Uzviz, but if you want to sit down for a bit, the place next door to Bulgakov's house is worth trying out (Andriyivsky Uzviz 11; tel: 044 416 5123). The restaurant has no name so as to reinforce its mysterious nature, but the building is recognised by the black metal cat outside, with the tail of a snake – a character remembered from Bulgakov's *The Master and Margarita*. The chef is Armenian so of course the food is wonderful, and live piano and violin music adds to the semi-spooky atmosphere. A full meal costs around US$12–18.

Across the street is the **Kolesa Theatre** (Andriyivsky Uzviz 8; tel: 044 416 0422), a small avant-garde playhouse that already has an established following in Kiev. The upstairs theatre produces more well-known pieces (eg: Henry James, Ionesco, Flaubert) while the lower floor is a working café with interactive theatre every night of the week. Somehow or other, patrons will get roped into the performance art.

Last but in no way least is the delightful **Museum of One Street** (Andriyivsky Uzviz 2B; tel: 044 416 0398; open 12.00–18.00, closed Monday; entrance 3UAH) at the very bottom of the descent. Breaking away from the stifling mould of Soviet museums, the ingenious display recounts the story of this one street through a meticulous collection of objects gathered over the ages from each address. Simple treasures like old clothes, spectacles, dishes and books are arranged in artful installations to represent all that has happened in these homes during the past century. Visitors need not speak Russian to enjoy the visual history of the lives of this neighbourhood: the circus performer, the Orthodox priest, the Jewish rabbi, the composer, the writer and soldier. (Breaching inscrutability I will reveal that this is my favourite museum.)

Podil

Andriyivsky Uzviz and Kiev's funicular join the original 'upper city' with Podil, the Dnepr flood plain turned residential neighbourhood. To get there, take the funicular: the ride is fun, the view is good, and it only costs 50 kopecks. Pick it up behind St Mikhayil's Monastery of the Golden Domes or near the boat terminal. Otherwise, take the metro to Kontraktova Ploscha or Poshtova Ploscha, walk down the Uzviz, or take a taxi.

Long ago, Podil was the nitty-gritty part of Kiev where foreign merchants and craftsmen lived and laboured far away from the more refined churches and palaces on the hill (hence the river port, Contract House and large market spaces). The cosmopolitan flair of yesteryear is still in place and a visit to Podil allows an honest impression of what the rest of Kiev used to look like before all the turmoil of the 20th century. What was once Kiev's fringe quarter now features some of its best architecture and most candid street scenes. Walking around Podil with the intent to sightsee is a worthy cause. In addition to the historic buildings (including the **Podil Synagogue,** merchants' homes and several smaller churches), there is the riverfront close by and a flurry of human activity.

Kontraktova Ploscha (contract square) is the central space in Podil. As in centuries past, this area is still an open market of sorts. On the south side stands the white colonnades of **Hostiny Dvor**, or Hospice's Court. The long shopping arcades are very similar to those you see on Nevsky Prospekt in St Petersburg, and were built at the very beginning of the 19th century. Further up Mezhigirska is the **Contract House,** once the offices of the market place where annual 'contract fairs' were held which took the form of large-scale swap meets between merchants from throughout the Russian Empire.

Podil is also home to **Kiev Mohyla Academy** (Kontraktova Ploscha 4; web: www.ukma.kiev.ua), probably the most prestigious place of learning in Ukraine. Founded in 1615, it was Kiev's first university, but was only reopened in the 1990s as a private liberal arts academy. Student life is vibrant around the main building and throughout Podil. However, as with all city quarters made famous by a university, few students can actually afford to live here any more. Arty and

Seeing the city

historic, Podil is becoming a gentrified neighbourhood for Kiev's newest professionals.

CHURCHES AND HOLY SITES

Detailing Kiev's hundreds of churches would require a multi-volume set of guidebooks, and then a few years later there might very well be a hundred more to write about. Wandering through Kiev, you will see tiny steeples and giant domes. Ask locals 'which church is that' and you will only sometimes get an answer. Through the ages, Kiev has been known for its hundreds of churches, and today that same legacy continues. Even if you think churches are not your thing, it would be a pity to miss what Kiev does best. For now, these are the sites that fascinate the majority:

Kievo-Pecherska Lavra

The 'Caves Monastery' is Kiev's number one tourist attraction both for Ukrainians and foreigners, and should be a priority for any newcomer to Kiev. The enormous ensemble of white church halls with green and gold rooftops has come to represent the spiritual heart of the country and symbolise Kiev's survival throughout a millennium of adversity. Officially, the monastery is defined as a government Historical-Culture Preserve, but this area – and the caves in particular – are a national religious shrine and the headquarters for the Ukrainian Orthodox Church (Moscow Patriarchate). Over 100,000 pilgrims come every year from all over the

KIEVO-PECHERSKA LAVRA

Church of Berestov Saviour

SICHNEVOHO POVSTANNYA

Church of All Saints

UPPER LAVRA

St Nicolas Church

Church of the Assumption (Uspensky Cathedral)

Museum of Historical Treasures

Museum of Books & Printing

Museum of Theatre, Music & Cinematography

Great Belltower

Main entrance

Troitskaya Church

Refectory & Chapel of Sts Anthony & Theodosius

Rear entrance

Residence of the Metropolitan (Museum of Ukranian Decorative Folk Art)

Museum of Micro-Miniatures

Khrestovozdyvzhenska Church (entrance to near caves)

TSYTADELNA

Free entrance

LOWER LAVRA

Anna Zachatiyevskaya Church (entrance to far caves)

N

Bradt

Far Caves Belfry

Church of the Birth of the Blessed Virgin

Dnepr

NABEREZHNE SHOSE

SICHNEVOHO POVSTANNYA

0   300m
0   300yds

© Bradt Travel Guides Ltd

Orthodox world to pray and worship and tourists should only visit in the spirit of reverence and modesty. That said, the Lavra is beginning to show signs of tourist-trap development that already detract from the mood, including abundant souvenir shops and multifarious money-making devices.

The history of the Lavra dates back to Prince Vladimir's introduction of Christianity as the new state religion of Rus. Following this event St Anthony of Lyubech left Mount Athos in Greece and settled in Kiev in 1051. He lived on the banks of the Dnepr in a man-made cave where he became known for his strict asceticism and spiritual powers. With the help of his devoted follower St Theodosius, Anthony was able to expand the caves by a series of tunnels and cells to accommodate more disciples – leading to the formation of an extensive underground network where monks spent entire lifetimes meditating, praying and writing. ('Lavra' means 'street' in Greek, which is an apt name for the city of tunnels through these hills.) Ukraine's (and Russia's) earliest historians, scholars and icon-painters were all attached to Kiev's Lavra, including the author of the *Chronicle of Bygone Years,* Nestor. This heritage, and the advent of a printing press in 1615, made Kiev the intellectual centre of Christian thought for all Slavic lands all the way into the age of the Tsars and the Russian Revolution. Today, the Lavra has a monopoly on producing Orthodox religious items: icons, crosses, vestments and the golden domes you see throughout Ukraine.

The stunning buildings on the surface were begun as early as the 11th century, and while a few exhibit the simple rounded domes of Byzantium, the majority of the

MONKS ON LINE

Before visiting the Lavra, it's a good idea to check out their official website: www.lavra.kiev.ua. Not only is the site informative, but its layout and choice of information will grant you a much clearer understanding that the Lavra is not merely Kiev's most touristy of sites, but rather a sacred centre for the Orthodox world and a leading destination for serious Orthodox pilgrims for almost a millennium. Amazingly, traditions have changed little. Besides a lengthy history of the monastery and its importance to Slavic and Christian civilisation, the website gives very clear instructions on what items a pilgrim must bring on his or her voyage:

- Icon of the Mother of God (the Virgin Mary)
- Icon of St Nicholas the Miracle Worker (patron saint of travellers)
- Prayer books
- A bottle to collect holy water from healing wells

To be received as a pilgrim at the monastery (meaning a free, but cold room and all the soup and bread you care to eat) you should also wear a cross around your neck and come with a written introduction from your home parish.

Churches and holy sites

architecture reflects mid-18th-century baroque styles employed to rebuild the monastery after a devastating fire in 1718. (The Mongol invasions of 1240 and 1480 and an earthquake in 1620 had already destroyed the older portions of the monastery in stages.) The area was made a cultural preserve in 1926 after the Soviet takeover, but long periods of neglect and the destruction of the war left a series of odd museums surrounded by rubble. Gorbachev returned the monastery and Far Caves to the Church in 1988, followed by the Near Caves a year later, while the Ukrainian government gained control of the upper churches after independence. Most of the glistening structures you see today were only recently restored.

A visit to the monastery and caves can be as short or as long as you want, however the ticketing system is as Byzantine as the architecture. General admittance to the Upper Lavra is 12UAH, but every church, exhibition and museum sells separate tickets – it does not take long to collect a pocketful of ripped paper. On occasion, foreigners are charged about ten times more and the right to take photographs costs an additional 12 UAH. If you find this troublesome, you can sometimes avoid the maze through a personal guided tour, which will cost around US$30. Freelance tour guides will approach you with lower prices upon entering, or you can make prior arrangements; tel: 044 290 3071. To get to the Pechersky Lavra, take the metro to Arsenalna, then cross the road and take trolley #38 or bus #20 to the fortification walls at Sichnenoho Povstannya (Ivana Mazepa) 21. *Marshrutka* #163 also travels between the Lavra and Khreschatyk. If you're not so keen to brave public transport, catch a cab from your hotel for around US$3–4. Drivers will know where to drop you. Any of Kiev's tour agencies will also be glad to arrange transportation and guided tours for you at the Lavra.

The Upper Lavra

If you are in a taxi or with a tour group, you will most likely get dropped off outside the light blue **Troitskaya Church**. Now used as a gatehouse, the original church was built in 1108 but now features classic examples of Ukrainian baroque. Before rushing inside, be sure to enjoy a long look at the murals of the outer walls, painted in 1900. These depictions also reflect the realist style of 'the wanderers'. The main path leads to the **Great Bell Tower,** the tallest Orthodox structure in the world at 96.5m in height, from which the four-ton bell is suspended. For 3UAH you are allowed to climb to the third-highest level and take in a fantastic view of all the domes, the park beyond, the Dnepr river and Kiev's left bank. The steps are precarious, as are the guardrails, so acrophobes beware. Directly across from the bell tower is the **Church of the Assumption (Dormition Cathedral** or **Uspensky Cathedral),** which is technically the oldest church (above ground) in the Lavra, completed in 1077 and symbolising the move of Kiev's monastic life from below ground and into the open, after Orthodoxy became the favoured religion of Kiev's princes. The original structure was blown up by retreating Soviet forces in 1941 and was only rebuilt in the year 2000 with its seven gold turrets and marvellously detailed design. Earlier visitors to Kiev will remember the original ruins and piles of stones still beautiful with the frescos of 900 years ago. To the north of the Church of the Assumption is the **Church of All Saints** built at the end of the 17th century by the Cossack *hetman* Ivan Mazepa, best known for its vivid interior of gold and painted portraits. Mazepa was an important patron for several of Kiev's churches and academic buildings, and you can spot his crossed arrow insignia on some of the buildings. To the south of the Dormiton Cathedral is the **Refectory**, built at the end of the 19th century when the community of monks was large enough to require such a large dining hall. The accompanying Byzantine dome is almost more impressive than the interior **Chapel of Saints Anthony and Theodosius**, although some of the original 19th-century frescos still remain. As the Lavra grew in importance and popularity, so did the number of monks who lived here, and the size of the very decorative refectory hall shows that mealtime was an extensive affair.

The rest of the Upper Lavra is comprised of several remarkable buildings housing slightly unremarkable national museums. Each is open from 09.00 to 17.00, most are closed on Tuesday, and cost less than 5UAH. The **Museum of Historical Treasures** is in the far rear of the Lavra and shows all the jewellery and metalwork from the Scythians to the present. Directly behind the Dormition Cathedral is the early-17th-century print shop that now houses the **Museum of Books and Printing** which exhibits some unique illuminated manuscripts dating back to Kievan Rus. The **Museum of Theatre, Music and Cinematography** is located at the back of **St Nicholas Church** with the star-studded blue dome. The exhibit is mostly nostalgic paraphernalia from Kiev showbiz days. Directly south of the bell tower is the **Residence of the Metropolitan** where the head of the Ukrainian church once lived. Today it is the **Museum of Ukrainian Decorative Folk Art** that is slowly accumulating its collection of national costume and crafts. Directly across is the **Museum of Micro-miniatures,** a remnant of the Lavra's Soviet period. There is little historical value in this off-the-wall display except maybe to better understand the Soviet cultural mentality of the 1970s. Through a row of microscopes visitors can view things like a chessboard on a pinhead, the word 'Peace' written on a human hair, the portraits of famous Soviet heroes etched into poppy seeds, or golden horseshoes on a dead flea. Several other halls are open and advertised as art galleries, however the exhibits consist largely of conveyor-belt paintings churned out and sold to tourists.

Visiting the caves

Sadly, most tourists wander for hours in the Upper Lavra looking for the caves and seeing everything but. What your guide won't tell you is that you can visit the caves on your own for free, since the entrance to the tunnels and the present-day monastery (the Lower Lavra) are holy sites that exist outside the realm of entrance fees. To get to the caves from the Upper Lavra, walk under the white flying buttresses of the old print shop and descend to the right and through the gate. This brings you to the Lower Lavra. To get to the caves from the street, walk down the long descent outside the fortification wall – this is where most of the Russian-speaking crowds will be headed.

THE BODIES OF THE SAINTS

After the monastery moved above ground, many of these caves became virtual necropolises – underground cities with marked 'streets' where the dead were laid. While some of these saints died nearly one thousand years ago, their bodies have been preserved without any form of embalming. The church claims this to be the miracle of saints, and pilgrims still come to touch the shrouded bodies and partake of this life power.

Soviet scientists were employed to disprove the miracle and deride any supernatural belief in the caves. Their studies concluded that the caves' total lack of moisture prevented organic decay. Now in the post-Soviet era, these same studies are being used to support the mystical power of the saints' relics. Supposedly, the Soviet scientists had also found that radiation from the bodies was emitted in elliptical patterns somehow linked to the magnetic poles of the earth. An experiment with wheat plants then proved the saints emitted a 'bio-physic' power that directly influenced the nuclear level of living matter. This

Both Far and Near caves are open to the public from 09.00 to 16.00. There is no admission fee, but it is customary to purchase a beeswax candle at the entrance to use as your light in the tunnels. Visitors are asked to whisper only, and women are asked to cover their heads and not to wear heavy make-up. Few research was especially useful following the Chernobyl disaster, when it was 'scientifically proven' that this holy radiation protected against atomic radiation, especially when prayers were offered to the saints.

Many other miracles are addressed to the bodies of the saints, but the biggest miracle is that the bodies are still there. Seventy years of atheist Soviet rule did much to destroy the Ukrainian church, but somehow the caves survived with their saints. There is evidence that many of the bodies were moved or hidden to confuse the authorities, however the accepted story is that the Soviet government tried to empty the caves and failed. After piling all the saints into the back of a truck, the driver found he could not start his engine. The officials tried everything, but they could not move the vehicle. The patriarch was summoned and told of the dilemma, to which he responded that try as they might, the saints' bodies would never leave the monastery. After three weeks of sitting outside, the bodies were brought back into the caves, the truck's engine started, and there was no more meddling with anything subterranean.

places in Ukraine grant a better view into Orthodox spirituality than these caves. Both church and lay people come to pray, to sing, to meditate and to pay homage to the oldest saints of Ukrainian Orthodoxy, whose bodies are preserved in the tunnels. Darkness, gold, incense, icons and skulls add to the solemn and mystical aura of the caves. As the popularity of this holy site increases, certain sections of the tunnels and underground chapels have been barred off for use of pilgrims only. These are usually the most beautiful and interesting parts of the caves, so be a pilgrim if you want and enter through the wooden doors; just be silent and circumspect.

The caves are divided into two separate networks, *blyzhny* (near) and *dalni* (far). The **Near Caves** date from the 11th century and contain the very sacred **Vedenska Church** with its gold iconostas. St Anthony built these tunnels for himself to find solitude from his original community that had expanded in the older caves. His tomb lies in these caves, as well as that of Nestor the chronicler. Once your eyes get used to the darkness, you can see the fragments of original frescos above most of the tombs. The entrance to the Near Caves is slightly hidden, since the real entrance is used for guided group tours only. If you are on your own, go to the **Khrestovozdvyzhenska Church** (18th-century). The entrance to the caves is in the forechamber, the exit is in the chapel.

The **Far Caves** comprise the original underground monastery from 1051 and centre around the **Church of the Annunciation** with its immaculate gold doors and incredible painting. St Theodosius is buried in his own chapel, as well as many other saints and those church leaders killed during the Russian Revolution. The Far Caves also join up with the legendary Varangian cave, where the Vikings hid their booty back in the 10th century. If you think you suffer from claustrophobia, think long and hard before entering the Far Caves. Most tunnels are fairly deep underground and barely measure six feet high and two feet wide. The influx of large tour groups can easily place over a hundred single-file people between you and the surface.

Entrance to the Far Caves is through the **Annozachatiyevskaya Church** at the furthest southeast corner of the Lavra. The green-roofed walkway connects the exit of the Near Caves to the entrance of the Far Caves. The towering gold-domed church across from the Far Caves exit is the **Church of the Birth of the Blessed Virgin** which was built in 1696. The only remaining painting inside dates from the 19th century, while the exterior uses examples of traditional Ukrainian folk art. Nearby is the **Far Caves Belfry** with its sharp spires and classic Ukrainian baroque style – this is one of the better-restored but least-visited buildings in the Lavra.

St Vladimir's Cathedral [2 A2]

Kiev's most artistic church is also one of its youngest constructions, built to commemorate 900 years of Christianity in Rus. Started in 1862, the cathedral took over 30 years to complete due to some overly ambitious architects and designers who continued to think bigger and better until this small project became one of Kiev's masterpieces. In one of his last displays of public duty, Tsar Nikolai II presided over the cathedral's christening in 1896. The final design reflects the basic Byzantine style of seven black domes, but the lemon-yellow exterior and colourful interior make this a much lighter and more decorative church than is typical in Orthodoxy. Stepping inside will trigger some very sincere 'oohs' and 'aahs'. Colossal paintings depicting Kiev's spiritual history cover much of the walls and

Churches and holy sites

ceiling, guaranteeing fulfilling moments and traveller's epiphany. On your right, upon entering, is the painting of Prince Vladimir's baptism in Chersoneus in Crimea. On the left is the baptism of Kiev, with the citizens of Rus descending into the Dnepr, and the Prince presiding with his cross. Facing backwards exposes a rather dark and ominous representation of Michael the Archangel in the Final Judgement. Most of the interior of St Vladimir's was painted by the Russian artist Viktor Vasnetsov who belonged to a 19th-century circle of artists known as 'The Wanderers' (*Peredvyzhniki*). Impressed by the political adventurism of the time, the Wanderers broke from the famed St Petersburg Academy, disenchanted by the rigid Western classicism advocated by aristocratic culture. They sought realism and contemporary culture in art, two things which they felt had been denied to subjects of the Russian Empire. The paintings of St Vladimir's express this search for sincerity, but do so using very spiritual themes. The faces and human figures reflect strong art nouveau and pre-Raphaelite influences, but the themes and composition are expressly Slavic (the dark colours look best in winter sunlight). One can spend hours crooking one's neck up at the walls and ceiling, moving from icon to icon, fresco to fresco.

St Vladimir's is the church most frequented by the citizens of Kiev and therefore the best place to experience an Orthodox service with the most beautiful music ever. There are daily services at 08.00 and 17.00, and on Sundays at 07.00, 10.00 and 17.00. The cathedral is located at Shevchenka 20 (tel: 044 235 0362) across from Universitet metro station; just a five-minute walk up from Khreschatyk.

St Sophia's Cathedral [1 C4]

Kiev's oldest standing church is also the most visible landmark in the city centre, thanks to the giant gold bell tower added in 1752. The original structure (through the baroque gates and to your right) was built in 1037 by order of Kievan Rus Grand Prince Yaroslav the Wise, who sought to thank God for defending Kiev against the Pecheneg invasion of 1024. As Prince Vladimir's son and heir, Yaroslav's wisdom is attributed to his knack at diplomacy, honest judgement, cultural leadership and his ability to join the various principalities of Rus together. He modelled and named the church after the greater Hagia Sophia in Constantinople, although today the resemblance is slightly cached beneath the external trappings of the baroque era, and the vast central compound which it inhabits. The original church was brought into the monastery during the 17th century, and later became the ecclesiastical centre for the Orthodox metropolitans (similar to archbishops). Miraculously, it was under Comrade Stalin's command that the place was turned into a 'cultural reserve'. In that same era, St Mikhayil's Monastery (just down the street) was blown to bits. St Sophia's was most likely preserved for its political connotations with a centralised 'Rus', allowing the Soviets to present their rule as a rightful continuation of Yaroslav's just autocracy. Not a consecrated house of worship, St Sophia's still retains its political symbolism today. St Sophia's cultural reserve is located at Sofiyska Square; open 10.00–18.00, closed Thursday. Tickets to get on the grounds are 2UAH; everything else is priced separately, although the main church is really the only building worth touring, entrance 10 UAH.

THE PLOT THICKENS

Upon entering St Sophia's Cathedral you will notice another grave, settled into the cobblestones and polished, often with flowers lain nearby. This is the final resting place of Patriarch Volodymyr, once head of the Ukrainian Orthodox Church allegiant to Kiev (as opposed to Moscow) who during his lifetime sought a Ukrainian church for the Ukrainians. Fully aware of the symbolism in so doing, the Patriarch's supporters brought the funeral procession to St Sophia's, insisting that he be buried within these walls. The Ukrainian government refused, stating a strict division of church and state, and that no favouritism be shown to one religious faction over another. A fanatical riot ensued, followed by a violent police crackdown, and a hasty burial of the Patriarch just a few steps outside St Sophia's. The controversy between these two versions of Ukrainian Orthodoxy continues today.

Visiting the 13-domed structure of St Sophia's requires attention to detail. Unlike many of Kiev's churches, which seek complete renovation and modern aesthetic appeal, St Sophia's is more of a museum-temple, preserving the city's past in layers. Pay close attention to the bare patches of the original church beneath the white-plastered buttresses, the glass panels in the floor showing the foundation, the ornate metal foot tiles inside, and the method of stone construction, with alternating layers and sizes (a feature clearly transported from Byzantium). Standing inside the central apse of St Sophia's offers the visitor the physical presence of the Kievan Rus that existed one thousand years ago. Hundreds of original frescos and some very well-preserved Byzantine mosaics have somehow withstood the ages, giving small clues about the spiritual and everyday life of Kiev's first royal family. The sarcophagus of Yaroslav 'The Wise' is located in the north chapel (along with his bones) and both Russians and Ukrainians visit his grave with the reverence owed a model statesman. At one time, many other Kievan Princes were buried here, including that of Vladimir Monomakh, seen as the last just and kindly ruler of Kiev.

St Mikhayil's Monastery of the Golden Domes [1 D4]

This sky-blue sanctuary rises up in a pyramid of bright domes directly east from St Sophia's bell tower. Several different monasteries stood on this spot from the 12th century onwards, but this newest version was only just completed in 2001. During Stalin's destructive wave of 1937, St Mikhayil's was completely blown up and the lot left empty until Ukraine's president supported its reconstruction. The complex is the headquarters for the more nationalist Ukrainian Orthodox Church (Kiev Patriarchate), meaning that this is one of the few places in Kiev where you'll actually hear Ukrainian being spoken in church. Both architecture and artwork are true to Ukrainian style and few churches in Kiev are so delicate and bright.

Churches and holy sites

The actual church is on the right from the bell tower entrance, rising up with clear blue walls and topped with seven gold domes. The interior lacks the ancient décor that the original church once featured, seeing as these 'frescos' were only painted in 1998, yet modelled after the originals. Still, St Mikhayil's does function as a monastery, and it is one of the best churches to visit to get a feel for Orthodoxy in the everyday life of Ukrainians. The monks of St Mikhayil's are busy with their duties, and the devout come here regularly to pray. Regardless of religious affiliation, Kievans feel endeared to St Mikhayil's, as it symbolises the rebirth of Ukraine's culture and beauty after the severe repression and destruction of the Soviet era.

As this is a working church and monastery, there is no entrance fee, but visitors should enter and move about quietly. The grounds are large, and there is a good view of the Dnepr from the rear.

Two meaningful monuments stand just outside the monastery's walls on Mikhayilivska Ploscha. To the left is the iron and stone cross that forms the shadowed outlines of a human, remembering the victims of the Ukrainian famine of 1932–33. The larger white marble sculpture shows Princess Olga in the centre with the Apostle Andrew on her right-hand side, and the founders of Slavonic literacy, St Cyril and St Methodius, on her left. None of these characters was ever alive at the same time, but the figures represent Kiev's spiritual, political and artistic forbears united.

Vydubytsky Monastery [5 G1]

According to legend, Vydubytsky was founded upon the spot where the pagan effigy of Perun floated to the surface after having been dumped into the water upriver. After baptising Kiev into Christianity, Prince Vladimir had cut down the idol and ordered it dragged by horse into the river, where it should have sunk. Despite their newfound faith, the Christian converts ran along the Dnepr banks following their pagan God downriver, until Perun floated to shore. They decreed this a place of holy remembrance, for which the monastery was built. Others claim the monastery existed far earlier than the 10th century, and that the monks kept themselves and their religion hidden away in the caves. As this was the narrowest spot of the Dnepr, and the chosen spot for crossing the river, the monastery is named 'Vydubytsky', a word that incorporates the roots for 'sailing' and 'oak tree' from which skiffs were once fashioned. Throughout much of Kiev's history, the monastery controlled the Dnepr ferry that crossed here, and was an important centre for writing the chronicles from which all of early Russian/Ukrainian history is known.

For a period during the 16th century, Vydubytsky was handed over by the Poles to the western-Ukrainian Greek Catholic faith, which led to intense protest from the Ukrainian Orthodox branch. After the Cossacks drowned the monastery's superior, the Poles closed all of Kiev's churches, but finally returned the monastery to the Orthodox community.

Like many of Kiev's churches, the monastery suffered destruction by fire, flood and political turmoil. During the Soviet era, the buildings were used first to house a carpenters' union and workshop, followed by the Soviet Institute for Archaeology. At the height of Stalinist repression, the famous 17th-century linden wood Vydubytsky iconostas was ripped from inside the main cathedral and burned to ash by Communist youth activists. It was only in 1998 that the monastic community was returned into full activity, now housing less than a dozen Orthodox monks who prefer the quiet hillside retreat to the larger and busier Caves Monastery.

Lovers of art and architecture should definitely take the time to visit Vydubytsky. Even with all the destruction that has taken place, this small cluster of buildings and gardens reveals a far more undisturbed piece of Ukraine's history and religious life than many of the city's recently renovated examples. **St Michael's Church** was built in 1070 and features some stunning mosaics and early frescos. The rough-hewn doors, intricately formed doorknobs and ancient architecture are like none other in the city. Look carefully, as some of the walls hold inscriptions (holy graffiti of sorts) that date back to the 12th century.

St George's Cathedral features a more classical design of the Kiev renaissance, built in 1701 and resembling many of the churches you'll see at the Caves Monastery. The white walls, green roof and gold domes are also typical throughout Ukraine, as is the odd number of towers and domes, five for St George's. Sadly, the interior does not reflect the artistic glory attributed to this cathedral in historical accounts, but some original frescos remain.

The monastery's **Refectory** is next to the main entry gate to the monastery, built at the time of St George's in a clear neo-classical form, and painted inside with exquisite, baroque depictions of the final judgement and second coming of Christ, as well as St George's triumph. Ironically, the clarity of these paintings dates to their timely restoration during the Brezhnev era of the Soviet Union.

Vydubytsky is a little outside the main tourist circuit, so you may just want to take a taxi straight there (around US$3 from the centre); address: Vydubytsky 40; tel: 044 295 4713. You can also take the metro to the Druzhby Narodiv station, although this is a long walk – or you can take a shorter walk from the Caves Monastery/Motherland complex. In the thick green forest of the summer, you can spot the monastery on the banks of Dnepr by searching for the dark-blue bell tower painted with seven-pointed gold stars.

Pokrovska Convent [Kiev A1]

On the city's north side, the pink Pokrovska Convent is Kiev's best exhibit of the undefiled St Petersburg style inherited from the Russian Empire. The pink, decorated cake-like **Pokrovska Church** (1889) is strikingly similar to the Kazan cathedral just off Moscow's Red Square, and the blue, white and green intricacies of **St Nikolai's Cathedral** (built in 1911) are purely Russian. The similarities make sense, seeing as the convent was founded by the sister-in-law of Tsar Alexander II, following her miraculous recovery at Kiev's Caves Monastery. Hidden away from the city's centre, the church survived the political turmoil of the revolution, and was a famous hiding place during the Nazi occupation. To visit the convent, take the subway out to Lukyanivska, or hail a cab to Bekhteryevsky 15; tel: 044 211 3825.

Churches and holy sites

Jewish sites

Much of the historic fascination with Kiev is linked to the importance of Jewish heritage in this city. One of the oldest documents to come from Kiev, which makes reference to the city in the 9th century, was written in Hebrew. Some believe that Kiev's Jewish population was a remnant of the Khazar Khaganate (Khazaria) – a Judaic-Turkic kingdom in the northern Caucasus that died out around the 11th century. Others suppose the Ashkenazi Jews reached Europe by passing through Crimea, and into the trading capital of early-12th-century Kiev. The Kiev community thrived for nearly 700 years and produced several eminent cultural, political, religious, and scientific leaders. With a history like that of Kiev, it is impossible to estimate the exact percentage of the city that was Jewish, but it is safe to say that the community was large and prominent, and that in 19th-century Ukraine, the Jews numbered in the millions. Like most minorities however, Kiev's Jews became easy targets in times of turmoil.

Cossack leader Khmelnytsky sought to destroy the Jews in his attack on Kiev, as they were perceived to collaborate with the Polish occupiers. After blaming intellectuals in St Petersburg for the revolutionary uprising in 1905, some of whom were Jewish, Tsar Nikolai II sent his Black Hundreds to Kiev with the specific task to terrorise and kill Jews. During the Russian Civil War, the Red and White Armies targeted Kiev's Jews as the city flip-flopped between the two forces. Stalin did not take kindly to the Jewish intellectual elite, and 'purged' much of Kiev's Jewish leadership in the 30s. And then, days after the Nazi forces occupied Kiev, they launched a systematic genocide of the city's Jewish population.

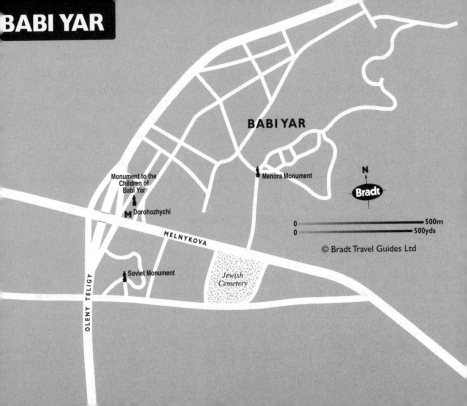

Just prior to World War II, there were over 150,000 Jews in Kiev who made up 20% of the city's population. Before the Nazi advance reached Kiev in 1941, some 100,000 of Kiev's Jews had already fled deep into the Soviet Union, many of them into Central Asia and Siberia. It was the Nazi Einsatzgruppen who ordered all Jews to report for relocation on September 29 1941. Kiev's older generation clearly remember the papers posted to telephone poles and glued on walls, demanding Jews report with their belongings to one of the outer train stations. Non-Jews were made to believe that the Jews were simply being deported to Israel. Instead, thousands were brought to a forested ravine that lies just outside the city limits, called **Babi Yar**. After lining them up at the ravine's edge, the captives were ordered to undress and line up in groups, after which they were shot en masse. On that last September day, 33,771 Jews were shot, and throughout the occupation, Babi Yar continued to be used for executing Ukraine's gypsies, nationalists, communists and more Jews. Few outside occupied Europe knew of the tragedy until after liberation. During the 1950s a solemn Soviet monument was erected to the 'Soviet citizens' who perished, and the massacre was remembered in the famous poem by Yevgeny Yevtushenko *Babi Yar*; however, it was only in 1991 that the construction of a Jewish memorial was allowed permission, followed by another monument in 2001 dedicated to the children who perished there.

Visiting Babi Yar is a sobering experience. To get to the area, take the metro out to Dorohozhychi metro station (at the end of the green line). Crossing Melnikova and walking south across the park will bring you to a shallow meadow and the austere Soviet memorial. Or, exit from the north side of the metro station (which goes right into the park) and you will see the very sad-looking **Children's Memorial.** Walk two park blocks north, then take the path to the right, and continue to the **Menora Monument.** The memorial is placed at the top of Babi Yar ravine, and marks the spot where the actual massacre took place.

Not far away from Babi Yar is the largest Jewish cemetery in Kiev, although it is not so commonly known as that today. Continue down Melnikova (about 600m) and the gates will be on your left side.

Today there are an estimated 100,000 Jews living in Kiev, which make up about 40% of Ukrainian Jews, but only about 3% of the city's population. There are no longer any marked Jewish neighbourhoods, however, some key properties have been returned by the government to the community, and are now open as places of worship. The **Central Synagogue** (Shota Rustavelli 13; tel: 044 235 9082) was built in 1898 in the very heart of the city. The building is often referred to as the Brodsky Synagogue, named after one of the city's key sugar magnates, Lazar Brodsky. For the duration of the Soviet regime, the building was used as a puppet theatre, and it was only reopened in the year 2000. Next door to the synagogue is a popular kosher restaurant and market where Jews from all over the world seem to mix.

The slightly older **Podil Synagogue** (Schekavytska 29; tel: 044 416 2442) was completed in 1885. The façade was built to look like a semi-detached duplex home with a clandestine entrance in the rear. Like many of Kiev's synagogues, the one in Podil was gutted and partially destroyed during the Nazi occupation, however, it was the first (and only at the time) to be rebuilt immediately. The Podil synagogue is an important centre for Jewish life in Kiev today, featuring a matzo bakery, *yeshiva* and *mikva*.

Closer to the central synagogue is the birthplace of **Golda Meir**, the former prime minister of Israel (Basseina 5A). Her father and mother had rented a set of rooms in this building, but left Kiev for America in 1903. A plaque and bust of the politician marks their home. For more information on Jewish life in Kiev, be sure to visit the Museum of One Street (see *Museums*), which has a few displays dedicated to the city's Jewish community prior to the revolution. Not far outside Kiev is also the birthplace of **Sholom Aleichem**, famed Jewish writer and storyteller, whose stories inspired the Broadway musical *Fiddler on the Roof*. (See *Chapter 11* on how to get there.) A statue remembering him is at Rognidynska 3.

MUSEUMS

Kiev's museums are typically run by pleasant ladies and old men who normally did some related degree at a Soviet university and now earn kopecks managing the displays. Ask a question and you'll be astounded by the knowledge you gain. You'll find that authoritarian attitudes thrive within museums and you'll be vehemently commanded where to go and what to look at. Free wandering is a no-no and if you skip a room or go in the 'wrong' direction you will face the wrath of a cultured *babushka* who will happily point out the glazed tiles you missed. Due to a lack of funds, there is rarely any heat inside museums and the attendants will not turn on the lights until you walk into a room. Some museum attendants will be selling their own souvenirs or museum booklets that help to supplement their meagre incomes.

The Great Patriotic War Museum

Sichnevoho Povstannya 44; tel: 044 295 9457 [3 G4]; entrance 5UAH

In Russia, World War II is remembered as the great patriotic struggle for the motherland. The *Rodyna Mat* (The Nation's Mother, or 'The Motherland') is the titanium goddess that towers above Kiev's right bank with a sword and shield in hand, bearing the hammer and sickle and commemorating the defence of one's country. Don't even think about comparing it to the Statue of Liberty, although there are elevators going up inside and a staircase to a viewing platform in her right hand (Brezhnev built it). The museum is located inside the pedestal and an adjoining hall, telling the story of Soviet Ukraine's victory over the Nazis in panoramic displays that transcend the need to understand the Russian-language descriptions. A separate exhibit details the struggle of socialism in the Soviet wars of the Third World, including Angola and Afghanistan. The letters, pictures and old uniforms are sobering.

The surrounding park is a popular place for strolling and offers a great example of vast Soviet public space and socialist realist statuary. Paths lead past the Eternal Flame, in remembrance of World War II, the Tomb of the Unknown Soldier and two heavily graffitied tanks tied together in peace. An underpass brings you past larger-than-life sculptured depictions of Kiev's defence and liberation. Over-muscled men (and women) carry cannons and machine guns, throw grenades and charge the

OF STEEPLES AND SWORDS

Following Ukraine's independence in 1991, the citizens of Kiev were allowed to shift focus from the Soviet symbols of their city and concentrate on the ancient, spiritual history of Kiev. In so doing, the faithful citizens realised that the sword tip of the very Soviet *Rodyna Mat* statue was indeed higher than the cross atop the gold-domed bell tower of the Kievo-Pecherska Lavra. Decisions were made, action was taken, and the motherland's sword was shortened to its present dagger-like length.

enemy. Outside the underpass is a display of Soviet aircraft, tanks and rocket launchers. On the west side of Pechersk are the ruins of the **Pechersk Fortress** (Hospitalna 24A; tel: 044 224 1970), the main Tsarist defence for Kiev in the 19th century, and its own museum today. Much of this original fortress area has been built over, but some of the original ramparts are still in place. The military function of this part of the city granted the closest metro station its name Arsenalna – after the Tsar's arsenal that was located here.

Getting to the *Rodyna Mat* is just a few more bus stops from the Caves Monastery. Go to Arsenalna metro station and take bus #20 to the very end, or else a *marshrutka* or taxi to 'Rodyna Mat'. Grand tours of Kiev will normally include this area in their tour of the nearby Caves Monastery.

The Museum of Folk Architecture and Life

Pirogov; tel: 044 266 2416; open daily 10.00–17.00; entrance 10UAH.

Of all the recreated village-museum preserves in Ukraine, the assembly near Pirogov is the largest in size, the broadest in culture, and the liveliest. Over three hundred original pieces of folk architecture have been gathered to represent every traditional region of Ukraine and now comprise a national 'village'. Visitors are allowed to roam freely and enter the wooden churches, windmills, thatched cottages and barns. The attention to detail on the inside is impressive, as are the craft displays. Costumed peasants play the part and answer questions. During warmer months traditional craftsmen work in the open and sell wild honey, woodcarving, pottery and embroidery. The outdoor fairs (in late spring and early autumn) are a lot of fun if you can time it right.

Visiting the outdoor museum should be a priority, as Kiev is Kiev, but 'the real Ukraine' is a strikingly different world of rural survival. The wooden wells, windmills, ancient churches and thatched huts were Ukraine's reality until very recently, and in some parts of Ukraine, what you see here continues to be reality. Wandering through the fields, you will pass through 'villages' from Galicia, the Carpathians, Podillya, Polissya and other regions of Ukraine, ending with the 'socialist village' showing grand examples of modern regional adaptations on the traditional Ukrainian *khata* (cottage). Perhaps not so intended these days, the museum still functions as an example of Soviet efforts to meld Ukrainian traditions into the communist logic.

Most people visit the museum with a group tour ordered through any local travel agent. Plan on at least four hours to really enjoy the place. Pirogov (Pyrohiv) village is directly south of Kiev on the right bank of the Dnepr, and thus outside the reach of most public transportation. On your own, take bus #27 from metro station Libidska to the village of Pirogov (Pyrohiv in Ukrainian). Or take the metro to Respublikansky Stadion and then take *marshrutka* #156 for a 20-minute ride to the village. The ride takes about 30 minutes. Otherwise, you can choose to spend your money on a cab or an organised tour (around US$15 either way).

The National Museum of Art
Hrushevsky 6; tel: 044 228 6429 [2 D1]; open 10.00–18.00, closed Friday; entrance 5UAH

This classical building was once the museum of history, and any art on display was a mere illustration of the past. Later, all artwork was nationalised by the Soviet government, leaving the museum with the largest collection of Ukrainian art in the world. Establishing a well-rounded display that defines the country's art has been difficult. For now, you can see medieval icons, 18th- and 19th-century romantic art (some Shevchenko sketches) and some of the most well-known pieces of Soviet-era socialist painting, including original poster art from the revolution.

The Kiev Museum of Russian Art
Tereschenkivska 9; tel: 044 224 6218 [2 C2]; open 10.00–17.00, closed Wednesday and Thursday; entrance 4UAH

Housed in the luxurious mansion of Kiev sugar-millionaire Fyodor Tereschenko (after whom the street is still named), Kiev's greatest collection of Russian art includes paintings by Vrubel, Levitsky, Repin, as well as the very famous 15th-century icon of St George slaying the dragon. Touring the museum takes less than an hour and gives a glimpse into the bourgeois home and lifestyle of Kiev's pre-revolutionary days.

The Art Museum of Bohdan and Varvara Khanenko

Tereschenkivksa 15; tel: 044 225 5269 [2 C2]; open 10.00–17.00, closed Monday and Tuesday

Another bourgeois mansion-cum-art museum, the Khanenko gallery includes a vast collection of post-Renaissance, western-European painting. Recognisable portraits by Rubens, David, Reynolds and Velazquez hang on these walls, and the house and furniture are an exhibit by themselves.

National Chernobyl Museum

Provulok Khorevy 1; tel: 044 416 3068 [1 C2]; open 10.00–18.00, closed Sunday; entrance 5UAH

One of Kiev's newest museums, the Chernobyl display in Podil explores the human side of a most devastating nuclear tragedy. Probably the most haunting sight in the museum are the hundreds of old signs from cities that were made ghost towns after evacuation. A model of the reactor and a detailed pictorial account of the accident help explain the event to non-Russian speakers (at present there are no English tours offered). The rest of the exhibit deals with the pain and trauma of Chernobyl in a series of highly surrealist art installations. See also pages 269–75.

National Museum of Ukrainian History

Volodymyrska 2; tel: 044 228 6545 [1 C4]; open 10.00–18.00, closed Wednesday; entrance 4UAH

Ukrainian independence is the prominent theme of the exhibit, from pagan Slavic times to the political struggles of the last decade.

In the open square next to the museum lie the foundation stones outlining the first stone church in Kiev. The Desiatynna (Tithing) Church was built in AD989 in honour of Prince Vladimir's promise to give one-tenth of the state income to the new church; however, the building was razed by the Mongols in 1240 and never rebuilt. Shading the ruins is an 800-year-old *lipa* or lime tree, a plant revered by Ukrainians who use the leaves and flowers as a cure-all.

Museum of One Street (see Andriyivsky Uzviz, page 234)

Andriyivsky Uzviz 2B [1 C3]; open 12.00–18.00, closed Monday; entrance 3UAH

PARKS

So many parks to choose from, and all of them so charming. **Khreschatyk Park** between the street and the river makes a good beginning for a walk above the

Dnepr. The road and path connect to over five different parks, including the exquisite **Marinsky Park** once used for Tsarist military manoeuvres. In the lower end of the city (right bank) are the expansive **National Botanical Gardens** near Vydubytsky Monastery, with broad chestnut forests and diverse species. Another public, forested space closer to the centre is the **Academic Botanical Gardens** behind the metro station Universitet.

The feel-good Soviet recreation zone **Hydropark** can be reached by the metro station of the same name. Spanning two long islands, the park is comprised of small forests, marshes and natural sand beaches, constantly reshaped by the Dnepr. Plenty of trails allow for some interesting walks and views of the city, and in summer, the place is filled with sunbathers, swimmers and ice-cream vendors – reminiscent of beachside amusement parks. In winter, the islands are an offbeat but strategic spot to see the gold domes of Kiev, to watch the ice-fishing and to step out on the ice yourself.

Parks

11 Beyond the City
OUTSIDE KIEV

There are plenty of interesting destinations just outside the city limits, and a few that are a bit further but can none the less be fitted into a pleasant one-day excursion. **Pereyaslav Khmelnytsky Переяслав Хмельницкий** was a vital city in Kievan Rus and a seat of its own principality, however the town went down in history in 1654 when Bohdan Khmelnytsky came to this spot and swore allegiance to the Tsar, fatefully tying Ukrainian lands to Moscow. Today the town brings in tourists interested in the Cossacks, ancient Kiev and the Pereyaslav agreement. The entire town and adjacent countryside now makes up the Pereyaslav Historical Preserve, which includes the Museum of the History of Ukrainian Folk Architecture, similar to the one in Kiev (Pirogov) and St Michael's Church. In contrast to big urban Kiev, a day trip to this left bank settlement offers a fair introduction to the old country and a taste of everyday modern life in rural Ukraine.

Pereyaslav is also the birthplace of Jewish writer **Sholom Aleichem** (Solomon Rabinowitz) whose famous stories candidly portrayed *shtetl* life in Tsarist Russia. A principal character in these tales was one Tevye the dairyman, and collectively these writings formed the plot for the musical *Fiddler on the Roof*. The home where the writer was born is part of the preserve and now houses a museum of his life. On the road to Pereyaslav from Kiev, you will pass near Voronkiv, the village where Sholom Aleichem attended school and later based his fictional town of Kasrilevke

(Anatyevka in the musical). Travel to Pereyaslav takes about one-and-a-half hours and is best done by bus (which leave periodically from the central *avtovokzal*) or taxi (prices vary, but around US$20 each way). Most tour agencies also offer Pereyaslav as a day trip.

Bila Tserkva Біла Церква is another town made famous by Bohdan Khmelnytsky when he signed his treaty of Bila Tserkva with Poland in 1651, cutting back on Cossack rights and allowing Polish gentry to regain their lands. Khmelnytsky broke the treaty within the year, eventually driving the Poles out. Bila Tserkva (literally 'white church') is a popular day trip for its quaint (white) churches and pleasant tree park. Travelling to Bila Tserkva is easy since it falls on the well-travelled southern route from Kiev to Uman and Odessa. Joining an organised tour of the town can be done with any Kiev agency and there are plenty of direct buses from the central bus station on their way to Uman. The drive takes just under an hour.

CHERNOBYL Чорнобиль
The site of the world's worst nuclear accident now tops the curiosity of tourists who probably knew about the event before most Ukrainians ever did. For all there is to see and do in Ukraine, Chernobyl is on its way to becoming the country's leading 'I was there' destination outside of Kiev. Practically every Ukrainian tourist agency offers a day trip into the 'zone', trading the would-be environmental attractions of Polissya for a post-apocalyptic view of a tainted landscape.

The town of **Chornobyl** (in Ukrainian) lies 20km south of the Belarus border on the Pripyat river. Few foreigners realise what a giant operation Chernobyl was and how central a role it played in the region. A massive artificial lake was formed to cool the four reactors and nearly everyone living in the nearby town of **Pripyat** was somehow connected to making the nuclear energy that kept Kiev's metro running and streetlights shining.

Unfolding the fateful events of April 26 1986 now sounds like a too-often told campfire tale: the number four reactor of the Chernobyl nuclear power plant was to be shut down for routine maintenance and it was decided to test the electrical system to determine if it could keep the reactor's regular cooling system running in the event of a power loss. Obviously, the experiment failed, and this was exacerbated by the fact that the emergency cooling system had been shut off, allowing the overheated system to continue to overheat. The initial explosion at Chernobyl was actually pressurised steam in the cooling system, followed by a genuine nuclear detonation a few seconds later. Two plant workers were immediately killed by the blast. Open to the air, the burning reactor shot nine tons of dematerialised waste a mile skyward, followed by a giant radioactive cloud of xenon and krypton gases.

Chernobyl's real heroes were the very first firemen sent in. A lack of preparedness and a general failure to grasp the seriousness of this type of accident led to the firemen receiving lethal doses of radiation within a couple of minutes. For two weeks, the reactor continued to burn while workers tried to counteract a myriad of chemical fires. A modern monument to the 31 firemen who died was recently erected in the town.

The double tragedy of Chernobyl was the Soviet Union's attempt to keep it quiet. The towns close to Chernobyl were only evacuated two days after the explosion, and the Ukrainian public were not notified until nearly a week after Swedish scientists had identified the radioactive cloud blowing north. Contaminated rain fell on southern Belarus soon after the explosion, so that this and the environment around Pripyat are considered the worst-hit areas. Soviet logic deemed Polissya a safe place for a nuclear plant due to its low population density and relative proximity to Kiev. The Pripyat marshes and woodlands of Belarus and Ukraine are still considered an exceptionally rare ecosystem, but the woods around Chernobyl will be forever poisoned. The famous '**red forest**' surrounds the southern and western sides of the site and forms a creepy landscape of barren trees sprouting from thick sand that was imported to stop ground radiation. All the small mammals died within the year after the accident and new fauna has only recently ventured into the area. As Chernobyl's cooling system once flowed directly into the Dnepr, the water has higher than average radiation levels that decrease as you move downstream (this is the real reason you shouldn't eat river fish from the markets).

For Ukrainians, the most direct consequence has been a jump in thyroid cancer among children, as well as the thousands of stillbirths and deformities in newborns following the first year after the accident. Since then, thousands more deaths have

Chernobyl

been blamed on the nuclear disaster, but it is hard to prove any correlations. The government supports involved compensation schemes with discounts and regular health treatments for registered 'invalids', but sadly, Chernobyl has become the national excuse for any form of malaise.

After repeated requests and cash payments from the EU and the United States, Chernobyl's last reactor was shut down permanently in the year 2000. Thousands remain jobless. Over 120,000 inhabitants were permanently evacuated, and to house them the government built the town of **Slavutych** on the northern banks of the Dnepr. For those keen to see Ukraine's youngest town, Slavutych is not in the 'zone' and can be reached by bus from Kiev or Chernihiv. Chernobyl is still an open wound for Ukraine, so that many Ukrainians still don't know how to react to a rise in travel interest. International agencies and the government hope that frank and open tours to the site will take away some of the stigma at home and abroad.

Visiting Chernobyl

You will not become sterile or get cancer by visiting Chernobyl. In fact, you are more likely to ingest radioactively contaminated foods in Kiev (like mushrooms, berries and vegetables) than to be negatively affected by the site. The restricted exclusion 'zone' is cordoned off by two concentric circles of 30km and 10km from the derelict plant. The only thing to see in the zone is that there is little to see. Landscapes are barren and overgrown, and the villages eerie and empty. A few diehards (literally) have returned to their country homes, but for the most part, things are left as they were at the time of evacuation. Entering an area frozen in 1986 USSR feels a lot like time travel.

Anyone is allowed to contact the appropriate government ministry and apply for the necessary passes to get into the 'zone', but going through a private tour agency is a lot less hassle. Getting to Chernobyl is not so tricky if you're with a group. The drive from Kiev takes two-and-a-half hours and passes checkpoints at the 30km and 10km zone (the guards' posturing and flustered paper-checking is a bit of show to recreate that special Soviet mood). Although clearly unnecessary – except for the obvious dramatic effect – visitors are fitted with special jumpsuits and shoes at the 10km checkpoint, then periodically checked with a Geiger counter during the tour.

A visit to the site comes down to staring at the giant concrete sarcophagus that supposedly stops the 180 tons of festering nuclear fuel from harming anyone. As a rule, you must stay at least 100m from the building. Organised trips tend to include a sobering tour of the ghost town of Pripyat and other villages where radioactive buildings were buried under mounds of earth, and children's toys abandoned in the streets. Most tours also require a feel-good luncheon when visitors are expected to engage in limited dialogue about nuclear safety and world peace.

Organised trips leave out all the bureaucracy, and make it a lot easier to plan from abroad. Large groups of ten or more tend to get deals charging US$30 per

Chernobyl

person, but if you are on your own, expect to pay at least US$150. Trips also have to be planned three to five days in advance as tour agents must apply for clearances beforehand. The company **SAM** (Ivano Franka 40B, Kiev; tel: 044 238 2060; fax: 044 238 6952; email: main@samcomp.kiev.ua; web: www.sam.com.ua/eng) is the best-known provider for Chernobyl and charges around US$200 for a one-on-one private guided tour, decreasing as group numbers increase (a group of five costs US$60 each). **New Logic** (Mikhailivska 6A; tel/fax: 044 462 0462; email: incoming@newlogic.kiev.ua; web: www.newlogic.com.ua) caters to young and professional travellers and can do a private day trip for US$120. Another trusted company is **Sputnik Kyiv** (Pushkinskaya 9; tel: 044 228 0938; fax: 044 464 1358; email: income@sputnik.kiev.ua; web: www.sputnik.kiev.ua).

If you are one of those fiercely independent types who wants to discover Chernobyl on your own, you are free to go the government route, although it takes longer and you will be without your passport for a few days while you are 'processed' (document clearance requires a minimum of seven days). Ukraine's **Ministry of the Chernobyl Catastrophe** has a much longer name in Ukrainian and carries an official mandate of dealing with requests to visit the 'zone' and the site; Velyka Zhytomyrska 28; tel: 044 216 8472; fax: 044 216 8546. You can also contact **Chernobyl InterInform** directly, based at the actual site. They can issue passes and arrange for a longer stay if you want. Write (in English) to: Director of the State Department and Administration of the Exclusion Zone, Chernobyl, Khmelnytskovo 1A; tel: 029 352 553; fax: 029 352 205. There is no public transport to Chernobyl, so independents will have to arrange their own (which means additional documentation for drivers, etc). An alternative to all the trouble is to visit the Chernobyl Museum in Kiev (see pages 255–6).

KANIV КАНІВ

The poet Taras Shevchenko – Ukraine's ultimate hero – requested that he be buried near this tiny village on a bluff overlooking the Dnepr river. His desire was fulfilled after his death and now visitors stream in from all over the world to see his grave at this very serene location. Kaniv itself was founded as one of the original fortresses marking the line between civilisation and the open 'wild field' and later became an important Cossack stronghold. Before the Russian Revolution and throughout Khrushchev's USSR, Shevchenko's grave was a popular site for clandestine meetings of nationalists and intellectuals. The **Taras Shevchenko Literary Museum** is on top of the main hill near his grandiose grave; tel: 04736 223 65; open 09.00–18.00; entrance 5UAH. The poet lived for a while in the smaller restored cottage in the woods behind. Just three miles south of the village is the **Kaniv Nature Preserve**, founded in 1926 to protect natural Ukrainian plant species. The park is open for walking and enjoying some very lovely views of the river. The main office is in the village (tel: 04736 230 47). Kaniv can be reached by car or bus from Kiev (2 hours) or Cherkasy (1 hour), and most Ukrainian tour agencies offer boat excursions to Kaniv as a day trip from Kiev.

Kaniv

UMAN УМАНЬ

It is sad to think that some travellers take in Ukraine's largest city but miss the very heart of the country. Uman is the right place to come and get a glimpse of small-town Ukraine without going through the business of getting stranded in a tiny village. The strange-sounding town is considered the gateway between west and central Ukraine and is named after the Umanka river which joins the Kamyanka river and forms a natural barrier against the south. The natural landscape inspired the Polish *rzeczpospolita* to station a regiment here in the 1600s that proved effective in warding off the Tatar invasions but failed to stop the Ukrainian Cossacks and the rebel peasant bands of the 18th century as they headed for Kiev. Taras Shevchenko's famous poem *Haidamaky* tells the story of the 1768 Uman massacre in which 20,000 people were killed – most of them Jews seeking protection from the Poles. The extremely wealthy Pototsky family ruled Uman until 1834 and their greatest contribution was the extravagant garden covering the northeast side of the town. The contrast of boundless luxury in such common environs has made the exceptional park a major attraction for Ukrainians. The town itself is honest, if not slightly bare. If you find you're trying to kill time in Kiev, Uman makes a distinctive day trip into rural Ukraine.

Getting there and away

Uman's fame means several tour agencies run day trips from Kiev with return coach travel included. The train station is located at Maidan Gagarina in the southwest corner of the town. There is a daily train to Kiev, but the other trains to Cherkasy and

Vinnytsya are very slow and inconvenient. From Kiev's central *avtovokzal* there are two daily buses and the trip takes three hours. Uman is the primary junction for road trips to Odessa from Kiev so the long-haul luxury buses are the quickest and most comfortable way to get there on your own. A Kiev–Uman ticket should cost US$6.

Where to stay/eat

If you choose to stay the night, the austere **Hotel Uman** on Maidan Lenina is the most likely choice with a fairly decent restaurant. The annual influx of Jewish pilgrims has established a steady market for staying with locals. Ask around for anyone with a room (*komnata*) or flat (*kvartira*). Depending on what time of year you are there, a room for the night will cost US$10–20. A few cafés line Sadova on the way to the park and for food essentials there is the central market (*rynok*) at the bottom of Radyanska.

Sofiyivka Park

Back when Imperial Russia had an inferiority complex against France, a common expression stated that 'Sofiyivka is no worse than Versailles!'. The lavish gardens occupy a quarter of Uman and bear no resemblance to French symmetry and splendour. Instead Sofiyivka is designed in the romantic style aiming to imitate natural landscapes. Trees, rocks and water are the prominent features and the original architects redirected the Kamyanka river in order to fill the artificial pools and miniature waterfalls that cut through the gardens.

Uman

Count Felix Pototsky began construction of the gardens in 1798 as a gift to his new bride, the legendary beauty Sofia. Greek by birth, Sofia had been sold into slavery by her parents as a 12-year-old girl. The Polish ambassador to Turkey bought her in Istanbul as a present for the Polish King Stanislaw August, however while travelling back through Ukraine she met the son of the Polish army commander Jozef Witte, who fell in love with the 15-year-old and bought her from the ambassador. The newly married Madame Witte quickly became a celebrated society figure among the Polish gentry. She soon took up delivering diplomatic mail and was rumoured to use the opportunity for spying for the Polish king as well as for Catherine the Great. Sofia eventually left her husband and two children but was soon remarried to the Polish Count Pototsky in Uman. He adored Sofia and designed the park as a memorial to her beauty incorporating the mythology of ancient Greece: the 400-acre park has its own isle of Lesbos, a terrace of the muses, red poppy 'Elysian' fields, a Cretan labyrinth and an underground stream called Styx. Sadly, long before the park was finished, the Count uncovered an affair between his son from his first marriage and his young wife. Broken-hearted, he grew seriously ill. Sofia supposedly spent two days on her knees begging to be pardoned but the Count died without forgiving her. She finished the park herself during a brief affair with the Russian Count Potemkin, then lived out her days in melancholy. The fact that a freak earthquake actually pushed her grave out of the Uman churchyard has the locals convinced that she was a witch.

The park is well maintained and it is easy to spend up to a day walking the paths; entrance costs US$1. The best time to visit is in September, when the colours are extraordinary and the white swans are still about, but the park is open all year and is still worth a trip even in the dead of winter. Horseback riding tours can be arranged at the park, and there are boat tours through the river Styx and on the largest lake. A taxi from the train station is US$2 and the park is an easy walk from the bus station.

Uman's rabbi

The Breslov movement of Hasidism was inspired by Rabbi Nachman who was himself the great-grandson of the founder of Hasidism. Born in Medzibezh in 1772, the Rabbi spent most of his life in the village of Bratslav (near Vinnytsya; from which comes the term 'Breslov') where he preached a religion based on joy and spiritual freedom. Modern-day Breslov-Hasidic Jews follow a principle of living life to the fullest and practise a unique form of free-flowing prayer where the devotee 'chats' openly with God for one hour each day. Rabbi Nachman died young of tuberculosis having expressed the desire to be buried in Uman, next to the victims of the 1768 massacre. In his writings he promised to pray for the success of any pilgrim that came to his graveside and recited the ten psalms of the *Tikkun K'lali*. Breslov-Hasidic Jews feel the need to make the journey to Uman at least once in their lifetime, which usually takes place on the Jewish New Year, and the commonly heard Breslov chant is 'Uman, Uman, Rosh Hashanah'. Uman's local Breslov community has quickly recovered in spite of decades of near extinction and the yearly pilgrimage is now the crowning event for the town. The Rabbi's grave is located in the Jewish cemetery on the corner of Belinskovo and Pushkina.

12 Language

Ukrainians speak Ukrainian and Russian, both Slavic languages. In the EU and many post-colonial nations of the world, people speak a lingua franca like English or French. For Ukrainians, the 'international language' (until recently) was Russian. Aside from Ukrainian, the older generation all speak Russian because they grew up in the Soviet Union. Many studied and can speak some German. You will find the younger generation speaks a fair amount of English, but not enough for you to get away with not learning some of the language.

Ukrainian is an Indo-European language of the Eastern Slavic family of languages. The original root language is now referred to as Old Church Slavonic, as it is still used in the Orthodox liturgy. Discernible versions of Russian, Ukrainian and Belarusian had emerged from Slavonic by the mid-12th century. Two Byzantine missionaries, St Cyril and St Methodius, travelled to Ukraine in the late-9th century and established a written language for the land, hence the Cyrillic alphabet, which combines Greek and Latin letters to fit Slavic sounds.

The Cyrillic alphabet scares most people off as you are essentially learning to read all over again. Learn it. Simply knowing the letters will enliven your trip, and speaking the very basics of Russian and Ukrainian (*please, thank you, excuse me*) allows you a better connection with the land and people.

After centuries of linguistic repression, it has become very important for Ukrainians to speak Ukrainian in a show of independence and solidarity. Everything is written in

Ukrainian and in most of western Ukraine, people will only speak Ukrainian. However, Russian is also an important language in Ukraine, and visitors will often wonder how similar/different the two languages actually are. The closest comparison to the relationship between Russian and Ukrainian might be Spanish and Portuguese. Ukrainians tend to have no problem understanding Russians, while the opposite is rarely true. Ukrainian sounds much softer and is much more poetic in some respects, while Russian has benefited from centuries of high culture and literature during which time Ukrainian was spoken mainly by the rural peasant population. Ukraine's politics of language is all very controversial right now, so it's best to learn a little of each. You'll find many people speak a fairly common mixture of the two, called *surzhyk*.

LANGUAGE POLITICS

A long time ago, Russian and Ukrainian were the same language, similar to Old Church Slavonic. History and geography separated the two groups and allowed enough improvisation and evolution to make them two separate languages around the 12th century. Foreign governance, namely by the Russian and Polish élite, meant for a time that the Ukrainian language survived among the lower, uneducated classes only. Strict suppression of the Ukrainian language from the 17th to the 19th centuries, and during the Soviet era, became synonymous with Ukraine's lack of independence and today, speaking Ukrainian has come to be an important political symbol of freedom and self-determination. Like all national movements, things can swing too far in the other direction, and Ukraine's many native Russian-speakers have begun to make their own linguistic stance. You'll find that certain areas of the country only speak Ukrainian, others speak Russian and some use both interchangeably. In Kiev, you can speak either Russian or Ukrainian. Also, keep in mind that urban areas may be Russian-speaking, but the countryside will speak Ukrainian. You will meet some people who are very fussy one way or another, and others who are happy to communicate however they can. Be sensitive and try to use whichever language they do.

THE CYRILLIC ALPHABET

The Ukrainian alphabet is not as daunting as it may look. Many letters are the same or use the Greek equivalent. If you think that learning a whole new language is not for you, so be it, but getting the alphabet down is key for finding your way around and enjoying your stay. A self-proclaimed non-linguist traveller recommends finding a video shop in Ukraine and spending an hour or so reading all the Cyrillic covers of movies you know. That's how he learned to read Ukrainian.

Letters		Ukrainian pronunciation
А	а	'ah' as in almond
Б	б	'b' as in boat
В	в	'v' as in vivacious
Г	г	'h' as in halo
Д	д	'd' as in doctor

Е	е	'eh' as in set
Є	є	'yeh'
Ж	ж	'zh' as in mirage
З	з	'z' as in zebra
И	и	'y' (short 'i') as in myth
Й	й	closes an 'ee' sound or '?'
І	і	long 'ee'
Ї	ї	'yee' as in old English 'ye'
К	к	'k' as in kitten
Л	л	'l' as in lemon
М	м	'm' as in man
Н	н	'n' as in nice
О	о	'o' as in Oh!
П	п	'p' as in pole
Р	р	'r'; short and rolled
С	с	's' as in sesame
Т	т	't' as in tight
У	у	'oo' as in moon
Ф	ф	'f' as in fruit
Х	х	'kh' (gutteral) as in 'Bach'
Ц	ц	'ts' as in bits
Ч	ч	'ch' as in cheddar

The Cyrillic alphabet

Ш	ш	'sh' as in shop
Щ	щ	'shch' as in fresh cheese
Ю	ю.	'yoo' as in you
Я	я	'ya' as in yacht
Ь	ь	soft sign, often transliterated as an apostrophe and used after 'hard' consonants д, з, л, н, с, т, ц. 'Soften' a letter by barely making a 'y' sound (as in yes) just as you stop saying the consonant.

Russian letters

Г	г	'g' as in go
Е	е	'yeh' as in yes
Ё	ё	'yo' as in yo-yo
Э	э	'eh', as in Ukrainian 'e'
И	и	long ee sound
Й	й	closes an 'ee' sound or 's'
Ы	ы	'y', like Ukrainian 'и'
Ъ	ъ	hard sign; causes an audible break in the word

Vowels are the main difference between Russian and Ukrainian sounds. Ukrainian vowels (and consonants) are always pronounced as written and tend to sound softer. Russian vowels change from long to short depending on where they fall in a word. Remember the key difference is to say the '*yeh*' found in so many Russian words, and saying the same letter 'E' as *'eh'* in Ukrainian. Always remember that 'ᴜ' (gamma) is 'H' in Ukrainian and 'G' in Russian.

Both languages are much more phonetic than English, so just sound the words out. Stresses are underlined. Test your knowledge of Cyrillic by covering the transliterations and reading down the column.

BASICS

	Ukrainian		**Russian**	
Good morning	Добрий ранок	*dobry ranok*	Доброе утро	*dobre oodra*
Hello (formal)	Добрий день	*dobry dehn*	Здравствуйте	*zdrastvwytye*
Hi (casual)	Привіт	*pryveet*	Привет	*privyet*
Good evening	Добрий вечір	*dobry vecheer*	Добрій вечер	*dobry vyecher*
Goodnight (farewell)	Надобраніч	*nadobraneech*	Спокойной ночи	*spokoiny nochee*
Goodbye	До повачення	*do pobachennya*	До свидания	*dasvidanya*
Yes	Так	*tak*	Да	*da*
No	Ні	*nee*	Нет	*nyet*
Please	Будь ласка	*bood laska*	Пожалуйста	*pazhawsta*
Thank you	Дякую	*dyakooyoo*	Спасибо	*spaseeba*
You're welcome	Нема за що	*nehma za scho*	Не за что	*nyeh za shto*
Excuse me	Пробачте	*probachteh*	Извините	*eezvineetye*
What's your name?	Як вас звати	*yak vas zvaty?*	Как вас зовут	*kak vas zavoot?*
My name is …	Мене звати	*mehneh zvaty*	Меня зовут	*menya zavoot*

Basics

	Ukrainian		**Russian**	
Nice to meet you	Дуже приємно	*duzhe pry'yemno*	Очень приятно	*ochen preeyatna*
How are you?	Як справи?	*yak spravy?*	Как дела?	*kak dyela?*
Fine, good	Добре	*dobreh*	Хорошо	*kharasho*
Bad	Погано	*pohano*	Плохо	*plokha*
Very	Дуже	*duzhe*	Очень	*ochen*
Attention	Увага	*uvaha*	Внимание	*vnimaniye*
Watch out	Обережно	*oberezhno*	Осторожно	*ostorozhna*
Help!	Допоможіть	*dopomozheet*	Помогите	*pamageetyeh*
I (don't) like …	Мені (не) подобається (ukr)	*mehnee (neh) podobayetsya*		
	Мне (не) нравиться (rus)	*mnyeh (nyeh) nryaveetsya*	мне (не) нравиться	*mnyeh (nyeh) nryaveetsya*

Questions

Do you speak …?	Ви говорите	*vy hovoryteh*	Вы говорите	*vy gavarityeh*
English-	по-англійськи	*pa anhleesky*	по-английский	*pa angleeskee*
Ukrainian	по-украшнсськи	*pa ukrayeensky*	по-украинский	*pa ukrainskee*
Russian	по-россіськи	*pa rosseesky*	по-русский	*pa rooskee*
German	по-німецьки	*pa neemetsky*	по-немецкий	*pa nyemetskee*
French	по-французьки	*pa frantsoozky*	по-французкий	*pa frantsoozkee*
Do you understand?	Ви розумієте	*vy razoomee'yeteh*	Вы понимаете	*vy paneemahyetyeh*
I do not understand	Я не розумію	*ya ne razoomee'yoo*	Я не понимаю	*ya nye paneemayoo*
Repeat,	Повторите	*povtoryteh*	Повторите	*pahvtareetyeh*

Language

	Ukrainian		**Russian**	
What?	Що?	*scho*	Что?	*shto*
Who?	Хто?	*khto*	Кто?	*kto*
Why?	Чому?	*chomoo*	Почему?	*pochyemoo*
How?	Як?	*yak*	Как?	*kak*
Where?	Де?	*deh*	Где?	*gdyeh*
on the left	на ліво	*na leevo*	на лева	*na lyeva*
on the right	на права	*na prava*	на права	*na prava*
straight ahead	прямо	*pryamo*	прямо	*pryama*
here	тут	*toot*	здесь	*zdyes*
there	там	*tam*	там	*tam*
far	далеко	*dalehko*	далёко	*dalyeko*
near	блізько	*bleezko*	близко	*bleezka*

Buying

How much?	Скільки	*skeelky*	Сколько	*skoylka*
What is it?	Що це	*scho tseh*	Что это	*shto ehta*
a lot	багато	*bohata*	много	*mnoga*
a little bit	трошка	*troshka*	чутьчуть	*chootchoot*
(too) little	мало	*malo*	мало	*mala*
How much does this cost?	Скільки це коштує (ukr)	*skeelky tseh koshtooyeh*		
	Сколько это стоит (rus)		*skolka ehta stoyeet*	

	Ukrainian		**Russian**	
## Needs				
I want ...	Я хочу	*ya khochoo*	Я хочу	*ya khachoo*
I need ...	Мені потрібно	*mehnee potreebno*	Мне нужно	*mnyeh noozhna*
I am looking for ...	Я шукаю	*ya shukayu*	Я ищу	*ya eeschoo*
May I ... ?	Можна	*mozhna*	Можно	*mozhna*
to sleep	спати	*spahty*	спать	*spaht*
to buy	купити	*koopyty*	купить	*koopeet*
to eat	їсти	*yeesty*	есть	*yehst*
to drink	пити	*pyty*	пить	*peet*
## Food and drink				
bread	хліб	*khleeb*	хлеб	*khlyeb*
cheese	сир	*syr*	сір	*syr*
sausage	ковбаса	*kovbassa*	колбаса	*kolbassa*
meat	мясо	*myaso*	мясо	*myasa*
fish	риба	*ryba*	ріба	*ryba*
sweets	цукерки	*tsookerky*	конфеті	*konfyety*
fruit	фрукти	*frookty*	фрукті	*frookty*
vegetables	овочі	*ovochee*	овощи	*ovoschee*
apple	яблуко	*yabluko*	яблоко	*yablako*
cherry	вишні	*vyshnee*	вишня	*veeshnya*

Language

	Ukrainian		**Russian**	
mushrooms	гриби	*hryby*	грибі	*greeby*
potatoes	картопля	*kartoplya*	картошки	*kartoshkee*
water	вода	*voda*	вода	*vada*
milk	молоко	*moloko*	молоко	*malako*
juice	сік	*seek*	сок	*sok*
sugar	цукор	*tsookor*	сахар	*sakhar*
tea	чай	*chai*	чай	*chai*
coffee	кава	*kava*	кофе	*kofye*
beer	пиво	*pyvo*	пиво	*peevo*
vodka	горілка	*horeelka*	водка	*vodka*

Useful words

book	книга	*knyha*	книга	*kneega*
map	мапа	*mappa*	карта	*karta*
money	гроші	*hroshee*	денги	*dyengui*
ticket	квіток	*kveetok*	билет	*beelyet*
train	поїзд	*poyeezd*	поезд	*poyezd*
bus	автобус	*avtoboos*	автобус	*avtoboos*
stamps	марки	*marky*	марки	*markee*
blanket	ковдри	*kovdry*	одеяло	*odeyalo*
room	кімната	*keemnata*	комната	*komnata*

Basics

	Ukrainian		**Russian**	
house	дім	*deem*	дом	*dom*
tree	дерево	*dehrehvo*	дерево	*dyerevo*
mountain	гора	*hora*	гора	*gora*
flower	квіти	*kveety*	цветі	*tsvyety*
wheat	пшениця	*pshehnytsya*	пшеница	*psheneetsya*
sunflower	соняшник	*sonyashneek*	подсолнечник	*pahdsolnyechneek*
rainbow	веселка	*vehsehlka*	радуга	*raduga*

Descriptions

small	малий	*maly*	маленкий	*malyenky*
big	великий	*vehlyky*	большой	*bolshoi*
new	новій	*novy*	новій	*novy*
old	старий	*stary*	старій	*stary*
beautiful	красний	*krasny*	красивій	*kraseevy*
important	важливо	*vazhlyvo*	важно	*vazhno*
cold	холодно	*kholodno*	холодно	*kholodna*
hot	горячий	*horyachy*	горячий	*gahryachee*
delicious	смачно	*smachno*	вкусно	*fgoosna*

Numbers

Ukrainian and Russian numbers are fairly cognitive. If you know 1–10 and the constructions, you can say any number in either language:

	Ukrainian		**Russian**	
0	нуль	*nool*	нуль	*nool*
1	один	*odyn*	один	*ah<u>deen</u>*
2	два	*dva*	два	*dva*
3	три	*trih*	три	*tree*
4	чотири	*cho<u>ty</u>ry*	четіре	*chye<u>ty</u>reh*
5	пять	*pyat*	пять	*pyat*
6	шість	*sheest*	шесть	*shehst*
7	сім	*seem*	семь	*syem*
8	вісім	*veeseem*	восемь	*<u>vo</u>syem*
9	девять	*<u>deh</u>vyat*	девять	*<u>dye</u>vyat*
10	десять	*<u>deh</u>syat*	десять	*<u>dye</u>syat*

11 through 19 are formed by adding the suffix 'надцять':

11	одинадцять	*odynatsat*
12	дванадцять	*dvanatsat*

20 through 40 are slightly irregular:

		Ukrainian	
20	двадцять	_dvat_sat
21	двадцять один	_dvat_sat _o_dyn
30	тридцять	_trih_tsyat
40	сорок	_sorok_
50	пятдесят	_pee_dehsyat
60	шістдесять	_shees_dehsyat
70	сімдесять	_seem_dehsyat
80	вісімдесять	_veeseem_dehsyat
90	девятннносто	devyah_nosto_
100	сто	sto
124	сто двадцять чотири	sto _dvat_sat cho_tyry_
200	двісті	_dvee_stee
300	триста	_trih_sta
400	чотириста	cho_tyry_stah
500	пятсот	pyat_sot_
1000	тисяча	tys_yacha_

Days and time

	Ukrainian		**Russian**	
today	сьогодні	s'_yoho_dni	сегодня	sye_vod_nya
tomorrow	завтра	_zav_tra	завтра	_zav_tra

	Ukrainian		**Russian**	
the day after tomorrow	післязавтра	*peeslyazavtra*	послезавтра	*poslyezavtra*
yesterday	вчора	*fchora*	вчера	*fchyera*
Monday	понеділок	*ponehdeelok*	понедельник	*ponyedyelneek*
Tuesday	вівторок	*veevtorok*	вторник	*vtorneek*
Wednesday	середа	*sehrehdah*	среда	*sryedah*
Thursday	четвер	*chetver*	четверг	*chetvyerg*
Friday	пятниця	*pyatnytsya*	пятница	*pyatneetsa*
Saturday	субота	*soobohta*	суббота	*soobohta*
Sunday	неділя	*nehdeelya*	воскресенье	*voskresenye*
What time is it?	Котра година?	*kotra hodyna*	Которій час?	*katory chas*
now	тепер	*tehpehr*	сейчас	*seychas*
hour	година	*hodyna*	час	*chas*
minute	хвилин	*khvylyn*	минута	*meenoota*

13 Further Information

BOOKS ON UKRAINE

A comparatively small amount has been written about Kiev in English, and the volumes that have been written tend to intimidate all but the most dedicated scholars. Really the only history written specifically on Kiev is the highly academic but biographical *Kiev: A Portrait, 1800–1917*, by Michael F Hamm (Princeton and University Press, 1995). The bible of Ukrainian history is Orest Subtelny's 700-page *Ukraine: A History* (University of Toronto Press, 1988). Since then, the noted Ukrainian scholar Paul Robert Magosci has also published an excellent (and longer) *History of Ukraine* (University of Washington Press, 1996) which incorporates the present context of independent Ukraine. The most current work on all things Ukrainian is Andrew Wilson's *The Ukrainians: Unexpected Nation* (Yale University Press, 2000). The work is a scholarly look at Ukrainian politics, economy and society, yet the chosen subject matter and writing make a good read. The book I do recommend for all those travelling to Ukraine is Anna Reid's *Borderland* (Weidenfeld & Nicolson, 1997). The author worked as a correspondent for *The Economist* during the early years of Ukraine's transition and artfully connects Ukraine's past with its present regions and people.

Very little Ukrainian literature exists in translation, but I would suggest Gogol's *Evenings on a Farm near Dikanka 1&2*. These dark but comic tales describe Ukrainian folklore like none other. Leonard Kent has edited a *Complete Tales of*

Nikolai Gogol (University of Chicago Press, 1985) with *Evenings*, as well as *Mirgorod*, which includes the famous story of the Cossack hero *Taras Bulba*. Most of Sholom Aleichem's work (translated from Yiddish) takes place in Ukraine and offers poignant insights into the relationships between the Ukrainians and Ukraine's former Jewish community. More modern literary explorations on Ukraine exist in the form of a powerful memoir *Honey and Ashes* by Janice Kulyk Keefer (Harper Collins, 2000). The book reviews the author's ancestry and her growing-up as a Ukrainian in Canada, with a poignant element of travelogue near the end.

For Ukrainian-language guides, the most comprehensive is *A Language Guide to Ukraine* (Hippocrene Books, 1994) by Linda Hodges and George Chumak, which does include some useful travel information. Lonely Planet also does a pocket-sized *Ukrainian Phrasebook* that can be very useful for travellers in western Ukraine and Kiev. LP also published a comprehensive guide to Russia, Ukraine and Belarus in 2000.

WEBSITES
On Ukraine

www.brama.com 'Brama' means gateway in Ukrainian, and this site keeps true to its name, providing an e-community for the Ukrainian Diaspora.

www.ukraine.com Up-to-date, modern, comprehensive directory on all things Ukraine-related.

www.cia.gov/cia/publications/factbook/geos/up.html CIA factbook on line with all the country's bare statistics.

Websites

www.rada.gov.ua Official website of Ukraine's Verkhovna Rada. Look up your favourite parliamentarian.

www.ukraine-international.com Ukraine International Airlines' official website.

www.online.com.ua Ukraine's 'Computer Information Agency'. Another Ukraine e-community for techies.

www.lonelyplanet.com/destinations/europe/ukraine Lonely Planet's website blurb on Ukraine.

www.ukraine.uazone.net Online Ukrainian news service.

www.travel.kyiv.org Amateur but colourful and informative website on travel to Kiev and Ukraine.

www.infoukes.com Canadian website for the Ukrainian Diaspora.

www.encyclopediaofukraine.com As the name implies, an online encyclopaedia of all things Ukrainian.

www.ukrweekly.com Weekly online publication on Ukrainian affairs.

www.un.kiev.ua The United Nations in Ukraine.

Kiev

www.kmv.gov.ua Official site of the Kiev government, in Russian, Ukrainian and English.

www.kyivpost.com Site for the *Kiev Post*.

www.uazone.net/Kiev.html An online guide to Kiev.

www.inyourpocket.com A quality, online city guide to Kiev that's good to check out before your journey.

www.relc.com/kiev Another small, homemade site on travel to Kiev.
www.dynamo.kiev.ua Official website of Kiev's famous football team.
www.biztravel.kiev.ua A business travel site for Kiev.

WIN £100 CASH!
READER QUESTIONNAIRE

Win a cash prize of £100 for the first completed questionnaire drawn
after December 31 2004.
All respondents may order a Bradt guide at half the UK retail price – please
complete the order form overleaf.

Have you used any other Bradt guides? If so, which titles? . . . .
. . . .
. . . .
What other publishers' travel guides do you use regularly? . . . .
. . . .
. . . .
Where did you buy this guidebook?. . . . .
What was the main purpose of your trip to Kiev (or for what other reason did you
read our guide)? eg: holiday/business/charity etc.. . . . .
. . . .

What other destinations would you like to see covered by a Bradt guide?

....

Would you like to receive our catalogue/newsletters?

YES / NO (If yes, please complete details on reverse)

If yes – by post or email?. . . . .

Age (circle relevant category) 16–25   26–45   46–60   60+

Male/Female (delete as appropriate)

Home country . . . .

Please send us any comments about our guide to Kiev or other Bradt Travel Guides.

....
....
....
....

Bradt Travel Guides

19 High Street, Chalfont St Peter, Bucks SL9 9QE, UK
Telephone: +44 1753 893444 Fax: +44 1753 892333
Email: info@bradt-travelguides.com
www.bradtguides.com

CLAIM YOUR HALF-PRICE BRADT GUIDE!

To order your half-price copy of a Bradt guide, and to enter our £100 prize draw, fill in the form below, complete the questionnaire on pages 298–9, and send it to us by post, fax or email. Post and packing is free to UK addresses. A list of other city guides can be found on the inside cover; the full range of titles and prices is on our website (www.bradtguides.com).

Title	Retail price	Half price
. . . .	. . . .	. . . .
Post & packing outside UK (£2/book Europe; £3/book rest of world)		. . . .
	Total	. . . .

Name. . . . .

. . . .

Address . . . .

. . . .

Tel. . . . .   Email . . . .

❏ I enclose a cheque for £ . . . . made payable to Bradt Travel Guides Ltd
❏ I would like to pay by VISA or MasterCard
   Number. . . . .   Expiry date . . . .
❏ Please add my name to your catalogue mailing list.

Pocket an expert!
More city guides from Bradt

Comprehensive coverage of a range of European cities, complemented by full-colour street maps.

Budapest Adrian Phillips & Jo Scotchmer
(published September 2004)
With its Parisian boulevards and illuminated bridges, Budapest is the most romantic of cities. This Bradt guide takes you from the castle and caves to the shops and spas, and provides all the practical details you'll need for a great short break.

Cork Linda Fallon *(published November 2004)*
Join the people of Cork as they celebrate their city's status as European Capital of Culture for 2005. Local writer Linda Fallon takes the visitor through the festivals, guided tours, pubs and restaurants, and even sporting events, that have brought Ireland's second city to prominence.

Dubrovnik Piers Letcher *(published December 2004)*
Piers Letcher brings his in-depth knowledge of Croatia to this historic walled town, fast becoming a popular short-break destination. Here is everything for that idyllic break, from nightlife and the best local restaurants to island retreats and nearby national parks.

Tallinn Neil Taylor *(published May 2004)*
Take a walking tour through the cobbled streets of old Tallinn with Estonia expert, Neil Taylor. With details of local excursions and cosmopolitan bars, cafés and restaurants this is the essential guide to Estonia's beautiful medieval capital.

Coming in 2005 *Riga, Vilnius, Ljubljana*

Available from all good bookshops, or by post, fax, phone or internet direct from:

Bradt Travel Guides Ltd
19 High Street, Chalfont St Peter, Bucks SL9 9QE, England
Tel: +44 1753 893444 Fax: +44 1753 892333
Email: info@bradt-travelguides.com Web: www.bradtguides.com

Index

Index

Left Woman selling fresh food at market

Above Detail in St Mikhayil's Cathedral

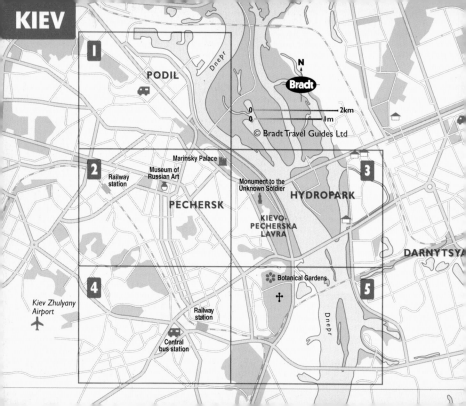

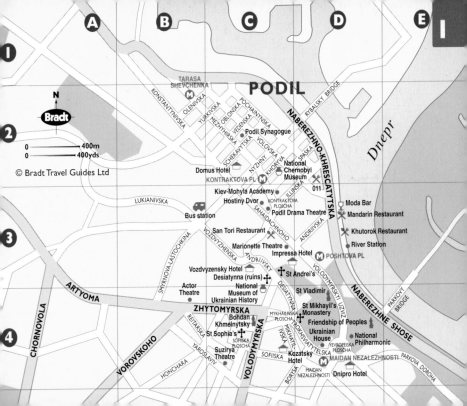

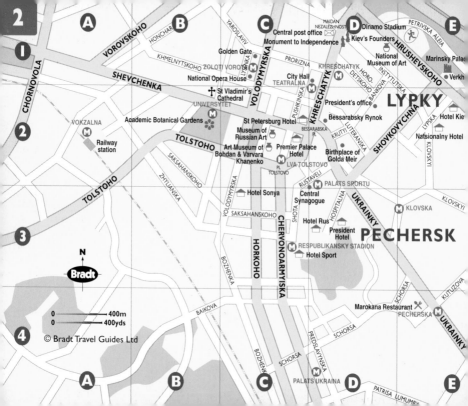

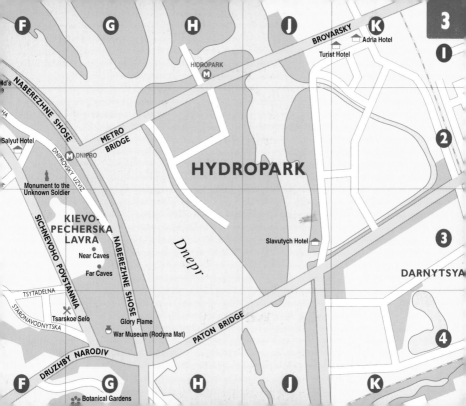

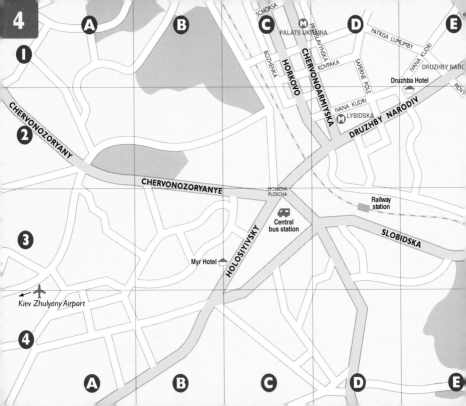

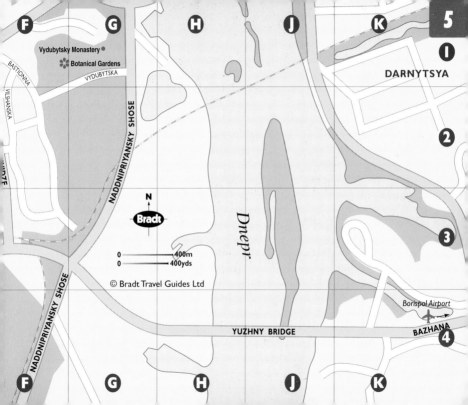

5

F G H J K

I

DARNYTSYA

2

BASTIONNA

VILSHANSKA

Vydubytsky Monastery

Botanical Gardens

VYDUBYTSKA

3

NADDNIPRIYANSKY SHOSE

N

Bradt

Дпепр

0 ——————— 400m
0 ——————— 400yds

© Bradt Travel Guides Ltd

Borispol Airport

NADDNIPRIYANSKY SHOSE

YUZHNY BRIDGE

BAZHANA

4

F G H J K

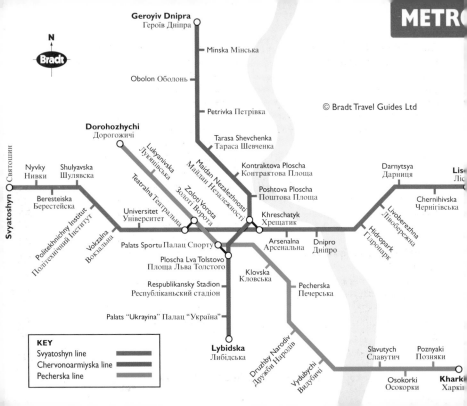

METRO

Geroiv Dnipra
Героїв Дніпра

Minska Мінська

Obolon Оболонь

Petrivka Петрівка

Tarasa Shevchenka
Тараса Шевченка

Dorohozhychi
Дорогожичі

Lukyanivska Лукянівська

Maidan Nezalezhnosti Майдан Незалежності

Kontraktova Ploscha
Контрактова Площа

© Bradt Travel Guides Ltd

Nyvky Нивки

Shulyavska Шулявська

Teatralna Театральна

Zoloti Vorota Золоті Ворота

Poshtova Ploscha
Поштова Площа

Darnytsya Дарниця

Lisc
Лі

Beresteiska Берестейська

Universitet Університет

Khreschatyk Хрещатик

Chernihivska Чернігівська

Svyatoshyn Святошин

Politekhnichny Instytut Політехнічний Інститут

Vokzalna Вокзальна

Palats Sportu Палац Спорту

Arsenalna Арсенальна

Dnipro Дніпро

Livoberezhna Лівобережна

Hidropark Гідропарк

Ploscha Lva Tolstovo
Площа Льва Толстого

Klovska Кловська

Pecherska Печерська

Respublikansky Stadion
Республіканський стадіон

Palats "Ukrayina" Палац "Україна"

Lybidska
Либідська

Druzhby Narodiv Дружби Народів

Vydubychi Видубичі

Slavutych Славутич

Poznyaki Позняки

Osokorki Осокорки

Kharki
Харкі

KEY
Svyatoshyn line
Chervonoarmiyska line
Pecherska line

N

Bradt